THIS BOOK IS DEDICATED TO THOSE
WHO LIVE THE HIGH COSTS OF THE
NATURALIZED PRIVATIZATION OF CARE.

UNDOING MONOGAMY

UNDOING MONOGAMY

The Politics of Science and the Possibilities of Biology

ANGELA WILLEY

DUKE UNIVERSITY PRESS DURHAM AND LONDON 2016

Designed by Heather Hensley
Typeset in Whitman and Trade Gothic Condensed by Copperline

Library of Congress Cataloging-in-Publication Data
Names: Willey, Angela, [date] author.
Title: Undoing monogamy : the politics of science and the possibilities of biology / Angela Willey.
Description: Durham : Duke University Press, 2016. | Includes bibliographical references and index.
Identifiers: LCCN 2015045617
ISBN 9780822361404 (hardcover : alk. paper)
ISBN 9780822361596 (pbk. : alk. paper)
ISBN 9780822374213 (e-book)
Subjects: LCSH: Non-monogamous relationships. | Monogamous relationships. | Sexual minorities—Sexual behavior. | Sexual ethics.
Classification: LCC HQ980.W555 2016 | DDC 176/.4—dc23
LC record available at http://lccn.loc.gov/2015045617

Cover art: Resa Blatman, *Aphrodite's Garden* (detail).
resablatman.com

Despite claims to the contrary . . . there are few signs that heterosexual monogamy is in terminal decline. The majority of adults continue to live in heterosexual relationships, while the normalization of homosexuality could be said to be working toward the heterosexualization of lesbian and gay lives. . . . In the process the norm of the "loving couple" as the ideal basis for adult life becomes even more fully entrenched. We should maybe heed the critical insights of those earlier feminists who warned that the concentration of love and care into couples and families impoverished the rest of social life.

—Stevi Jackson, "Love, Social Change, and Everyday Heterosexuality" (2013)

We need to know where we live in order to imagine living elsewhere. We need to imagine living elsewhere before we can live there.

—Avery Gordon, *Ghostly Matters* (2008)

CONTENTS

Acknowledgments xi

INTRODUCTION Politics and Possibility: A Queer Feminist Introduction to Monogamy 1

1 Monogamy's Nature: Colonial Sexual Science and Its Naturecultural Fruits 25

2 Making the Monogamous Human: Mating, Measurement, and the New Science of Bonding 45

3 Making Our Poly Nature: Monogamy's Inversion and the Reproduction of Difference 73

4 Rethinking Monogamy's Nature: From the Truth of Non/Monogamy to a Dyke Ethics of "Antimonogamy" 95

5 Biopossibility: Molecular Monogamy and Audre Lorde's Erotic 121

EPILOGUE Dreams of a Dyke Science 141

Notes 147

Bibliography 169

Index 191

ACKNOWLEDGMENTS

This book owes its materialization to the good humor, brilliance, and generosity of many friends and colleagues and to the support of several institutions.

I had the pleasure of working on this book full-time in Houston thanks to a Rice University Humanities Research Center fellowship, "Materialism and New Materialism across the Disciplines," in 2013–2014; thank you to my colleagues there, especially Sarah Ellenzweig, Lauren Kleinschmidt, and Jack Zammito.

Five College Feminist Science and Technology Studies Initiative reading and writing groups have provided intellectual grist and accountability as well as fun and sweetness over the last several years. Thank you to Kiran Asher, Aimee Bahng, Karen Cardozo, Christian Gunderman, Jennifer Hamilton, Rebecca Herzig, Jacquelyne Luce, Laura Lovett, Lis McLoughlin, Donna Riley, Britt Rusert, and Banu Subramaniam for making those spaces so generative and sustaining and for reading zillions of iterations of what would become chapter 5.

I am grateful to colleagues and students in my home department—Women, Gender, Sexuality Studies at the University of Massachusetts, Amherst—for their collegiality and intellectual generosity. Thank you to Kiran Asher, Abbie Boggs, Laura Briggs, Alex Deschamps, Tanisha Ford, Ann Ferguson, Linda Hillenbrand, Miliann Kang, Karen Lederer, Kirsten Leng, Svati Shah, Banu Subramaniam, and Mecca Sullivan. Kiran, Laura, and Kirsten gave valuable detailed feedback on sections of the book, and Banu gave generous feedback on the entire manuscript. Thank you to my graduate students—especially Claire Brault, Kevin Henderson, Alix Olson, and Cordelia Sand—for pushing my thinking about queer feminist politics and materialisms. And to my fall 2015 "Monogamy" class at the University of Massachusetts, Amherst, for thinking with me about which epigraphs to open with as I wrap up copyedits.

Thank you, too, to my colleagues and students in Gender Studies at Mount Holyoke College and Critical Social Inquiry at Hampshire College. Thanks in particular to my fall 2014 "Monogamy" class at Hampshire. Their creativity in imagining the scope of a "critical monogamy studies" blew me away. And thank you to all of the Five College undergraduate students with whom I've codesigned queer feminist science studies research projects and practicums. Thinking with these students has made this book more imaginative.

Sara Giordano and Lynne Huffer have been generous interlocutors through many stages of this book's coming into being over the last decade and also gave feedback on each and every chapter. Thank you to Lynne and to Pamela Scully, the kind and brilliant codirectors of the dissertation from which this book grew, and to Sander Gilman, whose tutelage has had a profound impact on my thinking about monogamy science. Thanks are due, too, to my master's thesis advisor, Claire Hemmings, for encouraging me to pursue my interest in monogamy. I also want to thank my undergraduate women's studies professors, Mary Bosworth, Susan Berger, Nicole Fermon, Fawzia Mustafa, Nina Swidler, and Irma Watkins-Owens, for introducing me to feminist theory in so many different ways.

I owe a special thank you to Sara Giordano, Jennifer Hamilton, and Banu Subramaniam, close collaborators from whom I have learned to think in new ways, whose intellectual interests and styles have marked this book in unquantifiable ways, and without whose friendship it wouldn't yet be done.

Thank you to fellowships from Interdisciplinary Studies at the University of Massachusetts, Amherst, and Crossroads in the study of the Americas at the Five Colleges, both of which provided support and community for developing parts of this book. Thanks to Sue Dickman and Nate Therian at Five Colleges for all of your support. Thanks, too, to the Five College Women's Studies Research Center. Under the direction of Karen Remmler and Darcy Buerkle (in my years here) the center has been instrumental in making western Massachusetts a vibrant place to do feminist scholarship.

I wrote chapter 1 in the company of a lovely community of historians of sexual science at the Leslie Center for the Humanities at Dartmouth College over the summer of 2013. Thank you to my colleagues there: Sanjam Ahluwalia, Aimee Bahng, Chiara Beccolosi, Pablo Ben, Michael Dietrich, Veronika Fuetchner, Doug Haynes, Kit Heintzman, Rainer Herrn, Rebecca Hodes, Rachel

Hui-chi Hsu, Ishita Pande, Ryan Jones, and Kurt MacMillan. Charlie Beckler was my fabulous research assistant on that chapter.

Thank you to Larry Young and members of his Emory University laboratory for generously sharing their time and knowledge.

Thank you to friends and colleagues with whom I've thought about monogamy, nonmonogamy, and social belonging over the years, especially Bailey, Caitlin Childs, Sara Giordano, Onni Gust, Julie Kubala, Christina Leddy, Kerrie Lynn, Meghan Martiniere, Louisa Merchant, Sreerekha Mullasery, John Pisani, Uditi Sen, Traci Schlesinger, Arjun Shamlal, and Josephine Wilson. And to those beyond my local cohort with whom I've thought about what a queer feminist critical materialist science studies (or some such) might look like, especially Moya Bailey, Cyd Cipolla, Laura Foster, Kristina Gupta, Durba Mitra, Anne Pollock, Deboleena Roy, David Rubin, Harlan Weaver, and Veronica Sanz.

The kindness and community of many more friends helped me to write this book. Thank you to Lisa Armstrong, Arlene Avakian, Martha Ayres, Bethany Baylies, Jen Bertasi, Catherine Boswell, Barbara Cruikshank, Janice Irvine, Amber Krebs, Cathy Luna, Toni Mead, Lynn Morgan, Sonny Nordmarken, Shannan Palma, Jacob Speaks, Nina Swidler, and Shruthi Vissa.

Thank you to Kim TallBear and Jennifer Terry for reflecting back to me the feminist political desires that animate this project in your generous comments on the manuscript. I couldn't have asked for better readers. Courtney Berger has been a thoughtful and dedicated editor. Thanks to both Courtney and Sandra Korn at Duke University Press for being incredibly helpful throughout this process. Thanks, too, to Claudia Castaneda, who edited my book proposal and chapter 1.

Thank you to librarians in general, and in particular, to Beth Lang, Laura Quilter, and Charlotte Roh at the University of Massachusetts, Amherst, and Julie Adamo and James Gehrt at Mount Holyoke College. Beth and Julie helped me find things I read for this book, Laura and Charlotte educated me on fair use, and James prepared my images.

For making literal and metaphorical space for me to write this book (from building this desk I'm typing at to providing beverage service to making chalk boards, pencil cases, and other writerly gifts to waiting and listening patiently) and for celebrating all the little bitty steps in this very long process with me, I thank those most intimately involved in the writing of this book (in chronological order from the date my business started being yours): Gail Willey, Joe Willey, Traci Schlesinger, Sara Giordano, Coltin Fulk, Hunter Fulk, Tabitha Fulk, Tyler Fulk, Cloe Fulk, Erika Kate MacDonald, Bailey, and Jake Guimont.

Some of this book's most interesting ideas germinated in thinking and imagining with Cloe, Tyler, Tabby, Hunter, and Coltin. They've taught me tons about relational inventiveness.

Of course, no one thanked here is liable for flaws, mistakes, or omissions that remain.

Finally, despite having a lovely desk at home, I confess to having written much of this book in cafés. Among them I would especially like to acknowledge Doshi House in Houston and Café Evolution in Florence, Massachusetts.

Portions of this book have appeared elsewhere in various forms. An earlier version of a section of chapter 3 titled "Universalizing Polyamory Discourse" is included in "'Science Says She's Gotta Have It': Reading for Racial Resonances in Woman-Centered Poly Literature," in *Understanding Non-monogamies*, edited by Meg Barker and Darren Langdridge, 34–45 (New York: Routledge, 2010). Most of chapter 5 and a section of the introduction titled "The Possibilities of Biology" appear in "Biopossibility: A Queer Feminist Materialist Science Studies Manifesto, with Special Reference to the Question of Monogamous Behavior," *Signs* 41, no. 3 (2016). Thank you to *Signs* for permission to republish the content of this article.

INTRODUCTION

POLITICS AND POSSIBILITY

A Queer Feminist Introduction to Monogamy

The dyad, for so long opposite sex and now increasingly also same sex, is portrayed as the fundamental unit of love and family.

—The Critical Polyamorist, "Couple-Centricity, Polyamory and Colonialism" (2014)

The family is the best way to advance capitalism, as the base unit through which capitalism distributes benefits. Through our reliance on the marital family structure . . . we allow the state to mandate that only some relationships and some forms of social networks count.

—Yasmin Nair, "Against Equality, Against Marriage" (2010)

So, nature is not a physical place to which one can go, nor a treasure to fence in or bank, nor an essence to be saved or violated. Nature is not hidden and so does not need to be unveiled. Nature is not a text to be read in the codes of mathematics and biomedicine. It is not the "other" who offers origin, replenishment, and service. Neither mother, nurse, nor slave, nature is not matrix, resource, or tool for the reproduction of man. . . . Nature is a topic of public discourse on which much turns, even the earth.

—Donna Haraway, "The Promises of Monsters" (1992)

"Creationists and evolutionists don't agree on much, but they both believe that monogamy is the most natural form of reproduction for the human species." In this opening line of an op-ed published in the fall of 2012, legal historian John Witte Jr. named a Christian and (neo)Darwinian consensus on monogamy's naturalness.[1] His remarks suggest that they arrived at this conclusion independently and corroborate one another only due to the facticity of the claim. Just weeks beforehand, Missouri congressman Todd Akin had been met with a firestorm of bipartisan attack for being "unscientific" when he declared that a woman can't get pregnant if she's raped, because her body "has ways of shutting that whole thing down."[2] The assumption that the link between monogamy and reproduction is human nature, according not just to God but also to *evolution*, is at the heart of Akin's ill-considered speculation about the womb's capacity to recognize rape-sperm.[3] If indeed we are here to reproduce in the bonds of coupledom, it stands to reason that bodies have mechanisms for ensuring that destiny. The entrenched scientific naturalization of dyadic family structures is deeply implicated in antifeminist sexual politics. It is also ubiquitous, as my epigraphs from The Critical Polyamorist and Yasmin Nair suggest, and informs most research on human sexuality. As Avery Gordon reminds us, if we are to imagine living elsewhere, we must know where we live.[4] We must then understand the politics of pervasive assumptions about human nature and coupling. Nature is, as Donna Haraway so eloquently instructs, a discourse on which so much turns, including possibilities for other worlds. Refiguring monogamy's nature is the work of this book.

This book intervenes in assumptions about human nature and biology that underlie discourses that reinforce monogamy's compulsory status *and* the framing and practice of alternatives in the contemporary United States. Attempts to imagine human nature as nonmonogamous, however marginalized, often reproduce the logics underlying monogamy's naturalization: that we are fundamentally sexual beings, that sexuality is indeed something discrete and knowable, and that the structuring of human relationships and society around sexuality is natural. The book demands a critical reorientation toward the monogamy question in the natural sciences, social sciences, and humanities. It offers a radically interdisciplinary exploration of the concept of monogamy in U.S. science and culture, propelled by queer feminist desires for new modes of conceptualization and new forms of belonging.

I take those concepts and forms as imbricated with one another in ways that make disciplinary ways of knowing themselves an object of critical inquiry. This book borrows from feminist and queer theory, the natural sciences, philosophy, anthropology of science, critical science studies, history, and literary and cultural studies to explore monogamy's meanings *and* the materiality to which they are attributed as *co-constituted*. Through a genealogy of monogamy as a bioscientific object, ethnographic fieldwork in a neuroscience laboratory, and critical feminist readings of documents from genomics to comics, I show how challenging the lens through which human nature is seen as monogamous or nonmonogamous forces us to reconsider our investments in coupling and in disciplinary notions of biological bodies.

Through its analyses of the limitations and possibilities of naturalizing and denaturalizing queer feminist challenges to monogamy, the book introduces a new set of questions: What resources might we cull for thinking beyond the nature/culture binary? What modes of conceptualization might enable new forms we cannot yet imagine? What approaches might enable us to hold the politics of science and the possibilities of biology in the same frame, such that our new conceptions of materiality reflect the breadth of feminist and other contributions to knowing bodies? Reading early twentieth-century sexology, contemporary science journals, news journalism, polyamory literature, lesbian comics, and theory as sites of knowledge about bodies, the book proceeds from the insight that knowledge and power are not only always enmeshed with one another but also always implicated in possibilities for new becomings. That is to say, *living elsewhere* and *becoming otherwise* are entangled processes. The politics of science and the possibilities of biology are not then separate sets of concerns, but questions we must work to integrate.

The naturalness of monogamy—for individuals, groups, or species—is persistently posed as a "true" or "false" question: are we or are we not wired for monogamy? I reframe the question, asking instead, what is the relationship between how we imagine social belonging and how we understand human nature? I argue that to imagine how we relate to one another differently is to open up new possibilities for how we understand what we are biologically. Narratives in which humans are imagined as complementary sexually dimorphic populations made to pair off are in fact at the heart of neo-Darwinian frameworks that shape how we understand not only relating but also biology and behavior in general.[5] Diverse claims about the human as a monogamous species—a species that pairs off to rear its young—establish tight relationships between sexual desire, reproduction, and parenting. In a context in which the heterosexual, reproductive, nuclear family is understood as the building block of a culture and economic system that seem inevitable, these claims "make sense." They have certainly not, however, gone unchallenged. Claims that the human is *not* a monogamous species, that the cultural ideal of monogamy is a distortion rather than an expression of our true nature, proliferate. For decades feminist science studies scholars have shown us that science is not a mirror held up to nature but rather processes of knowledge production that reflect and reinforce political and cultural norms.[6] Contestations in scientific narratives are conflicts in culture. In the chapters that follow I uncover assumptions about biology, sexuality, difference, and belonging as the shared conditions of intelligibility for these seemingly antagonistic stories about monogamy.

When we refer to monogamy, we refer to phenomena—sexual fidelity, the ideal of coupling, pair bond formation—made intelligible through various disciplinary and disciplining modalities. Monogamy is not *either* biological *or* cultural and historical; neither is it simply *both*. We live in what Donna Haraway has called a "naturecultural" world where what we *know* and what *is* are intimately enmeshed and co-constituted. Feminist engagements with embodiment as a naturecultural or material-discursive phenomenon have radical potential for transforming science and the worlds it helps materialize. I ground the book in this conception of matter as powerful, meaningful, and always political, by integrating *critical engagement* with the knowing that precedes us with attention to the *materiality* those disciplinary knowledges purport to explain in often startlingly unimaginative ways.

Theorizing Compulsory Monogamy

Historically, feminists have had a vexed relationship with monogamy, from debates over polygamy and patriarchal marriage in feminist movements of the late nineteenth century to contemporary debates over monogamy, polygamy, and polyamory.[7] An exciting and undertheorized body of feminist writing on monogamy has sought to extend earlier feminist challenges to naturalizing assumptions about sexuality, bonding, and forms of belonging. Adrienne Rich's critique of compulsory heterosexuality in her seminal essay "Compulsory Heterosexuality and Lesbian Existence" is a paradigmatic example of those early challenges to the naturalized ideal of heterosexual marriage.[8] In her essay Rich argued that rather than being natural or innate, heterosexuality is naturalized by making alternatives to it invisible. Over two decades later, contemporary feminists critical of monogamy have drawn on Rich's strategy to make both heterosexuality and monogamy visible as culturally entrenched norms. Elizabeth Emens's groundbreaking essay "Monogamy's Law: Compulsory Monogamy and Polyamorous Existence" is a particularly compelling example of this later generation of feminist work. In "Monogamy's Law," Emens argues that the "twoness" requirement of marriage is as deeply embedded in U.S. culture and law as the "different sex requirement."[9] Rich articulated heterosexuality as a problem for feminists by arguing that it perpetuates the social and economic privilege of men and separates women from one another. Feminist critics of monogamy have similarly put monogamy on the map for feminism. These thinkers have passionately articulated the asymmetrical expectations and costs of monogamy for women and men and critiqued constructions of women as property.[10] They have explained how overinvestment in one person can make it difficult to leave an unhappy relationship and can contribute to the devaluation of friendships and communities.[11] Others have written about monogamy vis-à-vis bisexuality, trans, and asexuality studies. Collectively, these thinkers have made a powerful case for understanding monogamy as compulsory and compulsory monogamy as a problem for feminism.

These broad and diverse feminist engagements with monogamy defy easy categorization. It is tempting to try to break the literature down into (Marxist) materialist, psychoanalytic, and philosophical perspectives. However, while certain authors have various commitments to these and other primary disciplines, most of the analyses are interdisciplinary.[12] And although the literature spans decades, it cannot readily be organized chronologically. It could be argued that the earliest critiques came out of middle-class straight women's dissatisfaction with being trapped in patriarchal marriages that left them isolated and dependent while their husbands worked, and that later critiques came out of a succession of sexual liberation and identity movements. The former has been more or less subsumed into a reductive narrative about second wave feminism's critique of patriarchy.[13] Meanwhile the latter—especially queer critiques of the reproductive family and social science research on gay male dating and social movements—has received far more attention as a locus of resistance to compulsory monogamy.[14] This schema oversimplifies the deep interconnectedness of straight and queer feminist critiques of monogamy, ignoring the ways lesbianism as a way of life was explored as an alternative to straight monogamous marriage and how both heterosexual and same-sex marriage remain important in feminist critiques of monogamy.[15]

I would like to reclaim here a critical feminist response to monogamy as a queer feminist legacy. In so doing, I organize my discussion primarily around feminist concerns with monogamy's relationship to compulsory hetero/sexuality and its institutionalization in marriage. I end this section with a briefer discussion of feminist accounts of the roles of homophobia, biphobia, and transphobia in maintaining monogamy as "the only way."[16]

Feminists concerned with challenging or transforming the institution of marriage have had to look at monogamy. Since the personal became political, marriage has been a problem at the center of the project of creating new relationships and types of social and political organization. In the original *Our*

Right to Love: A Lesbian Resource Book (1978), one contributor described the centrality of monogamy to "the problem" thus: "One of the most significant rules imposed on this relationship [marriage] is that of monogamy, an extremely well-entrenched code, completely supported by law, religion, and custom. Upon this framework, taught by parents, schools, churches, synagogues, the law, medicine, and reinforced by the media, women and men are expected to build their lives."[17] As many have noted, this code serves patriarchy, literally, by allowing patrilineage.[18] If a woman has more than one (male) partner, paternity is uncertain.[19] In the context of little or no public support, being able to make formal and informal financial demands of "fathers" has been important for mothers. Many have argued that earning potential and economic vulnerability in general are key to the imperative for women to marry and thus to understanding their investments in monogamy.[20]

Given these conditions, monogamy "promotes the practice of women seeing each other as property."[21] As one critic concisely put it: "Both *monogamy* and *non-monogamy* name heteropatriarchal institutions within which the only important information is: *how many women can a man legitimately own?*"[22] Indeed adultery laws have historically applied only to women's extramarital sexual relations, not men's, and "husband-swapping" was never a term with wide currency.[23] Women belong to men, while the reverse is not (with some notable exceptions) true. These practices are often reinforced by gendered constructions of desire: while men are said to have "drives," discourse around women's sexuality is centered on notions of romantic love and belonging, to which monogamy is central.[24]

The security that monogamy offers is not only economic but is linked to the need for other types of protection. Many have pointed out implicit and explicit links between monogamy and rape culture. Girls are inculcated with fear from the time they are quite young and learn that part of being sexually responsible is learning where to go, when, and with whom: how to avoid rape.[25] The protection of a man, from both physical assault and damage to one's reputation, thus becomes highly valued: "By allowing one man full access to her body, a woman can obtain his protection from other men."[26] Offering the protection of a partner as an alternative to control over one's own body and sexuality, "monogamy becomes a central element in sexual power relations."[27] Many have argued that for young girls and grown women alike, the most efficient way to negotiate the ever-present risks associated with being seen as promiscuous and/or a lesbian is to "settle down" with one boy or man.[28] Monogamy, then, though it is repeatedly left unsaid, is an absolutely central feature of femininity. Compulsory monogamy is thus deeply raced and classed, as it is the subject most estranged from normative femininity's white and middle-class coding, most vulnerable to violence, and thus most in need of monogamy's protection.[29]

If monogamy is central to femininity, another central concern of especially lesbian feminist critique is the ways men have benefited from monogamy to women's collective detriment.[30] Athena Tsoulis articulates the gendered power dynamics inherent in the rhetoric of romantic love: "Monogamous love, eulogized in our society, is the tool by which women are controlled. The familiar idealised pattern of falling in love and living with the man of our dreams for ever and ever (we hope) has infiltrated our thinking. It is no accident that 'love is blind' and leads women into an irrational loss of control. It leads us to *making men the centre of our world, re-directing our energies and severing ties with others* in an all-consuming fashion."[31] According to this view, the romanticization of exclusivity and the fantasy that there is one person "out there" who will fulfill most if not all of our needs undermines the importance of women's relationships with one another and depoliticizes their shared interests by individualizing them. Women's overinvestment in a single relationship, emotionally and in terms of their labor, typically works to men's advantage, providing them with the support and free time to focus energies on career, personal growth, and/or other relationships.[32] This "overinvestment" results in women's constrained ability to "develop other parts of ourselves" and often makes leaving an abusive or unfulfilling relationship extremely difficult.[33]

Since at least the 1990s, feminists concerned with subjectivity have moved beyond foci on safety and economics to consider various psychosocial investments in monogamy. Christine Overall, for example, describes women's often naturalized investments in monogamy in terms of identity formation. She argues that women, more than men, are encouraged to construct their identities relationally and that "because in Western culture sexual relating is defined as the ultimate form of intimacy, the result in women's romantic/sexual relationships is often an expansion of the sense of self to include those with whom they have sexual relationships."[34] This pressure is reinforced, she argues, "by the definition of the heterosexual couple as the building block of the culture."[35] Thus a woman is likely to experience her partner having a new sexual partner as more threatening than a new friend, hobby, or other commitment (Overall uses vegetarianism as an example), which may also take up a partner's time and energy. One partner having a new sexual partner forces what Overall calls "the monogamous partner" to expand her realm of intimacy and may thus be experienced as violent.[36] Hence women's greater investment in monogamy.

The reification of sex as the most important kind of relating underlies this overinvestment. Queer feminists have critiqued monogamy for its privileging of sexual desire as a basis for structuring relationships and have sought to challenge the designation of particular types of relationships as distinct and hierarchically organized. Becky Rosa explains: "For monogamy to exist there needs to be a division between sexual/romantic and non-sexual love, with the former prioritized over the latter."[37] Challenging this hierarchy inherent in the ideal of monogamy can lead to the revaluation of friendship and at the same time challenge what Rosa refers to as "compulsory sexuality," that is, the way sex is seen as essential to healthy adulthood, romantic love, and future-oriented relationships.[38] Sociologist Kristin Scherrer argues along similar lines that monogamy is such a sex-centric concept that asexual long-term relationships become difficult to imagine within its logics.[39] What counts as a monogamous relationship, in terms of what partners share (and do not), both with one another *and* with other people, is complicated by asexuality in ways that render monogamy's conceptual limitations quite pointedly problematic. Asexual relationship paradigms posit distinctions between romantic/aromantic and sexual/asexual. That is to say, a romantic partnership may be an explicitly nonsexual one. In this way, asexuality poses a problem not only for monogamy's compulsory sexuality but also for its conflation of sex and romance. The special status of sex, implicit in discourses of both monogamy and nonmonogamy, will emerge as a central preoccupation of this book.[40]

Some feminist critics of monogamy have extended concerns with the coformation of monogamy and heteronormativity to ways homophobia, biphobia, and transphobia function to reinforce compulsory monogamy. Some have argued that in a homophobic society wherein lesbians are seen as already transgressing norms of femininity, they are under greater pressure to be monogamous.[41] Possibilities for fulfilling relationships seem to be limited by the pervasiveness of this ideal: "We [lesbians] want to honor each other, and to do that we believe we need to use the model of the heterosexual imperative. That is the married, monogamous one."[42] Gay men are not immune to these pressures and are often under intense pressure to respond to gendered assumptions about sexuality that presume first that all gay men are male, second that relationships among males are necessarily nonmonogamous, and finally that male libido is particularly dangerous among gay men, where it leads to sex considered high risk.[43]

Bisexuality studies of the 1990s was an important site for the theorization of compulsory monogamy and its relationship to control of women's sexuality. Many theorists of bisexuality have argued that compulsory monogamy is exacerbated for women by "biphobia" in both lesbian and heterosexual communities. Stereotypes of bisexuals as nonmonogamous, or as incapable of monogamy, have created an increased pressure for them to *be* monogamous, to prove that they *can*.[44] In her explanation of this dynamic, Murray explores the concept of "safe" people—those who are explicitly off-limits sexually. Due to pervasive assumptions about the nature of sexual desire, it is assumed that sexual feelings are either absent or present depending on the location of this safety net. For example, straight men and women are often thought incapable of being "just friends," whereas gay men and straight women are assumed to make the best of friends. Another assumption embedded in these stereotypes is that sexual feelings get in the way of friendship. This makes bisexuals dangerous, as they are assumed to be attracted to everyone. It seems that the assumption with nonmonogamous bisexuals (real or imagined) is that no one is out of bounds. The object of desire is not understood simply as "*anything* that moves," as one bisexual magazine's title put it, but *everything*! The nonmonogamous bisexual is never "safe," even when partnered. Some celebrate this as a radical challenge to the "love laws"; others are concerned with the ways it can engender "polyphobia" and reinforce compulsory sexuality.[45] Because sexuality is often inferred on the basis of the gender of one's partner, a monogamous bisexual woman is likely to be read as either a lesbian or as straight.[46] As Hemmings points out, "it is a present with only one lover of only one sex . . . that poses the most problems for a bisexual identity."[47] The conflation of bisexuality and nonmonogamy in the popular imagination may then be attributed as much to the assumption that all desire must be embodied or actualized as to stereotypes of bisexuals as immature or sexually voracious.[48]

While the connection between nonmonogamies and trans identities is not so deeply entrenched, in "Trans and Non-monogamies" Christina Richards illuminated trans parallels to these gay and bisexual critiques. She draws on survey data to show that some trans-identified folks find the freedom to relate sexually and romantically with more than one person validating of the complexity of their gender identities. She also notes the risk of this insight serving to further pathologize trans folks.[49] Her findings reveal the extent to which a monogamous model of relating presumes not only the complementarity of two dimorphic sexes but also, even in queer reconfigurations, the stability of gender and sexuality over time. Thus compulsory monogamy reflects and reinforces not only sexist schemas of heteronormative relating but also deep investments in the stability of gender itself.

This scholarship renders monogamy visible as a powerfully entrenched norm and makes it an object of critical inquiry. Working from these compelling queer feminist analyses, this book asks what else is at stake in the way we define, value, and resist compulsory monogamy. Monogamy's place in the production of normal and abnormal bodies is among my central concerns in the book. Marriage has been deeply implicated in regulatory schemas of race and nation,[50] and monogamy must be understood within this frame. This insight informs my decision to begin the book with a genealogy that reveals what I call "monogamy's nature"—that is monogamy as an object of scientific knowledge and a form of embodiment—as an artifact of colonial science and thus implicated in processes of racial formation and nation building.

While the book is not *about* gender or race per se, processes of gendering and racialization are integral to how we imagine not only monogamy but also nonmonogamous alternatives.[51] This project is shaped by queer-of-color critique and black and postcolonial feminist theories that provide critical resources for reading universalizing queer and feminist rhetorics of liberation whose logics reproduce race and class and indeed sexuality as we know it.[52] While "it has now become axiomatic to argue that race, gender and sex, that racial identity and sexuality, are inextricably linked through various discursive operations," as Celia Roberts notes, "theorizing [the specificity of those] interconnections between sexual and racial differences remains a core problematic within feminist theory."[53] As Nadine Ehlers argues, we must work from the knowledge that the deployment of sexuality is "always already racialized."[54] Indeed, we must constantly interrogate the invisible whiteness that purportedly race-neutral claims about sexuality and sexual difference belie.[55] The workings of racism's *erotic life* in monogamy discourse is indeed a "core problematic" in this book. My readings here are attuned to the specificity of assumptions about race and difference that shape configurations of "ideal" and "natural" sexuality. I am, throughout the book, committed to the use of feminist science studies as a vital tool for reading the interconnectedness of seemingly distinct formations of difference with histories in the biosciences.[56]

Indeed monogamy must be counted among those concepts whose intelligibility and power is inextricable from its biologization, from its emergence as *sexuality*. Concepts problematized by these feminist critiques of monogamy—

sex as the highest form of intimacy, the naturalness of jealousy, compulsory heterosexuality, and compulsory sexuality—are not only racially gendered social and religious norms. They also reflect the idea that humans are sexual, straight, reproductive, and designed and destined for certain roles and tasks. That is to say, these assumptions are also deeply embedded in naturalizing scientific discourse and continue to reproduce themselves there.

On the Politics of Science

While feminists have theorized monogamy as a powerful social norm, scientists study monogamy as a mating system or strategy.[57] Monogamy's normalized status cannot be disentangled from its scientific naturalization. Critical feminist science studies offers resources for illuminating the dynamic relationship between science and the contexts out of which its claims emerge and which they shape in turn. To understand compulsory monogamy, we must take an interest in the politics of science. Conversely, attention to the politics of scientific knowledges about bodies reveals the deep cultural importance of monogamy. In a culture where coupling is of paramount importance to how our lives and worlds are structured, monogamy will be important to science both as a category of analysis and as a set of implicit assumptions about how to think about the natural world. How we approach monogamy as an object of knowledge will enable and delimit new possibilities. In this section I consider the importance of feminist engagements with sciences of difference and their epistemological underpinnings to understanding and ultimately undoing monogamy.

In its most capacious sense, science is a project of trying to understand or explain the natural world, but not all theories about what nature is or how best to understand it or any of its aspects or parts are considered science. Science has rules, the criteria for what makes scientific knowledge scientific, for what knowledges constitute science. The basic rules are finite: scientific knowledge is based on the scientific method and is objective, that is, value neutral and therefore universal and reproducible. Philosophers of science have variously referred to this pretense as "the God's-eye view" or "the view from nowhere"; Haraway has called it "the God trick."[58] Feminist science studies scholars have argued that part of what this ruse disguises is that what usually counts as scientific methodology allows only for the study of what can be measured, thereby excluding from the realm of scientific inquiry phenomena that cannot readily be understood in terms of their component parts. Science as such thus demands conceptualizations of natural phenomena that minimize the complexity of its objects: here, monogamy.

The basis of the study of monogamy as a mating strategy is the evolutionary assumption that each individual organism, human or otherwise, has as its primary "goal" the perpetuation of its own genetic material through reproduction. A mating strategy evolves according to increased chances of species survival. It is widely accepted that for more than 90 percent of the animal kingdom, this means spreading genetic material as far and wide as possible.[59] Humans are counted among the small percentage of species considered naturally monogamous.[60] Monogamy, the story goes, evolves in circumstances where having two "parents" to feed and protect offspring increases their chances of survival and thus the continuation of the species.[61] While no evolutionary basis for sexual fidelity exists, *coupling* is considered normal for humans. Rather than an object of inquiry itself, monogamy is often an a priori assumption informing scientific research, as is the case in the laboratory on whose findings headlines announcing the discovery of a monogamy gene were based, which I take up in chapter 2's laboratory ethnography.

In studying monogamy, scientists generally look for different mating strategies in males and females and link these strategies to scientific descriptions of gametes: sperm are seen as plentiful and mobile, hence males optimize their chances of reproduction by spreading their genetic material around. Eggs in females on the other hand are represented as both immobile and finite, so females presumably maximize their genetic survival by selectively choosing how to make the most of their seed.[62] In an unusually transparent illustration of this logic, science writer Joe Quirk describes men and women as "sperm spreaders" and "egg protectors," respectively, in order to explain their different dispositions toward monogamy.[63] This "Victorian script" is at the heart of evolutionary understandings of human behavior.[64] Elizabeth Lloyd has famously shown how evolutionary explanations of female sexuality have misrepresented basic physiological processes by consistently beginning from heterosexual pair bonding as the essence of human nature. Female orgasm was for decades only intelligible as an evolutionary adaptation that rewards pair-bonded (monogamous) female primates for having frequent sex with their male mates. The linking of female orgasm to intercourse persistently renaturalizes female monogamy, as I will show again in my treatment in chapter 2 of the neuroscientific present. While biologically suspect, this link remains an unquestioned assumption underlying the formulation of a wide range of questions and experiments aimed at understanding sexual desire and relating.[65]

These scientific strategies and representations come to naturalize different gendered meanings for monogamy: monogamy is assumed a priori for females, while a variety of different theories emerge in different moments to explain male monogamy.[66] While scientific naturalizing stories about monogamy are geared toward illuminating the evolutionary mystery of male monogamy ("the monogamy gene" is indeed a male gene), the scientific naturalization of nonmonogamy requires that female monogamy be dethroned as a scientific myth. Both the gendered story of monogamy and attempts to correct its very Victorian sensibilities about the desires of ladies and gentlemen are also racialized. Feminist histories of science have provided resources for understanding how these gendered scripts mark investments in whiteness.

The simultaneity of black slavery in European colonies and North America and the formation of biological sciences led to the emergence of a science of racial difference, which, through an analogizing logic, became deeply enmeshed with the science of sexual difference.[67] Those racial and sexual categories that continue to shape formations of racial and sexual differences—black and white, female and male, gay and straight—coevolved. Through analogizing logics, they gained evolutionary significance vis-à-vis one another. In a culture deeply invested in racialized gender norms that posited European ideals of masculinity and femininity as complementary halves, sexual differentiation became an exemplary measure of evolutionary superiority.[68] The more distinct from one another "male" and "female" bodies of a given race (or species) were described to be, the more evolved that population was imagined to be. Through this logic, racialized groups became sexual and gender deviants, and "masculinized," "feminized," or otherwise "ambiguous" "sexes" became racialized as inferior biological types.[69]

Vital to understanding discourses of monogamous and nonmonogamous difference is the critical insight that the co-constitution of categories of racial and sexual difference did not simply create a giant underclass of *not straight white propertied men*. It produced a multiplicity of complexly gendered types. It placed some "races" closer to the feminine end of the spectrum and others closer to the masculine end of the spectrum, producing a multiplicity of "abnormal," deviant genders—for example, hypersexualized and strong (read masculine) black women, dangerous black men, meek Asian women, sexually passive Asian men, and so on. As Sally Markowitz warns in "Pelvic Politics," when we talk about the reproduction of "the gender binary," we always risk reproducing whiteness, because gender was never binary, never just two.[70] In the case of the science of love, we have to ask, whom do we envisage spreading his seed around, whom do we imagine protecting hers? When we talk about species-beneficial mating behaviors, who is the desirably reproductive model for this vision of monogamic bliss? And in the case of challenging inversions of this evolutionary claim, who is the romanticized "other" who stands in for a nature outside of or before culture? I engage these questions directly in chapters 1, 2, and 3, and they provide the critical grounding of my return to the embodiment/materiality of monogamy in the book's final chapters.

Feminist engagements with science have offered important analyses of the racism inherent not only in the science of gender but also in the epistemological authority of science. Feminist science studies scholars have argued that we must acknowledge the cultural specificity (Euro-American) of the epistemic, taxonomic, and biomedical models with which we take issue.[71] This insight is at the heart of my project here, a project of articulating a critically engaged materialism that explicitly and concertedly resists reinvoking a universalizing metaphysics. To engage scientific stories and make use of them, as this book does, and as feminists are increasingly likely to do, need not mean retreat from critique of science's epistemic authority.

For decades feminist science studies scholars have sought to theorize new ways of imagining "objectivity" or new criteria for evaluating knowledges about the natural world. The highly influential and often overlapping concepts of "strong objectivity," "situated knowledge," "agential realism," and "contextual empiricism" fuel this discussion.[72] While the authors of these concepts are not always regarded as having similar aims, their visions of feminist science share common elements: a recognition that knowledge is partial, situated, not universal; a desire to lay bare the political effects of all scientific truth claims; and most important, some vision of what it might look like to politicize scientific knowledge production in a way that allows for an answerability, an accountability, beyond the realm of internal critique, that science as we know it lacks.[73]

The conceptual terrain of dialogue about feminist science over the years owes much to Sandra Harding's concept of "strong reflexivity," wherein the producers of knowledge see themselves as broadly accountable and are committed to considering the blind spots imposed by their specific social locations. This reflexivity is the precondition for what she calls "strong objectivity." Strong objectivity is contrasted to the "weak objectivity" that the sciences employ. According to Harding, objectivity in science is not weak because it is flawed in method or avoidably biased but rather because it starts, inevitably, from the questions, concerns, and interests of scientists (people) and the institutions of which they are a part. Strong objectivity on the other hand begins from the "standpoint" of the lives of the most marginalized. That is, it presumes not the essentially epistemically superior position of, say, women but rather the benefit of attempting to generate and approach questions from different vantage points, whoever the asker. The multiplicity of competing truths produced within primatology, for Haraway, exemplifies the range of situated knowledges science *could* produce; these competing narratives provide us with additional resources for imagining "human nature" and making the world differently. Haraway argues that even as we challenge and remake its contents, we need science, our myth, just as we need all of the other creative means we have at our disposal.[74]

Karen Barad, like Haraway, frames her critiques of the concept of objectivity in terms of resisting a problematic subject/object split. It is impossible, she argues, drawing heavily on physicist Niels Bohr, to distinguish the object of study from "the agencies of observation."[75] According to Bohr, there is no "observation independent object," there are only phenomena—observation is part of any phenomenon. Barad proposed the concept of "agential realism" as a way of resolving the tension set up between "realism" and "social constructivism" ("real" object and subjective observation). In so doing, she asks us to think of science as "material-discursive" practices.[76] In this formulation, objectivity and agency are bound up with responsibility and accountability: we, producers of knowledge, are thus bound to consider the possibilities—both enabling and violent—of interacting with the world by studying it. In this sense we become responsible not only for the knowledge we seek, but for what exists. My project is shaped by this feminist understanding of agency. I am concerned with the role played by naturalizing claims not only in representing monogamy and nonmonogamy but also in making them "real."

Helen Longino, like Barad, wants to foreground accountability as she proposes ways we might politicize the production of scientific knowledge. She argues that science should absolutely be expected to "reflect the deep metaphysical normative commitments of the culture in which it flourishes"[77]—this does not make science "bad." Criticism of the assumptions that underlie scientific inquiry and reasoning should thus be considered an appropriate, necessary part of science. Longino has grounded her own vision of feminist science in an explicit rejection of the good/bad science formulation on which the vision of expelling science's bias is premised. For Longino, among others, reading for androcentric bias is not enough. We have to look at conventions, like passive voice and attributing agency to data, as well as at interpretive frames that limit the possibilities for what we might come to know. We have to insist that the frameworks we use are always political choices, whether or not we see them as such, and that they do not in fact "emerge" from data. Ultimately, like Harding, Haraway, and Barad in their own ways, Longino insists that we have to acknowledge our agency and our role as knowledge producers in shaping the course of knowledge. In practice, this means "alter[ing] our intellectual allegiances."[78]

For Harding, the project of implementing strong objectivity cannot be assimilated into the logic of research or dominant philosophies of science; it would supplant science as we know it. For Haraway, we cannot implement such changes to science without changing our lives—we will be able to imagine the natural world differently when we are able to structure our own lives in ways that are not premised on a logic of domination. The new myths of the natural world we are able to create will in turn foster and support new worlds as our old science myths have done. Barad's vision of accountability has implications for the individual choices we make as knowledge producers, whereas Longino's vision requires that the material conditions of scientific knowledge production be concretely addressed. Despite their differences, together these epistemological interventions suggest the absolute centrality of the *politics* of science to its potential as a resource for feminism.

In recent years, a growing body of scholarship has endeavored to reclaim the biological for feminism. Richer understandings of the world might be gleaned, they suggest, by taking into account the processes of "the body" rather than positing cultural explanations as a totalizing substitute for biological ones. Much scholarship in this field-in-formation directly or indirectly highlights the ways the nature/culture binary has worked to delimit feminist and nonfeminist approaches to the body and invites us to reconsider what we think we know about what bodies are and how they work.[79] This scholarship's resonance is powerful, because experience, however complexly mediated, is deeply embodied, and because feminisms need theories of what we are and might become, theories that upset and reconfigure the naturalized categories that operate to delimit what we can say, think, and imagine for our futures. It is my contention that if these possibilities of biology are to be realized, they must be grounded in critical feminist genealogies and accountable to feminist insights about the politics of science.

On the Possibilities of Biology

How do we (feminists) talk about the biology of monogamy? What would it look like to take "the body" seriously as a queer feminist scholar of monogamy? Feminist endocrinologist and science studies scholar Deboleena Roy provocatively declared that the body to which feminists long to return "doesn't yet exist."[80] Roy makes a case for our agency in bringing into being that body, that nature, for which we long. In this section I address the importance of *critique*—and the sorts of critical interventions I reviewed in the previous section—to that project. I am particularly concerned with the importance of maintaining a critical perspective on the *politics of science* in attempts to theorize the naturecultural, material-semiotic coming-into-being of new ontologies. New materialist *engagements with matter* have often been articulated as a project in tension with *feminist critiques of science*.[81] I contend that this framing of feminist materialism is not only misleading (as others have argued), but an obstacle to bringing into being materialities with which we are willing to live, to paraphrase Roy. Haraway describes as "naturecultural" a world beyond the nature culture binary—a world in which what we have come to think of as nature and what we have come to think of as culture have coevolved together. This section reflects on the challenges of thinking natureculturally, and specifically the risks of slipping into a renaturalizing mode that resolves those challenges too easily. These risks and challenges are at the heart of the book's methodological innovation.

Indeed, across science and nonscience disciplines, the utility and accuracy of the conceptual distinction between "nature" and "culture" as discrete spheres or phenomena has been profoundly challenged. In recent years, a "new materialism" has been said to have emerged, one that treats nature as vital and complex.[82] Feminist theory has been a highly visible force in this reclaiming of matter. Even as attempts to do naturecultural research have been led by feminists—perhaps most famously Donna Haraway, Karen Barad, and Elizabeth Grosz—new materialism is often staged as an intervention in critical theory in general and in feminist theory in particular, rather than as part of those traditions.[83] Sara Ahmed launched a lively debate in and beyond the pages of the *European Journal of Women's Studies* in her impassioned intervention into new materialism's "founding gestures."[84]

Ahmed argued that the emergence of this field is animated by a discursive move in which feminists attempting to reclaim "biology" for feminism position themselves in opposition to the "anti-biologism" of feminism. In this early parsing of the field as a distinct feminist project, Ahmed named Elizabeth Grosz, Vicky Kirby, Susan Squire, and Elizabeth Wilson among the most important thinkers "gathering" around this move to recoup the biological for feminism.[85] She argued that this move relied on an unfair and inaccurate representation of feminism: "I want to consider what it means for it to be routine to point to feminism as being routinely anti-biological, or habitually 'social constructionist.' I examine how this gesture has itself been taken for granted, and how in turn that gesture both offers a false and reductive history of feminist engagement with biology, science and materialism, and shapes the contours of a field that has been called 'the new materialism.'"[86] In her response, Noela Davis argued that Ahmed's counterexamples actually illustrate the problem: the importing of an old materialism, a stable albeit misrepresented body, into feminist projects.[87] She insisted on the importance of taking feminism to task for critiquing science in such a way that biology and culture are allowed or made to seem separate.

I am indebted to insights on each side of this split and want to hone in on a slippage that I believe happens on *both sides*, making it difficult to chart a path that takes both sets of insights seriously. "Biology" refers here not to the science but rather to the body "itself." This slippage is important because it makes it appear as though the science of "biology" were an unmediated representation of "the body itself," a fallacy whose debunking is at the heart of feminist science studies.

In both Ahmed's assessment of new materialism and Davis's rebuttal, Elizabeth Wilson's work figures as an exemplary site of intervention into a feminist theory inhospitable to integration of the biological. In Ahmed's assessment, this supposed intervention names an "imaginary prohibition" against engaging biology. In Davis, Wilson's work articulates cogently a difficult and necessary intervention that Ahmed's "deflationary logic" obscures. As the framing of the relationship between feminism and materialism in Wilson's work has been such productive terrain for this debate, I return to two often-cited passages from her work and then back again to Ahmed's critique in order to illustrate this slippage on "both sides."

In the introduction to *Psychosomatic: Feminism and the Neurological Body*, Elizabeth Wilson asserted that "feminist theories have usually been reluctant to engage with *biological data*: they retain, and encourage, the fierce *anti-biologism* that marked the emergence of second wave feminism."[88] Here "anti-biologism" is the cause of feminist reluctance to engage with data. Feminist reluctance to engage with *data* is in fact well supported by feminist engagements with the processes by which it is produced, in feminist science studies. Yet the term "anti-biologism" suggests a reluctance to thinking about embodiment that obscures a long history of lively feminist debate about how to talk about the leaky, bleeding, desiring body.[89] In another frequently referenced passage, in the introduction to *Neural Geographies: Feminism and the Microstructure of Cognition*, Wilson referred to feminism's "distaste for biological detail," "despite an avowed interest in the body."[90] Here, "biological detail" takes on a very narrow meaning, one confined to the kind of *detail* only accessible through very specific scientific disciplinary approaches that privilege reductionist explanations over others. Bodies, then, are reduced to this detail through the positing of an inconsistency in an "avowed" commitment to the body and a "distaste" for data. In this move, feminist theories of embodiment and corporeality are represented as disingenuous—theories not really of the body but of something else, ostensibly the body's outside: culture. In this interchangeable use of "biological detail," "the body," and "biological data," there is no conceptual space for engaging feminist skepticism about *science* and its privileged epistemic status. All critiques of science are rhetorically subsumed into the category of "anti-biologism," where they serve as implicit evidence of the hypocrisy of feminist claims to care about the body.

At the same time, Ahmed's reclamation of those feminisms that she argues Wilson's interventions overlook does not resist this slippage but rather reiterates it. She points to examples of feminist health materials researched and disseminated in the 1970s and 1980s that drew directly on scientific research, as well as to feminist science studies scholars who helped to revise our biological knowledge. Both Wilson and Ahmed enact a slippage between biology as the *study of* the body—or the body produced in the context of scientific inquiry—and biology as "the body itself." With this slippage in mind, I argue that we must insist on some distinction between feminist critiques of *science* and feminist refusals to engage *the body* that are rightly critiqued by Wilson and others. This will necessitate drawing a distinction between "engaging data" and asking new questions about the body, and then carefully accounting for the interface between data and new modes of conceptualization. This will in turn necessitate a certain kind of resistance to disciplinary divides that despite the widespread institutionalization of some forms on interdisciplinarity remain quite fixed.

In this book, I seek to undiscipline approaches to bodies and make space for invention.[91] Key to this methodological intervention is the interruption of stories about a progression *from critique* (of politics) to *engagement* (with biology).

The slippage between the body (bodies?) and science is such an easy one to make because it emerges from disciplinary ways of knowing that have kept nature and culture separate and cultivated them as discrete disciplinary objects. Feminist critique enables the possibility of "new" sorts of engagements with and understandings of matter. We cannot afford to reduce feminist critiques of science to some flattened category of "social constructionism"—a now familiar narrative, summarily echoed by Stacy Alaimo and Susan Heckman in the introduction to their collection *Material Feminisms*: "Initially, feminist critiques of science focused on the androcentrism of science—the masculine constructions, perspectives, and epistemologies that structure scientific practice. Following the social studies of science, feminists argued that scientific concepts constitute the reality they study, that science, like all other human activities, is a social construction. Despite the persuasiveness of this position, however, questions began to arise about the viability of this approach."[92] This is a common progress narrative, telling as it does a story that takes us from the bad old days of feminist critiques of science to feminist new materialism.[93] We see here again that problematic slippage between science and its objects. Let me repeat a sentence: "Feminists argued that scientific concepts constitute the reality they study, that science, like all other human activities, is a social construction." What does it mean to say that scientific concepts "constitute the reality they study"? The reading of the insight that science is a representational practice, not a window on "nature itself," as a statement about the very existence of nature, is not a very accurate or helpful one. In the move to represent "feminist critique of science" as comment on the inherent nature of its object, a slippage occurs that reveals more about the politics of new materialist frames than about the "critics" from whom they ostensibly break.

The citational practices of many new materialist thinkers calls up a genealogy of European philosophers—beginning with Lucretius—invested in offering ultimately totalizing scientific explanations of the world and our place in it, toward the ultimate goal of replacing "god" as an explanatory regime.[94] Colored as it is by an implicitly Judeo-Christian worldview that allows us to imagine nature as law-governed and by an atheistic proto/modernity that separates the rational from the irrational, this genealogy is an uncomfortable one for a feminist materiality.[95] This narrow genealogy also comes at the expense of recognizing a breadth of resources we might cull in service of a radical materialist vision, some of which have been relegated to the status of "feminist antibiologism." We need our theories of the naturecultural world to be grounded in critical genealogies, such that we are thinking expansively about

TABLE I.1 Slippery Rhetorics of Nature and Culture

Object	Nature ("The body itself")	Culture ("Nature"/history/discourse/corporeality)
Disciplinary site	Science ("Scientific data")	Humanities (Theories of subjectivity and embodiment)

how to generate new approaches, spaces, and languages for representing it.[96] Rather than claiming the unreality of the world it seeks to know, critique of science problematizes the *special status* of scientific ways of knowing when and wherever knowledges can claim that status. If "nature"—in problematizing scare quotes—is in fact always already *culture*, as Vicki Kirby argued in her highly influential reading of Judith Butler,[97] then it would seem that removing the scare quotes has only returned us to a natureculture that was always already *nature*, the proper object of science. That is to say, if we run the risk of reducing the naturecultural to culture, as Kirby suggested, we run a similar risk of reducing it to nature.

Influenced as I have been by the pedagogies of science writing, I made a little chart to help map the persistent rhetorical conflation of natureculture's constitutive objects with the disciplinary homes to which they traditionally belong (table I.1). I map these distinctions because I am concerned with *what happens* in those moments when feminists trying to productively reimagine the world naturecultrally use "materiality," "matter," or "nature" or "the body" "itself" when they are actually referring to scientific data. These slippages between "the body" or "nature" and "science" constitute a conflation of objects and disciplines, or topics and methods, that paradoxically reinscribes the nature/culture binary with which we have long wrestled and which a *feminist* materialism ought to offer us new resources to navigate. The case for engaging scientific methodologies and ways of knowing *must be made* with regard to our queries about the naturecultural world, not presumed self-evident. And how we make that case matters. The increasingly axiomatic claim that we (feminists and/or humanists) must engage with "science" in order to bring the material body into our knowledge-making takes for granted that scientific data is the source of uniquely direct knowledge of vital bodies. It is my contention that we cannot productively engage data without explicit attention to the politics of *science*.

It is important to recall that the stories of the biosciences have been broadly and vigorously critiqued by academics and activists alike for abstraction, inaccuracy, and irrelevance with respect to illuminating questions of import about embodiedness.[98] Much of what we (I am most certainly including scientists here) *know* of our species-life, human interconnectedness with the nonhuman world, treatments for ailments, and the strange agencies of the nonanimal world has indeed been generated outside of laboratories and outside the province of "Science" with a capital *S*.[99]

Let me be clear that my perspective in this book is not that feminist uses of scientific concepts and/or data are to be avoided. It is, on the contrary, that nuanced and careful narratives about relationships between feminism, science, and the body enable the work of producing newly accountable knowledges about the materiality of the naturecultural world. We cannot develop new approaches when we are linguistically trapped by notions of disciplinary proper objects that continually dissolve "natureculture" back into *either* of its old constitutive parts. We need "critique" to help us remember that "the body" is *still not* "scientific data," nor is "biology" flesh "itself"; it is, rather, a field of study, a discipline, a discourse on the body, in Haraway's famous formulation.[100] The naturecultural world in its perpetual becoming is real. Sciences and the humanities offer a variety of tools—and, so importantly, not the only tools—for understanding, representing, and shaping our worlds.

Dyke Materializations

My aim in the book is to approach monogamy as a naturecultural object: one with histories, contexts of intelligibility, and embodied realities. This means first that monogamy's status as an object of scientific knowledge must not be taken for granted but rather situated in time. I do this in chapter 1, which offers a genealogy of the debate in turn-of-the-century sexology over whether or not monogamy was natural, showing that monogamy's twentieth-century status as a facet of human nature was ultimately dependent on the evidence of a colonial archive, which is thus the legacy of contemporary non/monogamy. In chapters 2 and 3 I examine competing contemporary stories about monogamy's nature. In chapter 2 I analyze the dominant narrative, that it is natural, and in chapter 3, that it is not (at least not for everyone). Chapter 2 is based on ethnographic fieldwork in a neuroscience laboratory on whose research reports of the discovery of a monogamy gene were based. This chapter demonstrates how assumptions about human monogamy are naturalized and shape notions of the normal (sexual/social/pair-bonded) and the abnormal (asexual/asocial/promiscuous) that are built into the modeling of gene-brain-behavior connections in contemporary neuroscience. In chapter 3 I examine feminist challenges to the prevailing naturalization of monogamy in the form of often quite marginalized claims about the naturalness of *nonmonogamy*. There I show how these stories present certain kinds of challenges to compulsory monogamy and at the same time leave intact many of the assumptions about sexuality, biology, and difference underlying the naturalization of monogamy. In chapter 4 I turn to lesbian feminism and develop a *dyke ethics* that engenders more nuanced thinking about both monogamy and embodiment. This dyke ethics considers monogamy and nonmonogamy within a broader schema of friendship and community valuation. It also supports a theoretical and ethical disposition of respect for the simultaneously political and embodied nature of desire.

The book's engagement with the politics of science and the naturecultural reality of desire culminates in a "re/turn" to the molecular "matter" of monogamy attuned to the multiplicity of modalities, methods, and systems for knowing bodies. That is to say, as it participates in the reimagining of ontology as open-ended "becoming," it refuses the *privileging* of the scientific body as a resource for that re-visioning.[101] In chapter 5 I read Audre Lorde's "Uses of the Erotic: The Erotic as Power" as a *biopossibility of the erotic* to "dis-organize" the non/monogamous body at the molecular level and to offer instead a vision of a materiality of human bodies that decenters sexuality, and even sociality, to make way for new forms of being and belonging.[102] Rather than asking how the science of monogamy might inform feminist engagements with it, the book draws on a wide range of insights and approaches to make sense of monogamy in ways that engender possibilities for materializations with which we can live.[103] In the epilogue, I consider the potential contributions of the book's engagements with monogamy to larger questions about possibilities for approaches to the material grounded in genealogies of radical critique: of the normal, of science, and of the idea that what exists is all there is.

1 MONOGAMY'S NATURE

Colonial Sexual Science and Its Naturecultural Fruits

> Creationists and evolutionists don't agree on much, but they both believe that monogamy is the most natural form of reproduction for the human species.
>
> **—John Witte Jr., "Why Monogamy Is Natural,"** ***Washington Post*****, October 2, 2012**

> A Martian zoologist visiting planet Earth would have no doubt: *Homo sapiens* carries all the evolutionary stigmata of a mildly polygamous mammal in which both sexes have a penchant for occasional "extra-pair copulations."
>
> **—David P. Barash, "Monogamy Isn't Easy, Naturally,"** ***Los Angeles Times*****, November 22, 2009**

> The emergence of sexuality as a possible candidate of scientific comprehensibility was *global* to begin with, and not a concealed Western project in which places of a distanced Other played no role in the early phases of its conceptual formation.
>
> **—Howard Chiang, "Historicizing the Emergence of Sexual Freedom" (2009)**

Even as monogamy enjoys the status of the normatively desirable, its *naturalness* is contested terrain. While Witte imagines human nature in harmony with the ideal of monogamy, evolutionary psychologist David Barash offers a counterpoint. Coauthor with psychiatrist Judith Lipton of *The Myth of Monogamy: Fidelity and Infidelity in Animals and People* (2002) and *Strange Bedfellows: The Surprising Connection between Sex, Evolution, and Monogamy* (2009), Barash speaks on behalf of those who argue against the idea that monogamy comes naturally to humans. Its merit as a social institution notwithstanding, humans—both male and female—he argues, are not by nature monogamous. These are more or less the sides in an increasingly popular multidisciplinary scientific debate about monogamy's nature—a debate in which questions about the efficacy of the institution of marriage, who should parent and how, and whether and to what extent participation in non- or extradyadic sexual relationships should be condemned loom large. Whatever the precise meaning evoked in the term's scientific deployment, the stakes of the debate over monogamy's naturalness are high.

This chapter is a genealogy of monogamy as an object of sexual scientific knowledge and is, as such, an exploration of "monogamy's nature." I read historic contest over monogamy's nature through the dependence of that debate on a colonial archive, that is to say, on knowledges of the cultures of colonized populations as evidence. The naturecultural fruit of this history, monogamy's nature must be understood as fundamentally entangled with the politics of race and nation. When we begin from data, the conditions of intelligibility for the measured bioscientific object "itself" are obscured. A queer feminist critical materialist approach to bodies requires a long memory.

Like contemporary discourses around heterosexuality, homosexuality, bisexuality, trans identities, intersex, and instinct itself, those on the nature of monogamy and nonmonogamy are prefigured in and enabled by late nineteenth- and early twentieth-century sexual science.[1] And like other European sexological knowledges of this era, as Chiang suggests in my third epigraph, the emergent debate over monogamy's naturalness was always transnational. Fin-de-siècle sexology marks a shift that characterizes twentieth-century thinking about sexuality as human nature—what Foucault called sexuality as the truth of the self.[2] The twentieth-century subject, Foucault famously remarked, is the sexual subject. Locating monogamy in late nineteenth- and early twentieth-century sexology can help us to understand how monogamy became sexuality and thus monogamy's importance to the modern self and to contemporary debates over monogamy's meanings.

Theorizing Monogamy in the History of Global Sexual Science

Scholars of the history of monogamy and marriage have shown that monogamy was well established as religious and legal doctrine early in the long nineteenth century.[3] By the early twentieth century, however, monogamy was understood not simply as marrying once or marriage to one partner, as its roots suggest, but rather as a manifestation or perversion of human nature.[4] The collusion of colonial political interests and their attendant imaginaries alongside the coterminous emergence of sexological authority created the conditions of possibility for imagining monogamy as a facet of human nature, and thus for a scientifically legitimated secularization of Christian marriage. That is to say, monogamy made a decided shift from being (just) a system of marriage endorsed, promoted, and policed by European legal and religious doctrine to an object with another kind of status. Specifically, it became an object of liberatory discourse that sought to free (natural) monogamy from (Christian) marriage. In this transition it retained every bit of its moral import, but discourses surrounding it began to take on the authoritative quality of *science*.

Rather than analyzing disparate local knowledges about monogamy and nonmonogamy, or when, where, and how European discourses around non/monogamy were embraced, resisted, or otherwise negotiated, I consider narratives about monogamy in canonical sexological texts produced in a world made global by colonial and imperial projects. Here I am concerned in particular with the global nature of the European sexological stories that have made debates about monogamy's nature scientifically intelligible.

As scholars of postcolonial sexuality studies—perhaps Ann Laura Stoler most famously—have by now established, the history of sexuality is also the history of colonization, and indeed, sexual sciences are deeply enmeshed with processes of racialization. Sexology must be understood as part of the colonial project and its experts' fantasies about geographically distanced Others as constitutive of its knowledges. I use the language of both Edward Said's concept of the imaginary and Joan Scott's concept of fantasy, the former to highlight the largely inventive nature of European projections onto the non-West, and the latter to gesture to the depth of investment in those fantasies about other lands and people.[5] It is not only racialized sexual knowledges but psychic investments in their reality that shape contest over monogamy's meaning in sexology. What the stories we tell about "them" enable "us" to imagine about ourselves lends those knowledges a certain "truthiness."[6] Indeed, European investments in both the patriarchal family and the egalitarian couple are at the heart of the imperial projects that constituted the context for the emergence of monogamy as a sexological object.

In *Imperial Leather* Ann McClintock contends that "after the 1850s, the image of a natural, patriarchal family, in alliance with pseudoscientific social Darwinism, came to constitute the organizing trope for marshaling a bewildering array of cultures into a single, global narrative ordered and managed by Europeans."[7] Hers is a powerful comment on the role of the patriarchal family in linking scientization, racialization, and domination. While it captures the integral importance of coupled forms of belonging to processes of colonization, her use of "pseudoscientific" suggests an instrumentalism in the deployment of scientific authority. From a science studies perspective, the distinction between "scientific" and "pseudoscientific" obscures the fact that science is always of culture. The use of "pseudoscience," in an effort to displace claims that harm, uses the same epistemic logic that gives these claims their power in the first place. In light of the epistemological interventions of science studies, I would revise McClintock's assessment slightly by saying that the image of the nuclear family—and sometimes an expressly *anti*patriarchal vision of it—in alliance with *the consolidation of epistemic authority within a paradigm of the scientific* not only contributed to but was *made possible by* this racist organizing trope (the marshalling of many cultures into a global narrative of difference to be controlled by Europeans). This flexible global narrative provided the substance of a usable colonial archive of evidence in service of a wide range of stories about sexuality.[8] In this subtle revision of McClintock's assessment of coupledom's import to nineteenth-century colonial projects, I suggest that the scientization of monogamy discourse is itself part of the problem and worthy of attention.

Foucauldian approaches to the history of sexuality alert us to the productive nature of contestations over the authority to define the normal and the abnormal, that is to say, over what counts as science.[9] Contest over what counts as "real science" also reifies a hierarchy of ways of knowing that has historically been deeply raced, classed, and gendered, in addition to being decidedly Eurocentric.[10] Sexological knowledge of the late nineteenth and early twentieth centuries was a mix of disciplinarily and generically diverse proclamations produced by a wide range of political actors with varied access to biomedical and scientific authority, due to training, gender, geography, and other mediating factors. Questions about what sexological knowledges *count*, when, where, and why, is part of the project of rendering intelligible a history of global sexual science. I am less concerned here with the various uses or epistemic specificity of "Western science," as such,[11] and more concerned with how monogamy was rendered a candidate for scientific knowability through an already global epistemic regime. Thus this project does not retroactively condemn or recuperate sexological discourses about monogamy as "good" or "bad," "true" or "biased," scientific or pseudoscientific but rather seeks to understand the conditions of their intelligibility *as science*.

European knowledge of geographically distanced Others forms the content of sexology's legitimation through scientization at the turn of the century, such that when we refer to the emergence of what we call "sexuality" we are referencing an "epistemic modernity" rendered through the evidence of a colonial archive.[12] The convergence of geographic and temporal alterities, where "other cultures" represent other times, Chiang argues, is the epistemic condition of possibility for the scientization of sexuality in disparate locales. I build on Chiang's "double alterity" here by exploring how the geographically distanced Other—specifically through anthropological accounts of marriage and sexual practices—comes to stand in for the imagined *evolutionary past* in sexological discourse on monogamy. It is by now well established that in European sciences of the nineteenth century "the term 'savage' signified not only the European in 'ancient' time, but also those peoples in the colonized world deemed to be the contemporary counterparts of those 'ancient savages.'"[13] The arrangement and rearrangement of bodies along a temporal trajectory from them/there to us/here was at the heart of the co-constitution of racialized and sexualized difference.[14] Whether that past comes to represent the distance the "we" of the texts have traveled or our true natures, access to that temporal other-as-evolutionary-evidence through colonial knowledge-making allowed debates about marriage practices and politics to gradually take on the valence of science.

In the two sections that follow, I read monogamy discourse in the major works of two important sexologists widely acknowledged as key figures in the making of a science of sexuality: Richard von Krafft-Ebing and Havelock Ellis. Krafft-Ebing's and Ellis's works have become paradigmatic examples of the import of European sexology for contemporary sexual subjectivities.[15] Focusing in particular on the opening pages of Krafft-Ebing's *Psychopathia Sexualis* and Ellis's *Studies in the Psychology of Sex*, volume 6, *Sex in Relation to Society*, I trace monogamy discourse in their respective works to locate monogamy within the historiography of sexual science. I focus on the narratives that emerge about monogamy in these texts, and on key aspects of the contexts that constituted their intelligibility, rather than focusing on the tellers themselves.[16] That is to say, while their positioning as pivotal figures in the history of sexuality matters, I sideline specific questions of authorship, intent, and consistency in argumentation to focus instead on the kinds of stories they tell about monogamy. My analysis is concerned in particular with what this "archive of discourse" can tell us about the scientization of monogamy.[17]

My reading is shaped by a Foucauldian paradigm in which "liberation" and "pathologization" are not opposites but rather co-constitutive discourses that produce us as sexual subjects. That is to say, claims about whether or not, or to what degree, human nature is monogamous share in common epistemic conditions of intelligibility. These conditions include the convergence of temporal and geographic otherness that allowed claims about marriage practices and sexual mores across cultures to stand in as evolutionary claims. In Krafft-Ebing, monogamous marriage marks the superiority of "Christian nations." In Ellis the capacity to redefine monogamy in accord with nature, not Christian doctrine, marks the superiority of "civilized races." In both cases, monogamy is bound up in implicitly and explicitly racialized notions of superiority, utterable within the cultural, political, and economic logics that animate a colonial worldview. This pair of discursive moves both establishes its own authority from within the logic of colonial discourse and bolsters that discourse by lending it greater scientific relevance and credibility.

"Especially Islam": On the Importance of Christian Monogamy

The content of Krafft-Ebing's *Psychopathia Sexualis* has received a great deal of attention for the work his categories of perversion do to render the modern sexual subjects that shape contemporary understandings of sexuality.[18] While his case studies are indeed rich, far too little attention has been paid to their framing. In the book's opening pages Krafft-Ebing mobilizes the vague specter of "Islam" repeatedly to establish the "we" of the text. "We"—the Christian nations—are monogamous. Monogamy is what separates "us" from "them." In *Psychopathia Sexualis*'s English-language translations, monogamy is the national characteristic that separates the civilized from a generic racialized Other, and "especially" from Islam. Islam stands in as an exemplary threat to a "Christian" worldview and way of life; *Christianity* stands in for whiteness, Europeanness, and modernity.[19]

To elucidate the work of the "especially" in Krafft-Ebing's formulation, I draw on Fernando Bravo López's tracking of early twentieth-century uses of the term "Islamophobia." López argues that these early uses offer a way of thinking about the ambiguities and flexibility of the phenomena to which this term refers today: racism, religious intolerance, and/or fear of religion in the public sphere. According to López, in their work *Le pelierinage a la maison sacree d'Allah* (*The Pilgrimage to the Sacred House of Allah*, 1930), Etienne Dinet and Silman ben Ibrahim describe two aspects of "Islamophobia"—"pseudo-scientific" (racial) and "clerical" (religious), united by a common conception of Islam as an enemy and threat to Christianity that must be fought.[20] These two conceptions work in concert—as "Islamophobia"—to vilify Muslims as a monolithic and threatening type. Indeed eugenic concerns with the future of the race ("pseudo-scientific") and concerns with Christian morality ("clerical") are "married" in sexology by a naturalization of Christian mores through a discourse of sexual selection: where the stakes of heterosexual courtship are precisely the eugenic *quality* of the next generation.[21] The melding of these racial and religious meanings into one salient signifier—"Islam"—in sexological discourse both serves to legitimate sexual science as part of the imperial project and in turn adds epistemic weight to its endeavors through a scientization of its imaginaries.

In her illuminating essay "Not a Translation but a Mutilation," Heike Bauer observes that much of the explicitly sociobiological and nationalistic language found in English-language translations of *Psychopathia Sexualis* reflects the context of British imperialism.[22] This is vitally important context for my reading. The English translation certainly had a life of its own and indeed had an imperial political life that exceeded the possibilities of its original German content. The language of "degeneracy" and "colonisation" that spatter the translations must be read in the context of British and U.S. imperialism that produced them and in which both Ellis's work and Krafft-Ebing's translations were circulating in the English-speaking world in the first decades of the twentieth century. And still the English translation cannot be fully appreciated without reference to the German text and context. Frequent mentions of Islam recall Germany's colonial relationship to Turkey and to the Ottoman Empire and indeed how Krafft-Ebing imagined the project of sexology and its stakes vis-à-vis those relationships. Likewise, although his ideas on those stakes may be overemphasized in translation, many of Krafft-Ebing's core concepts—like the heritability of dispositions toward sexual anomalies—were Darwinian ideas, and he was indeed seen by contemporaries as a subscriber to Darwinian evolutionary theories.[23] This context reminds us not only that Krafft-Ebing's categories and cures were not innocent of the imperial implications of their English language translations, but specifically that generative deployments of "Islam" were present in the original volume and have deep roots in anthropological thought on sexuality. Sir Richard F. Burton, for example, included most of the Muslim world in his "sotadic zone" of sexual inversion.[24] Indeed, Islam has long been used as an exemplar of sexual otherness.[25]

In the opening pages of *Psychopathia Sexualis*, Krafft-Ebing uses the specter of Islam to operationalize monogamy as the distinguishing feature between the subjects of sexual science for whom sexual normality (and pathology) are even possible from the necessarily degenerate. Connections established among Christianity, monogamy, and whiteness form the foundation for Krafft-Ebing's readers' subsequent understanding of deviant desiring and, importantly, the stakes of its study. He states: "The love of man, if considered from the standpoint of advanced civilization, can only be of a monogamic nature. . . . From the moment when woman was recognised the peer of man, when monogamy became a law and was consolidated by legal, religious and moral considerations, the Christian nations attained a mental and material superiority over the polygamic races, and especially over Islam."[26]

Krafft-Ebing makes two important distinctions here. He separates "the love of man" from that of animals and, among men, "advanced civilization" from the rest of humankind. He understands *civilized* human love as romantic love between men and women, positing heterosexual monogamy as the normal sexuality against which all other desire is construed as perversion. This passage places monogamy at the heart of a theory of European superiority. The juxtaposition of the categories "Christian nations" and "polygamic races" designates polygamy as a naturalized racial characteristic and situates the Christian nation as a stand-in for monogamy and racelessness, or whiteness.[27] Polygamy is represented both as a marriage practice allowed by Islam and prohibited by Christianity *and* as a manifestation of atavistic sexual tendencies of the biologically inferior. This seeming conflict between cultural and biological explanations for real and imagined differences reflects and invigorates an emerging scientization that links the social and the biological in ways that support social control as a means of bettering the race, and biomedical intervention as a means of improving society. As we turn later to the politics of contemporary stories about monogamy's nature, we must remember that biological determinism is not the only legacy of race science. It is the flexible invocation of nonmonogamous peoples/practices/religions that opens *Psychopathia Sexualis* that marks it as a project of empire and in so doing establishes it as a work of political consequence.

The work monogamy does to legitimate sexology is evidenced in another passage in the book's opening pages, wherein Krafft-Ebing invokes one of the most powerfully Orientalizing images of Empire: the harem.[28] "The Mohammedan woman," he says, "is simply a means for sensual gratification and the propagation of the species; whilst in the sunny balm of Christian doctrine, blossom forth her divine virtues and her qualities of house wife, companion and mother. What a contrast! Compare the two religions and their standard of future happiness. The Christian expects a heaven of spiritual bliss absolutely free from carnal pleasure; the Mohammedan an eternal harem, a paradise among lovely houris."[29] The use of "Mohammedan" has served historically to construct distance between Christianity and Islam. As opposed to translations of Allah as "God," which situates both religions as monotheistic believers in one god, the use of "Mohammedan" is a rhetorical move that situates Muslims as followers of the prophet Mohammed *rather than* subscribers to a belief in God.[30] This use of language contributed to perceptions of Islam as a threat to Christianity and helped intensify missionary zeal for converting Muslims, which in turn fueled "civilizing" projects in Egypt, the Sudan, Libya, Morocco, Syria, Lebanon, Palestine, and Iraq. This idea of the harem in the afterlife is a very old and still vitally productive stereotype of Muslim identity.[31] It has served to construct Muslim men as naïve, superstitious, licentious, and dangerous while relegating Muslim women to the status of passive victim.[32] This type of "Orientalist Islamophobia," as Ramon Grosfoguel and Eric Mielants point out, was and is always undergirded by an epistemic racism that positions as reliable knowers "an artillery of experts, advisers, specialists, officials, academics, and theologians that keep talking about Islam and Muslim people despite their absolute ignorance on the topic," while other "epistemologies and cosmologies are subalternized as myth, religion, and folklore."[33]

In the introduction to *Psychopathia Sexualis* the story of monogamy is plainly racialized and overtly hierarchical. The modern "we" is monogamous. The premodern figures of the licentious, superstitious, and barbaric Mohammedan man, his "lovely houris," and his poor wives are the foils that render the stakes of the sexological project plain. Monogamous modernity is civilized, egalitarian, and oriented toward "progress." Turn-of-the-century Islamophobia, marrying as it did scientific and cultural discourses of difference, made "Islam" an *especially* flexible and generative tool for legitimating sexology as science through its positioning as a nation- and empire-building project that separates colonizing from colonized populations as ostensibly distinct types: Christian nations and polygamic races.

Despite the text's powerful racialization of monogamy and mobilization of cultural investments in defending it, and even as the text plays a vital role in establishing the importance of Christian monogamy as marker of superiority and mechanism of colonial change, its formulations are haunted by an empirical problem: the problem of Christian polygamy. At the end of the book's first (and lengthy) footnote, Krafft-Ebing briefly acknowledges this empirical inconsistency in the tidy schema that juxtaposes "Christian nations" and "polygamic races." He says: "Polygamy, which is distinctly recognised in the Old Testament . . . is nowhere in the New Testament definitely prohibited. In fact many Christian princes (*e.g.* the Merovingian kings: Chlotar I., Charibert I., Pippin I. and other Frankish nobles) indulged in polygamy without a protest being raised by the Church at the time."[34] The existence of Christian polygamy was widely known and therefore necessary for Krafft-Ebing to acknowledge, but its implications for his argument are nowhere elaborated. This fissure makes the ideal of Christian marriage visible. It lays bare investments underlying the colonial politics of monogamy and attendant claims about difference. But later this visibility is obscured by a process of secularization through scientization that consolidates such challenges within its logic. In Ellis we see a reemergence of these categories of "monogamy," "polygamy," "Christianity," and "civilization" in a distinctly and authoritatively scientific narrative.

Projections onto the Ostrich: On the Importance of Natural Monogamy

Unlike Krafft-Ebing, Ellis and his translators are often framed as progressive social actors, using sexology to undermine rather than police the status quo. Ellis's celebrated activism, interdisciplinarity, and objectivity are often contrasted with characterizations of sexologists like Krafft-Ebing whose writings were both explicitly pathologizing and arguably less popularly accessible in their day.[35] Indeed Ellis, alongside thinkers like Emma Goldman, Friedrich Engels, and Edvard Westermarck, is remembered as an advocate of "free love"—that is, the liberation of coupled love from its institutionalization in Christian marriage and state regulation. Ellis's reputation as a radical thinker and in particular the importance of his marriage to a lesbian, Edith Lees, to the historiography of his sexological thought undoubtedly shapes my reading. In this sense, my engagement with Ellis's treatment of monogamy might be described as something of a "disappointing" archival encounter.[36] I had hoped to find more critical resources for undoing monogamy in the pages of his books. Instead, I came to see the colonial logics that linked politically oppositional sexological stories about monogamy's nature.

In Ellis, the temporal and geographic construction of monogamous and nonmonogamous types that emerges in Krafft-Ebing is reimagined. Ellis achieved this departure not by challenging the idea of monogamous and nonmonogamous types but through a deepening of the scientization of monogamy. To imagine, as Krafft-Ebing's formulation did, that polygamy is safely contained "there" and "then," is, in Ellis, to refuse to see the truth of sexuality:

> It must be said that the natural prevalence of monogamy as the normal type of sexual relationship by no means excludes variations, indeed it assumes them. The line of nature is a curve that oscillates from side to side of the norm. Such oscillations occur in harmony with changes in environmental conditions and no doubt with peculiarities of personal disposition. . . . In those parts of the world in which polygamy is recognised as a permissible variation a man is legally held to his natural obligations towards all his sexual mates and towards the children he has, by those mates. In no part of the world is polygamy so prevalent as in Christendom; in no part of the world is it so easy for a man to escape the obligations incurred by polygamy. . . . Our polygamy has no legal existence. The ostrich, it was once imagined hides his head in the sand and attempts to annihilate the facts by refusing to look at them; but there is only one known animal which adopts this course of action and it is called Man.[37]

At the end of this wordy passage on non/monogamy Ellis offers an evocative enlightenment metaphor—we, humans, exercise a willful ignorance about reality. He captures the will to this metaphorical blindness not only in the image of heads in the sand but also in his corrections regarding the scientifically inaccurate projection of denial onto the ostrich. What distinguishes the ethical from the unethical here is "truth." When we acknowledge the existence in nature of deviations from monogamy, then we must account for them in our systems of recognition, he argues, lest they lead to harm. It is in "Christendom," therefore, where the valuation of monogamy as an ideal leads man to ignore its "variations," that "polygamy" is threatening. Ellis's critique recasts traditional Christian monogamy as clandestine polygamy, a familiar strategy among free love advocates. While the bodies to whom the stigma is attached has shifted, the affective power of this rhetorical strategy relies in part on the widespread racialization of polygamy of the sort found in *Psychopathia Sexualis*.[38]

Ellis's statements about monogamy and marriage, not only across his career but even within *The Psychology of Sex*, are eclectic. What remain consistent are his sense of the importance of marriage and his commitment to understanding its grounding in human nature as distinct from its institutionalization in law. Bringing law and social mores surrounding monogamy into harmony with nature was an important project for Ellis, and one that was dependent on his expert authority. Rather than reading Ellis's words here as (just) a radical intervention in the sort of Christian pro-monogamy discourse found in Krafft-

Ebing—as a liberatory, social constructionist, or interdisciplinary departure from approaches that pathologize nonmonogamy—I read them as part of a complex renegotiation of the meaning of monogamy.

Ellis's work performs and reveals a process of secularization—through scientization—of monogamy, where the authority to define it shifts from the church and state to the expert discourse of science. This secularization is part of a much more widespread epistemic and cultural shift, in keeping with the economic demands of nineteenth-century liberalism. It is also part of a process of rendering implicitly Christian religious values invisible as part of the fabric of modern secular-scientific epistemic regimes. The meaning of monogamy for Ellis is not, as it is for Krafft-Ebing, Christian religious doctrine enshrined in law. For Ellis, this is not true or natural monogamy, and natural monogamy cannot exist under the tyranny of its rule. The monogamy enshrined in law and claimed as Christian is, according to Ellis, a primitive monogamy: "The marriage which grew up among animals by heredity on the basis of natural selection, and which has been continued by the lower human races through custom and tradition, by the more civilized races through the superimposed regulative influence of legal institutions, has been marriage for the sake of the offspring. Even in civilized races among whom the proportion of sterile marriages is large, marriage tends to be so constituted as always to assume the procreation of children and to involve the permanence required by such procreation."[39] This primitive monogamy was the natural state of animals and "lower races," where "marriage" had the sole purpose of producing and facilitating the survival of offspring. Among "civilized races," however, marriage exceeded procreative functionality, as a project of personal fulfillment and self-actualization. This distinction rendered regulative demands for monogamy anachronistic and decidedly premodern.

Ellis conceded that other scholars of sexuality had rightly recognized in human nature the impulses that gave rise to the ideal of monogamy enshrined in law and custom.[40] He then parted ways from the consensus that Christian marriage was the natural expression of our nature, arguing that we mistakenly conflated those natural impulses with an ethics of regulation: "It is necessary to bear in mind that the conclusion that monogamic marriage is natural, and represents an order which is in harmony with the instincts of the majority of people, by no means involves agreement with the details of any particular legal system of monogamy. Monogamic marriage is a natural biological fact, alike in many animals and in man. But no system of legal regulation is a natural biological fact."[41] While in Krafft-Ebing we encounter a narrative in which civilization required the institution of monogamy to control base instincts and the institution made Europeans superior, in Ellis we find a narrative that suggests that our nature is self-regulating and that the superiority of the civilized lies not in their systems of formal governance but in their nature: "Under free and natural conditions the inner impulse tends to develop itself, not licentiously but with its own order and restraints, while, on the other hand, our inherited regulations are largely the tradition of ancient attempts to fix and register that natural order and restraint. The disharmony comes in with the fact that our regulations are traditional and ancient, not our own attempts to fix and register the natural order but inextricably mixed up with elements that are entirely alien to our civilised habits of life."[42]

Here, it is precisely the civilized nature of European subjects—subjects of Christian Nations—that makes the lifting of the "archaic" laws governing marriage not only safe but also ethical. Indeed, sexologists did not see all peoples as disposed to this sort of self-regulation. Some, Ellis explained, had no concept of love: "Some savage races seem to have no fundamental notion of love, and (like the American Nahuas) no primary word for it, while, on the other hand, in Quichua, the language of the ancient Peruvians, there are nearly six hundred combinations of the verb *munay*, to love. Among some peoples love seems to be confined to the women."[43] This highly gendered assessment of capacities for "love" invoked both the sexual double standard in the West and that common theme in turn-of-the-century colonial discourse, the brutishness of "primitive" masculinity. Among men, the kind of sensitivity required to navigate complex monogamy, unregulated by the state, was clearly the province of Europeans. In late nineteenth-century sexual science (well-to-do) European men were understood to possess a unique capacity for "sympathy," an affective state said to enable an actor to "transform basic impulses of pleasure or pain into a moral feeling that considers the social good."[44] The apex of evolutionary development, this notion of "sympathy" suggested a raced and gendered taxonomy of the capacity to practice free love.

In Ellis, designations of superiority and inferiority were not simply mapped onto "Christian nations" and "polygamic races"; rather, ever-proliferating categories, which recalled those divisions, became more deeply scientized. They were no longer couched in the moralizing language of Christianity; rather, the differences that were used to distinguish them emerged as a priori meaningful scientific categories. They became differences in biology, couched in a language of critical distance, rather than impassioned political motivation. These differences in nature suggested the need for different approaches to the governance of different raced and gendered human types. Ellis was a staunch advocate of the idea that monogamy was the height of evolutionary development and of the position that among the civilized, "the love relationship" must be free and unconstrained by law. On the other hand he is also well known as an advocate of the state's right and responsibility to control procreation.[45] The need for governance over procreation was in fact quite urgent and the stakes high for Ellis, as for many social reformers of his day.

The strong eugenic flavor of Ellis's approach to procreation was bolstered by his authoritative redeployment of stories about the geographically distanced Other to construct a new evolutionary story wherein Christian monogamy was *not* the apex of human development. In a dense passage worth citing at length, Ellis rewrote the dominant teleology that imagines human evolution as a march of progress from promiscuity to Christian marriage and replaced it with a more nuanced narrative. Rejecting, too, the story that higher primates, including humans, are and always have been monogamous, Ellis displaced strict monogamy's place in the evolutionary schema:

> Some assume a primitive promiscuity gradually modified in the direction of monogamy; others argue that man began where the anthropoid apes left off, and that monogamy has prevailed, on the whole, throughout. Both these opposed views, in an extreme form, seem untenable, and the truth appears to lie midway. It has been shown by various writers, and notably Westermarck . . . that there is no sound evidence in favor of primitive promiscuity, and that at the present day there are few, if any, savage peoples living in genuine unrestricted sexual promiscuity. . . . On the other hand, it can scarcely be said that there is any convincing evidence of primitive strict monogamy beyond the assumption that early man continued the sexual habits of the anthropoid apes. It would seem probable, however, that the great forward step involved in passing from ape to man was associated with a change in sexual habits involving the temporary adoption of a more complex system than monogamy. It is difficult to see in what other social field than that of sex primitive man could find exercise for the developing intellectual and moral aptitudes, the subtle distinctions and moral restraints, which the strict monogamy practiced by animals could afford no scope for.[46]

In this new narrative, animality was characterized not by promiscuity but by *strict monogamy*. Ellis's position that a freer system than strict monogamy was appropriate to civilized races is couched here in an evolutionary narrative suggesting that simple monogamy, of the type erroneously enshrined in religious and legal doctrine, is not only evidence of lower functioning, but indeed itself maladaptive. In this scientific formulation, marriage's separation from the simple demands of reproduction led to the development of the aptitudes we use to measure the distance between human and nonhuman animals. In other words, natural monogamy is not just *evidence* of evolutionary superiority, it is in fact its cause.

This shift constituted a scientific reversal of the moral order familiar in Krafft-Ebing. Here "complexity" was valued as both mechanism and evidence of humanness, and simple or strict monogamy stood in for rote reproductivity, the animal, and the inferior. Drawing extensively on ethnographic and historical works, Ellis rewrote pathologizing narratives about the sexual mores of geographically distanced Others as stories of complex systems from which Christian nations should endeavor to learn. For example:

> Mainly under the influence of the early English missionaries who held ideas of theoretical morality totally alien to those of the inhabitants of the islands, the Tahitians have become the stock example of a population given over to licentiousness and all its awful results. . . . It is noteworthy also, that, notwithstanding the high importance which the Tahitians attached to the erotic side of life, they were not deficient in regard for chastity. . . . The Tahitians were brave, hospitable, self-controlled, courteous, considerate to the needs of others, chivalrous to women, even appreciative of the advantages of sexual restraint, to an extent which has rarely, if ever, been known among those Christian nations which have looked down upon them as abandoned to unspeakable vices.[47]

This renarrativizing of the evolution of monogamy through a revision of prevailing assumptions about the sexual mores of the temporally/geographically distanced Other indeed destabilizes a powerful narrative of monogamy as sign and symbol of European superiority. It seems to contradict the logic of empire—where Europe civilizes its Others. At the same time, it functions not as a rejection of epistemic racism but as a *corrective* to negative racialized stereotypes that lends further credibility to the epistemic frames that give colonialism its power. Historian David Ludden reminds us that Orientalism is a system of knowledge that *makes knowable*, not to be confused with negative representation.[48] Similarly, science studies scholar Jennifer Reardon argues, but with special reference to *scientific* knowledge about race, that rather than celebrating as "true" those declarations that seem to represent the freeing of science from racial ideology, we should read all scientific pronouncements as Foucauldian "statements" that only make sense or gain support if they function within the moral, political, economic, and epistemological frames of the dominant society. So any and all scientific statements about the nature of difference should be read as part of the consolidation of authority to explain the nature and significance of difference.

Monogamy emerges as part of human nature, as an object for science, through the deployment of "expertise"—both pathologizing and recuperative—about the geographically/temporally distanced Other. Ellis's monogamy is not the colonial monogamy of Krafft-Ebing, relegating nonmonogamy to the evolutionary past, as represented by the licentiousness of "polygamic races." Ellis's complex monogamy is similarly couched in the language of evolutionary development, but unmoored from simple hierarchies. Ellis's monogamy remains an important factor distinguishing "us" from "them," albeit with a looser take on who might occupy those categories. Those individuals and populations for whom the practice of coupling constitutes more than a system for procreative efficiency are practitioners of a modern form of monogamy that requires and reflects "civilized" capacities. The secularization of Christian monogamy into a form of modern monogamy appropriate to civilized human developmental capacities places monogamy at the heart of negotiations of racial and national hierarchies.

Sexology, Evolutionism, and the Making of Monogamy's Nature

My readings of Krafft-Ebing and Ellis suggest the importance of evolutionary thinking to the secularization of monogamy. The rhetoric of evolution was essential to monogamy's becoming as a scientific object, something about which we might know, objectively, rather than the rule of Christian moral codes or state laws, with their obviously political interests in controlling subjects. Discourses of evolutionism in sexology—sometimes implicit, other times quite direct—produce developmental logic as foundational to our understanding of what sexuality is. Whether the polymorphous perversity of early childhood or the immodesty of early man, the fantasy of sexuality outside culture and history is the fantasy of a temporal before. Sometimes these discourses seem to celebrate the victory of "our" distance from the most base animal instincts. Sometimes they suggest the wisdom, in measure, of acknowledging this animality in our nature, and rethinking social norms accordingly. They often share in common reference to an evolutionary temporality that situates a nondyadic sexuality—whether construed as promiscuous barbarism or complex freedom—in the evolutionary past. Sexologists accessed what they took to represent the evolutionary past through historical, anthropological, and lay observations, by Europeans, of geographically distanced Others. Hence colonial imaginaries were not only apparent in the rhetoric of sexological discourses on monogamy, but were indeed the evidentiary condition of possibility for monogamy's scientization.

The evolutionary temporality imagined by Krafft-Ebing's positioning of monogamy as superior to the systems of social belonging represented in his and his readers' fantasies of Islam,[49] and by Ellis's reversal, which situates true monogamy as the nature of the civilized and its pretense in Christian marriage as an artifact of a backward time, enables monogamy to become an object of science and of scientific debate. In other words, racialized fantasies of the temporally distanced Other ground the naturalization of monogamy as a facet of human nature. Importantly, in moments where that temporality is disrupted, we see discourses that might challenge the naturalization of monogamy consolidated within the expert's discourse. The epistemic authority of the sexologist to define what is natural depends on and reconsolidates that of the scientist more generally to explain difference. Monogamy discourse in Krafft-Ebing reveals the importance of sexology's framing as a project of empire to its emerging legitimacy. Monogamy discourse in Ellis illustrates a definitive secularization of monogamy, one that scientizes existing associations between "monogamy" and developmental superiority.

The formation of evolutionism's temporal imaginaries in the nineteenth-century biosciences consolidated conflicting ideas about the nature and meaning of human difference within a racialized conception of human nature as progressing. The shift from polygenism to monogenism required a reconciliation of the new idea that we all share an evolutionary starting point with the old and deeply entrenched belief that human difference—real and imagined—is best understood as hierarchical. The two came together in an understanding of human types as representative of disparate points on a developmental *continuum*.[50] Science's task, then, was to explain not only how humans evolved from animals but also how Europeans evolved from other human types.[51] Sexology validated both the logic and substance of race science in its conflicting accounts of monogamy's nature.

The Fruits of History: Toward a Naturecultural Monogamy

Entangled in these debates over whether or not monogamy is natural, haunted as they are by their colonial legacies, are questions about how we understand embodiment. These questions tend to presume that a normative value is either natural and thus biologically wired in some fashion or, conversely, "merely cultural" and thus imposed on bodies, which operate more or less as canvases for scripts of power. A few words from one of Ellis's popular essays read through the lens of a twenty-first-century queer feminist science studies suggest the importance of history to a naturecultural reading of monogamy, that is, one attuned to both *the politics of science* and *the possibilities of biology*. Through this lens, the final lines of Ellis's essay "Marriage and Divorce" offer a fruitful metaphor for conceptualizing the entanglements of racism, sexism, and desire. They read: "The work of marriage in the world must depend entirely on the nature of that world. . . . Do not expect to pluck figs from thistles. As a society is, so will its marriages be."[52]

This deceptively simple passage does two things that interest me here. First, it troubles a bit the myth of science and religion as opposed and competing epistemic regimes—a central premise underlying scientific claims about monogamy's nature as distinct from Protestant claims about monogamy's morality. The popular biblical reference evokes a tension in the midst of these marriage reformers' rigorously scientized accounts, aimed at wresting the institution from the stronghold of Christian governance. The botanical metaphor is from Mathew 7:16. The King James Version reads: "Ye shall know [true prophets] by their fruits. Do men gather grapes of thorns, or figs of thistles?" In this passage, we can tell a true prophet from a false one by his teachings and behavior—we should not simply trust his claim but determine his authenticity on the basis of our own observations. *Fruit* serves as the evidence of the bearing plant's true nature. We know a grapevine or a fig tree by their sought-after fruits and could never mistake them for thorns or thistles, which bear no fruit at all. Christianity is not without its rules of evidence, nor science without its "Gods in the gaps"—and, most important, the contexts out of which their utterances flower, in any given age, are the same conditions of intelligibility. Not surprisingly, at the turn of the twenty-first century, God and Darwin tend to agree that we were made to marry, whether or not we engage in the occasional extra-pair copulation. In a neoliberal world characterized by the privatization of wealth and care, what other fruits might we expect to pluck?

This rhetorical query leads me to the main reason these lines captured my interest. In the midst of so much attention to the need to liberate the natural from the constraints of social rules, the claim about marriage's relationship to its contexts in these lines lends itself to naturecultural reflections on the complexity of monogamy. In his more literal prose, which I have critiqued in some detail, Ellis says that monogamy is natural and marriage is not, or that natural marriage is not the same thing as its legal institutionalization, which perverts that nature. In this fig-marriage metaphor, however, nature and society are not so separate. The wording suggests that different models of marriage—free and Christian we can presume—are the fruits of wholly different plants. What we desire is the fig-marriage, and the plants from which we are trying to extract that ideal simply cannot yield it. The plant is not biology but rather "the world." The separation of "world" and "society" lends itself to a reading of "world" as something more than either nature or culture. "The world" here might stand in for the dense entanglements that constitute the conditions of possibility for the growth of as yet unrealized forms of relating. Another plant/world could, the author suggests, yield the fruit of free love (the form for which he makes an ethical case through sexual science). From another angle, we can tell from the fruit-marriage we have that the bearing world/society is not a metaphorical fig tree. But the metaphor itself is still richer. Both types of marriage are fruit, neither more natural than the other.

Not natural or unnatural in this metaphor, marriage is both real and located. Not seed nor roots but fruit, always fruit. Fruit, which materializes only if and when conditions are right. Fruit, which varies in size and shape and sweetness and nutritive properties, depending on those conditions. Fruit that in different contexts yields different values and different uses. A staple or delicacy. A treat, a tonic, or a poison. Monogamous marriage is not one thing. If we turn from a biblical reading, where the fruit is the evidence that reveals the plant, to examine *the plant* in order to more carefully consider what we might make of the fruits or flowers it bears, we must turn to history. The compulsory coupling to which we are heirs certainly intimates marriage's haunted history, from its institutionalization of women's subordination to men to its place in the making of capitalist forms and to its use as a tool by which to separate citizen/subjects (white, propertied, straight) from their Others in any given moment.

Monogamy's nature has an important genealogy in late nineteenth- and early twentieth-century sexual science. Tracing this particular archive of discourse reveals the racial underpinnings of monogamy's nature. When monogamy appears in turn-of-the-century European sexology, it emerges as a contested facet of nature with which our individual and collective engagement is of paramount importance. It is through monogamy's explicit association with the politics of European nationalist and imperialist aims that it becomes sexuality, not just a descriptor of marriage forms but a characteristic of individuals, populations, and species.[53] It is thus through this lens that monogamy is figured as natural. It is through this same lens that monogamy is figured as *unnatural* and challenging it on those grounds is imagined as a liberatory project of modernity.

If we return to the fig metaphor, we might conclude that monogamy is neither natural nor unnatural but rather a familiar fruit, plucked of thistle. The thistle is not degeneracy, excess, or the sublime romance of sexual selection: it is "the world." The world of stories and serotonin, guts and ghosts, histories and hearts. Out of this haunted history,[54] entangled as it is with the potentiality of bodies and the limits of intelligibility, the fruits of monogamy and nonmonogamy are borne.

2 MAKING THE MONOGAMOUS HUMAN

Mating, Measurement, and the New Science of Bonding

> My research is really trying to understand the social brain, what makes us want to engage in social interactions and form social relationships. The way that I've been going about doing that is by studying these interesting little rodents called prairie voles . . . and what makes them so interesting is that, like people, they are monogamous.
>
> **—Larry J. Young and C. Smith, "Molecules That Mediate Monogamy" (2009)**

> In his *Love's Trinity*, the Victorian poet laureate Alfred Austin sums up the holistic view of love that has long held sway:
>
> *Soul, heart, and body, we thus singly name,*
> *Are not in love divisible and distinct,*
> *But each with each inseparably link'd.*
>
> Now researchers are attempting to isolate and identify the neural and genetic components underlying this seemingly uniquely human emotion. Indeed, biologists may soon be able to reduce certain mental states associated with love to a biochemical chain of events.
>
> **—Larry J. Young, "Being Human" (2009)**

For a century now, monogamy has been understood as a facet of human nature. While a wide range of animals have served as models for the study of the evolution of mammalian monogamy, at the turn of the twenty-first century, monogamy's nature entered public discourse through genomic research using "monogamous" prairie voles. The *New York Times*, the *Nation*, *Al Jazeera*, and various local papers, as well as *Late Night with David Letterman*, *The Daily Show*,

Dateline NBC, the National Geographic Channel, National Public Radio, and *Grey's Anatomy* have all mentioned vole research on monogamy. A sampling of early headlines on genetic links to monogamy read: "To Have and to Vole," "How Geneticists Put the Romance Back into Mating," and "Love Is a Drug for Prairie Voles to Score."[1] These reports cited the research of a neuroscience laboratory headed by Dr. Larry Young at the Yerkes National Primate Research Center in Atlanta. While much work on monogamy as a mating system has sought to explain why humans couple in more familiar evolutionary terms, the neuroscience of pair bonding promises to account for the importance of this "integral aspect of human sexuality . . . for both psychological and physical health."[2] Young's lab conducts research on the genetic and neurobiological mechanisms underlying complex social behaviors, specifically bonding, toward the end of treating disorders, like autism, whose diagnostic criteria include social deficits.[3] They use "monogamous" prairie voles (*Microtus ochrogaster*) as a neurobiological model of healthy sociality. Looking past the press to Young's laboratory's research, I find that monogamy is not so much "discovered" there, as popular "monogamy gene" coverage suggests; rather, it is an assumption about human nature from which the research actually begins. Monogamy is used here, as in *Psychopathia Sexualis*, as I argued in chapter 1, to mark the desirable. Its intelligibility as a proxy for healthy bonding capacities is dependent on the twin specters of promiscuity and asociality. That is to say, monogamy is modeled here as a presumptively exclusive and fundamentally sexual pair bond.

Young and his lab are not trying to prove that monogamy is natural; it is the a priori foundation on which they make claims about normal psychiatric development, specifically around "social interaction" or "affiliative behavior." As the premise of multimillion-dollar research on human sociality in particular and gene-brain-behavior connections more generally, "monogamy" is both conceptually important to emerging understandings of human nature and an exciting site for exploring those shifts. In the laboratory, as my first epigraph illustrates, humans as a species are presumed to be monogamous. My second epigraph shows how Young describes the same research both as the study of the social brain and as research on love (an important slippage) and elegantly reveals the lab's project as one of untangling nature from culture within a frame that imagines advancements in biochemistry as the key to unlocking the timeless mysteries of "love." Reducing the historically rich naturecultural concept of "love" to "a biochemical chain of events" has the twofold effect of naturalizing it and of putting it within the power of science to define.

I analyze the laboratory's publications *and* practices in order to hold the discursive production of difference and the material conditions of possibility for that production within the same frame. I examine slippages in terminology and choices about its deployment, models that code monogamy as a meaningful biological category, and experiments that measure it, in order to trace the material-discursive normalization of coupling, with all of its complex historical entanglements. Young's laboratory provides the perfect site for exploring these processes. First, the lab's high visibility has invigorated public discourse on the nature of monogamy, especially its gendered nature and its relative plasticity, themes to which I return in more detail in chapter 5. Second, the laboratory led a successful initiative to get the prairie vole genome mapped to aid its use as a model organism, which has important implications for understanding the scientific reproduction of links between monogamy and human nature.[4] My analysis of the laboratory's publications and practices, through rhetorical analysis and ethnographic fieldwork, suggests that the naturalization of monogamy depends on the imposition of sexuality as an interpretive grid for bonding behavior, suggesting that "monogamy" is not only not necessarily exclusive, it is not necessarily sexual. This analysis points to the remarkable power and flexibility of monogamy in the production of normal and abnormal bodies.

Conceptual Ambiguity and the Naturalization of Coupling

I begin by situating Young's laboratory in the recent history of biological research on monogamy. Biologists have historically studied mating strategies and family structures across species as a means of further elucidating the evolution of human relationships. The use of family models has naturalized both the idea of family and links between courtship, reproduction, and child-rearing.[5] Humans are among a very small percentage of mammals described as monogamous. Until the late twentieth century, scientists tended to use "monogamy" to describe some form of coupling, usually evidenced by biparental care, with presumed sexual exclusivity.[6] Scientists have argued that when and where there were more predators, monogamy was common among vulnerable animals because one parent needed to protect the young while the other collected food. With the widespread use of DNA testing in the late twentieth century, scientists discovered that the offspring these parents were feeding and protecting were often not genetically related to their fathers and that these fathers had genetic offspring elsewhere.[7] Thus sexual and social monogamy became necessarily biologically distinct categories.

This distinction is vitally important to the contemporary science of mating, as "monogamy" does not usually denote sexual exclusivity in science as it often does in more popular discourse. The concepts of "sexual" and "social" monogamy are, however, often used without clear definition. "Monogamy," unqualified, is now sometimes used to refer to "social monogamy" and sometimes to "sexual monogamy," or exclusivity. The term "pair bonding" is also widely used to refer to social monogamy. Young's laboratory, like others operationalizing these categories, uses "monogamy," "social monogamy," and "pair bonding" interchangeably. During my fieldwork interviews at the lab, "Researcher B," when asked how long the laboratory has been using the language of "monogamy," responded: "The voles were initially studied because they are monogamous. So as long as voles have been studied, the term 'monogamy' has been used. We [current researchers in the lab] are more careful in terms of how we talk about it. So we use that terminology—'pair bond'—instead of 'monogamy.' Most of the time. We also prefer the term 'socially monogamous' because that gets you away from the whole idea of fidelity. Of course nobody actually knows what that means in the public, but it makes us feel better, right?" (June 12, 2008). Both the scientific importance of these distinctions and the commonplaceness of slippages between them are marked by the researcher's discussion of being careful to use more precise language and at the same time her ambivalence. That ambivalence about the distinctness of the signifiers is captured by the lab's use of "monogamy" unqualified, by the fact that researchers now are only making the distinctions "most of the time," and finally in Researcher B's sense that the distinction is mostly symbolic, because "the public" will conflate the terms anyway. This collapsing of concepts of sexual exclusivity (or "fidelity"), coparenting, and long-term cohabitation into the term "monogamy" links them in ways that naturalize companionate hetero-reproductive coupling. I use the term "coupling" to mark my analysis of the ideal of "twoness" being naturalized in the slippage that marks their deployment of these various terms. When referring directly to a specific experiment or publication, I will use whichever term the researchers used in that instance; I use descriptive language to refer to the specific behavior being discussed when doing so serves to further clarify the processes by which monogamy is being naturalized.

The concept of "social monogamy" remains central to scientific understandings of human evolutionary development. However, a cogent evolutionary explanation for the sexual fidelity with which it is sometimes conflated no longer exists. As I said, scientists have found that among pair-bonding species that were once assumed to be sexually monogamous, extrapair copulation is widespread. Because sexual exclusivity is no longer essential to the definition of pair bonding and yet the two concepts are deeply enmeshed in the popular usage of "monogamy," the question of whether or not "the human" is biologically "monogamous" depends on which definition is being deployed. Some scientists say monogamy is not natural but we should still strive to be faithful to our mates: "There is no question about monogamy's being natural. It isn't. But at the same time, there is no reason to conclude that adultery is unavoidable, or that it is good. 'Smallpox is natural,' wrote Ogden Nash. 'Vaccine ain't.' Animals, most likely, can't help 'doing what comes naturally.' But humans can. A strong case can even be made that we are never so human as when we behave contrary to our natural inclinations, those most in tune with our biological impulses."[8] Here, David Barash, coauthor with Judith Lipton of *The Myth of Monogamy: Fidelity and Infidelity in Animals and People* (2001), refutes accusations that their research promotes infidelity by calling the biological basis of monogamy into question. Barash challenges the idea that the unnaturalness of (sexual) monogamy means humans should no longer aspire to it or are doomed to fail at it. He argues that reason and morality are fundamental human capacities that should trump our baser animal biology.

The research of Young's laboratory, however, realigns the morality and nature of monogamy by using "monogamy" to mean "social monogamy." Research that abandons the language of adultery and sexual fidelity and instead uses the terms "monogamy," "social monogamy," and "pair bonding" interchangeably to refer to coupling, without reference to sexual fidelity, seems increasingly common. That is to say, extrapair copulations are increasingly assimilated within scientific definitions of monogamy. In Young's laboratory and in interviews with the press, as well as in the *Nature* editorial I quote in my second epigraph, researchers working on genetic links to monogamy also refer to the concept of "love." In Helen Fisher's authoritative work on the natural history of monogamy, she describes "love" as one of the three distinct systems that have evolved to promote human monogamy: "lust," "love," and "attachment."[9] Lust, associated with testosterone and estrogen, keeps us on the lookout for a mate. Love, associated with dopamine, is the new relationship energy high that keeps members of a potential pair in one another's company for long enough to form an attachment. Attachment is associated with vasopressin and oxytocin and is what ostensibly keeps pairs together for long enough to get their offspring through critical stages of development. While the work of Young's lab addresses this latter system, the language of "love" finds its way into the research through slippages between the concepts "monogamy" and "love." In some places, Young says the lab is breaking "love" down so that we can understand what it is and how it works.[10] The lab also asserts that "love" has an evolutionary purpose—it is what makes coupling rewarding; it has evolved in humans because coupling increases our offspring's chances of survival.[11] Elsewhere, Young describes his lab's work as that of explaining what makes humans interact socially.[12] "Love" is both monogamy itself—analogous to healthy sociality as it stands in for the capacity to form attachments—and vaguely referenced as a "mental state" that reinforces monogamous behaviors. This unfixed referent constitutes a productive ambiguity. The invocation of "love," mysterious and ill-defined, serves to romanticize the "monogamy" Young's lab claims is evolutionarily natural for humans.

While the ambiguity of monogamy's meanings in general makes it possible to claim that monogamy either is or is not "natural" given the same findings, Young's lab claims that monogamy *is* natural. The use of "monogamy," unqualified, to refer to coupling consolidates extrapair copulation or sexual infidelity within the definition of monogamy. Ultimately, the laboratory is naturalizing a romantic, companionate, sexual *and* exclusive, but *not necessarily sexually exclusive*, form of coupling. This use of monogamy serves to stabilize the reproductive family, perpetuating the containment of would-be challenges to its status as natural. Affairs are indeed a constitutive part of the monogamy being critiqued as compulsory.[13] Rather than asking us to rethink what we know about monogamy, the deployment of "social monogamy" as "monogamy" only serves to reify the gendered status quo I discussed in the introduction, wherein men lying and cheating is deeply naturalized (they are sperm-spreaders, after all).

Engaging Scientists

Before moving into analysis of experimental models, let me describe the approach of my fieldwork in the laboratory. I title this section "engaging scientists" to refer simultaneously to both my decision to include firsthand engagements with scientists in my research on monogamy gene discourse and the "engaging" scientists who brought new questions to the fore of my research. The first was somewhat serendipitous. Popular press reports on the monogamy gene had led me to the lab's publications. I had been studying those publications for a few months with the assistance of a generous neuroscientist colleague and friend, Sara Giordano, with whom I later wrote about sexual dimorphism in the lab's research,[14] when the idea of contacting Young presented itself. Giordano spent long hours translating dense explanations and lent me a valuable library of textbooks in neuroscience and cell and molecular biology, thus beginning my engagement with scientists. This interchange was also the site of the spark of my initial curiosity about what was being measured, the "stuff" of the discourse, which would take shape later in the laboratory. This mutual engagement describes a hybrid relationship that spans the terrain of teacher/student and researcher/subject, at times venturing into the terrain of collaboration, as our mutual questioning generated its own questions.

Interested initially in the relationship between journalistic claims about genetics and monogamy and the research on which they were based, I contacted Larry Young in 2007 to ask what he thought of the onslaught of attention his laboratory's work had received in the popular media. I introduced myself as a graduate student, also working on monogamy, but in the humanities. He agreed to meet for coffee and talk about it. We met in his office and exchanged giant binders of popular press coverage of his laboratory, both discovering pieces we had missed. We commiserated over the photocopier, completing our respective archives before we began to discuss its contents. As far as accuracy, Young said he had few complaints beyond that persistent definitional confusion over monogamy: since sexual fidelity is not part of the laboratory's definition of monogamy but remains part of the popular definition, announcements about the monogamy gene have led to misunderstandings that a genetic basis for sexual fidelity has been found. Beyond this simple factual error, stemming from linguistic ambiguities, Young stated that the press had also missed the bigger picture: they only picked up on the sexy part—the part about "love," not what that capacity stands for in terms of mental health and, in particular, autism treatment.[15] Indeed the laboratory's funding comes largely from the National Institute of Mental Health specifically for researching oxytocin's potential links to autism. Months later, when I had started visiting the lab, I asked another researcher about what Young had observed. She predicted the imminent shift toward media attention to the autism connection:

INTERVIEWER/ME (I): Do you think that your research affects general views about monogamy? People aren't talking about the autism connection so much. I guess because it's a less sexy topic? But people are really interested in autism right now.

RESEARCHER B: Right. It will get picked up. So the autism side of things in voles is all academic at this point. As you noticed. But I think that with the increased awareness it will get picked up on—especially because people like [Researcher A] are doing studies that are immediately applicable to things like autism. And before this, it's been sort of this tangential link—like "Okay, let's study this [monogamous] species and social bonds are a problem you have with autism. . . . So maybe we can study this and figure out more." (June 12, 2008)

Researcher B explains the connection plainly here: prairie voles are monogamous, monogamy is a social bond, social bonds are a problem for people diagnosed with autism, so maybe studying monogamous voles can help us treat autism. Indeed, with time, increased funding (NIMH and Autism Speaks), and now proliferating clinical trials leading to pharmaceutical interventions, connections between autism and oxytocin are making headlines: "Novel Drug Modifies Core Autism Symptoms in Adults"; "New Study Indicates Oxytocin May Provide Treatment for Autism"; "Will Oxytocin Nasal Spray Treatments for Autism Really Work?"[16] The connection that Researcher B narrates in the foregoing passage turns out to be quite a complex one, which depends of course on how we understand both monogamy and autism. After my initial conversation with Young I became increasingly curious about this entanglement and about the process by which evidence of a biological basis for what was being called "monogamy," "pair bonding," and "love" was acquired. I asked to observe in the laboratory and conduct interviews with willing researchers.

In December 2007, Young invited me to meet with the lab of about fifteen researchers to discuss my interest in their research. They gave me a full hour to give a PowerPoint presentation, "Monogamy in the Humanities," that ended with a narrative about how I had encountered their lab's work, why it interested me, and what I hoped to learn from them. They sent me out of the room for a moment to discuss my pitch and invited me back in with an enthusiastic yes, with the agreement that individual researchers would opt in as time permitted and make arrangements with me directly. I kept in touch and solicited interest by emailing their listserv, and in the spring of 2008, I began interviewing researchers and visiting the lab. I had ongoing contact with three researchers, Young himself and two graduate students (whom I call

"Researcher A" and "Researcher B"). We scheduled meeting times in advance around various experiments that I had either requested to observe or that one of the researchers had suggested it might be helpful for me to see. In the main laboratory space, I spent time observing researchers pipetting genetic material into thousands of tiny test tubes to be sent out for sequencing and sifting through letters and charts that represented DNA sequences on the computer. I also observed the process of slicing, dyeing, and producing electronic images of tiny vole brains.

In the animal laboratory, where animals are housed and all live animal experiments are conducted, I observed behavioral tests and the "sacrificing" of voles, including the removal, labeling, and storage of brains and livers for other experiments (brains for imaging and livers for DNA testing).[17] My lab visits lasted for two to six hours and took place during April, May, and June 2008, for a total of approximately twenty hours. Follow-up with the researchers in the following months occurred mainly through e-mail. One of the things that interested me most over the course of my fieldwork was the tension surrounding what the research was "really about." Researchers always tempered their interest in and claims about "monogamy" with caveats about the bigger picture, that is, the use of monogamy as a model for healthy social behavior in general.

The Monogamy Gene: A Gene for Mental Health?

I argued at the outset of this chapter that Young's lab's deployment of terminology contributes to their naturalization of coupling. I have narrated my entrée into the laboratory and thus into a more nuanced understanding of the connections linking autism and monogamy. In this section, I ask what Young and his lab are actually saying about biology in their use of monogamy as a neural model for social and psychiatric health. This model implicates the naturalization of coupling in the production of normal and abnormal types—what Nancy Stepan calls "the biosocial science of human variation."[18] This is a logical system in which differences are imagined as both binary and analogous. Within this schema, evolutionary temporalities that target "population" stand in easily for developmentalist models that target individual difference, each operating on the premise of a normal/desirable state and an abnormal/undesirable one. In such a schema, the distance between them validates the social distance between normal (monogamous/social) and pathological (promiscuous/asocial) bodies and constitutes the ground that treatment should aim to cover.

The monogamy gene research is funded for its implications for treatment for autism and autistic spectrum disorder and sometimes, though less often, for drug addiction, a genetic link whose scientific logic I will explain more fully later.[19] The laboratory is using social monogamy as an assay—or model—to study these "disorders." Researchers argue that the ability to isolate a gene for coupling—and the potential for the transformation of behavior that this opens up—is important not exclusively for its implications for making men monogamous or keeping couples together, but for its implications for understanding human attachment and sociality more generally.[20] This is not to say that implications for coupling were not of interest to the researchers; indeed they were. I commented glibly to one of the researchers that coverage of clinical trials treating heterosexual couples in counseling with intranasal oxytocin read to me like something out of the popular satirical newspaper the *Onion*. She nodded, laughing, and then responded:

> Like you said, your initial reaction to this is "it's something out of the *Onion*," but if you look at the emotional effects of a poor relationship, of being in a poor relationship, having inadequate communication with your partner, they are huge. Ultimately it turns into a societal problem in that if you are in a relationship and things aren't going well you're probably not doing as well at work, you may become depressed. So actually these social interactions are a huge part of our lives, a huge part of our happiness, a huge part of how effectively we're working in society and so I do actually think that these oxytocin trials with couples counseling are a good idea. (June 12, 2008)

While inhaling a hormone cocktail before therapy might *sound* absurd to the uninitiated, its rationale follows a familiar logic. Coupling is essential to the health of individuals and society, and thus monogamy—the capacity to form a pair bond with a mate—is being researched not (solely) as an end in itself, but as a model for healthy relating. The model operates on the consensus that stable pair bonds are essential to the health of society. Monogamy is both the foundation and model for what the laboratory has variously called "social interaction," "attachment," and "affiliative behavior."[21] The opposite of monogamy in this model is not only promiscuity but also *asociality*.[22]

Asociality, the targeted deficit associated with autism, is at the heart of the reproduction of monogamy's nature in contemporary genetics. Asociality is also emerging in science and popular culture in ways that are marked by both masculinity and whiteness.[23] "The new autistic subject" is one who can be reclaimed as quirky and lovable through the lens of sexed brain theories of autism.[24] Importantly, the lovability of this asocial character depends on its domestication within a framework that normalizes it as an extreme form of a sort of masculinity associated with being unemotional and often remarkably gifted in math or science. He is figured not as someone for whom social bonding is not rewarding but as someone less successful at achieving those bonds *because* he is less empathizing (feminine) and more systematizing (masculine).[25] This formulation renaturalizes strong associations between love and femininity. It also naturalizes the idea that men, although they need it, too, are naturally incompetent at love.[26] Still, it does more than naturalize (white) gender stereotypes of nurturing women and hyperrational men. It also recoups autism from a history as a disorder of affect that situated its subjects as incapable of love, by making an idealized autistic subject a figure of bonding *potential*.[27]

This normalizing promise, that asociality, like supposed male communication and commitment phobias, can be improved on with the right research and in turn the right pharmacology, must be seen as part of this important shift in autism's meanings. Autism's *depathologization* in culture and in science (on television and in the DSM-5, for example) depends on the ability to imagine autism within the purview of definitions of the human as a monogamous species, or at least, a species for whom affective social bonds are essential. Moreover, autism's extraction from the "wrong side of eugenics" and linkage to the possibility of becoming "desirably reproductive" is racialized.[28] This bridge from abjection takes the form of a racialized affective capacity. It was the bonds of monogamy that separated the civilized from the uncivilized in the work of Richard von Krafft-Ebing, and it was the capacity for affective connection that exceeded reproductivity that distinguished the civilized from the animal monogamy of our ancestors in the work of Havelock Ellis. The intelligibility of a model that uses monogamous and promiscuous voles as the neural proxies for healthy and asocial humans, respectively, owes a debt to whiteness. Monogamy, a historic marker of European evolutionary superiority, is the model for human health. A model of neural plasticity aimed at shifting subjects measurably closer to that ideal, one that takes affective capacity as the measure of health for humans, is a normalizing model invested in an understanding of health that is deeply embedded in histories of racialized sexuality wherein the embodiment of European values is collapsed into their tacit medicalization as healthy behavior.

Reports of a monogamy gene are based on the claim that a section of microsatellite or junk DNA that is longer in some animals than others may correlate with social monogamy, or pair bonding.[29] Microsatellites are short sections of DNA with repeated sequences of base pairs. The variability in the number of these repeats is used as a molecular marker for genetic difference between individuals and in population and kinship genetics. These markers are also used to study larger evolutionary shifts.[30] Specifically, this lab argues that longer strands of this section of microsatellite DNA—that is, strands with greater repetition of these base pair sequences—correlate with monogamous behaviors.[31] It is worth noting that this section of DNA is not a discrete entity and that the repetition of base pairs varies widely—in other words, they come in lengths other than "long" and "short." These distinctions mark statistical significance in behavioral correlation, *not* distinct genotypes, and there is variation on either side of the line.

This microsatellite DNA region is said to modulate another section of DNA—the vasopressin receptor (V1aR) gene—that codes for a protein that functions as a receptor for the hormone vasopressin.[32] While the lab generally reports on this receptor function as if it were straightforward, I first learned in interviews that cross-receptivity in receptors means they cannot know for sure whether oxytocin or vasopressin is acting on the receptors in a given instance. (I return to this point in chapter 5.) The length of the microsatellite DNA is said to affect the distribution of vasopressin receptors in different regions of the brain, with the longer strands leading to greater expression of these receptors in the nucleus accumbens and ventral pallidum, closely connected regions of the brain associated with "reward" and often studied for their role in addiction.[33] The lab uses this monogamy gene as a model for the study of the social brain, because it appears to demonstrate a concrete connection between bonding behavior and neurochemical reward.[34]

This is how the model works: (1) there is a variation in a section of microsatellite DNA; (2) that variation modulates a coding region of DNA, or "gene" controlling the distribution of hormone receptors in the brain; (3) that distribution of receptors enables a neurochemical process with a behavioral outcome; (4) the behavioral outcomes of this neurochemical process are measured by a "partner preference" test (discussed in the next section), which identifies voles as monogamous or promiscuous; (5) the genetic commonality of these monogamous and promiscuous voles, respectively, is the basis for identifying them as two separate genetic types: normal and abnormal (see fig. 2.1). (I will return to number 3—those processes that link genes to behaviors—in chapter 5.) Researchers in the lab alter the genetically nonmonogamous types in a variety of ways to make them behave more like the genetically mo-

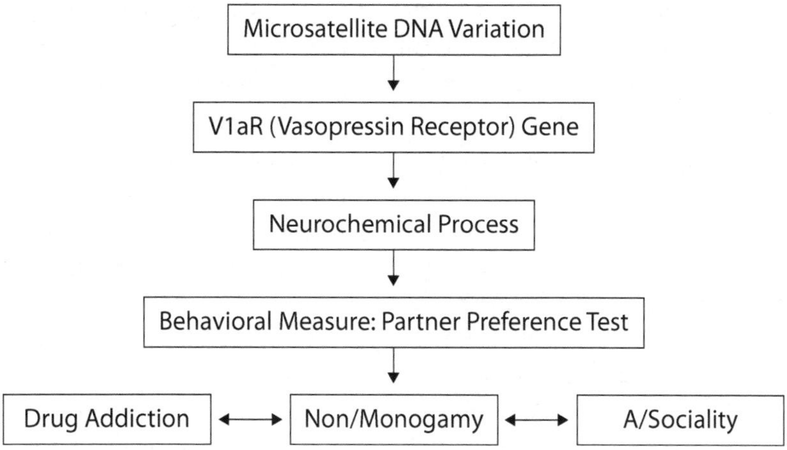

FIG 2.1 "The Monogamy Gene": From Genetic Variation to Behavior. Cocreated by Sara Giordano.

nogamous types. The ability to alter the neurochemical process that affects monogamous behavior and to make promiscuous voles monogamous is the basis for treatment of autism and other "asocial" behaviors.

The logic of the model lies in an understanding of genetic biomarkers as more or less causally linked to behaviors, in ways that matter despite in-group variation. The behaviors are said to be brought about by neurochemical processes, which, however internally complex, are enabled by the variation of certain "genes." The neurochemical process I have just described links a "gene" to pair bond formation. Again, scientists have been able to isolate and describe this process by using prairie voles because they are described as behaviorally socially monogamous.[35] The genetic variation that monogamous prairie voles possess causes the expression of vasopressin receptors in a region of the brain associated with reward. So when a hormone that will bind with these receptors is released, whatever experience or behavior led to that release will be reinforced. Researchers speculate that coupling behavior results in animals with this "gene" because a bond with a specific partner—what they sometimes call "love"—triggers the release of such hormones every time a vole (or human) sees the partner with whom they have bonded. Young and his team argue that this neurochemical reward mechanism—the same genetic variation, hormones, and pathway—is also what allows humans to interact socially and form attachments in general.[36] In this model, monogamy in voles is compared to social health in humans and promiscuity in voles to autism in humans.

Specifically, scientists use this genetic model to distinguish between monogamous and promiscuous vole types, to serve as models for the normal and the abnormal in human social bonding. The promiscuous meadow vole, with its shorter strand of microsatellite DNA on average, does not form pair bonds.[37] Researchers then use the correlation of this genetic difference with monogamy in voles to model the assumed neurochemical deficit of people with autism. The inability (real or imagined) to fall in love and sustain a bond is effectively coded as outside the purview of benign variation by this use of monogamy as a model for mental health. Conversely, autism is racialized by its association with promiscuity and failure to love. The lab defines both promiscuity and autism as asocial.

When I asked about the slippage between promiscuity and autism that happens in the translation from voles to humans, one of the researchers surmised that this parallel might sound funny to me because, as a nonscientist, I did not understand scientific proxy as the basis of animal modeling for translational research.[38] Proxy here is the substitution of one behavior or problem for another in a scientific model. Research on genetic links to behaviors is based on the substitution of other behaviors as models for ones that are difficult or impossible to measure.[39] Translational research is research considered directly relevant to humans, as opposed to "basic research," which may have long-term potential to *become* clinically relevant but has no direct or immediate implications for human health. Human brains and livers cannot be extracted for experimentation, and autism is a human concept—hence the need for an animal model. The failure to pair bond is the behavioral proxy for the lab's adoption of definitions of autism as social deficit.[40] Monogamy is the proxy for mental health based on the lab's interpretation of coupling as fundamental to healthy humanness. They understand promiscuity as evolutionarily normal and appropriate for the meadow vole and the model for something abnormal and "wrong" in humans.

The assumption that links healthy development to monogamy was formally institutionalized through the Vole Genomics Initiative, of which Young's lab was the primary sponsor. The Vole Genomics Initiative is a community of researchers and laboratories that mobilized to petition the National Human Genome Research Institute to map the prairie vole genome so that researchers could use the prairie vole more widely as a model for translational research. In 2009, a year after the proposal's initial submission, the initiative was successful, and the prairie vole was added to the institute's list of approved sequencing targets. The prairie vole genome was sequenced in 2012.[41] The proposal argues:

> The prairie vole (*Microtus ochrogaster*) has emerged as perhaps the preeminent animal model for elucidating the genetic and neurobiological mechanisms governing complex social behavior in vertebrates. . . . Prairie voles are highly affiliative, socially monogamous rodents that form enduring social bonds between mates (pair bonds) and display extensive biparental care. Other species within the *Microtus* genus are relatively asocial, uniparental, and fail to develop social bonds of any sort, providing an excellent opportunity for comparative studies focused on gene-brain-behavior relationships. . . . Biomedical research using the prairie vole model has important implications for human mental health and understanding basic human biology.[42]

According to this community of scientists, prairie voles are an exemplary model organism for translational research, and a better proxy for the human in a state of health than mice *because they are monogamous*. They present their difference from physiologically identical yet ostensibly *asocial* animals as an opportunity to understand difference (hence implications for mental health) and how genes are connected to behavior (hence the implications for basic biology). In her study of the standardization of animals for experimentation in the first half of the twentieth century, Karen Rader emphasizes how assumptions about particular animals and their likeness to humans inform their use as models in a given sociohistorical context.[43] It would seem that the move to using prairie voles as models for human behaviors marks an emerging understanding about monogamy as integral to healthy humanness. If the human is increasingly rigidly defined in terms of a racially gendered understanding of affective capacity of which "monogamy" serves as the exemplary model, we have to ask how this is working in the laboratory. Put differently, what *is* monogamy? In the next section, I explain the experimental model that measures monogamy.

Partner Preference and the Sexualization of Bonding

In the previous sections, I illustrated how the Young laboratory's deployment of "monogamy" naturalizes coupling and reinforces compulsory monogamy and how that naturalization of coupling hinges on the undesirability of nonmonogamy and autism. In this section, I go into the laboratory to ask how what they call monogamy, social monogamy, pair bonding, and sometimes love is actually measured. A major feminist critique of science has been the invisibility of its methods.[44] This lack of transparency with regard to methods promotes the myth that science exists as "something other than the activities of scientists."[45] Further, a major critique of feminism, especially its critiques of science, as I discussed in the introduction, has been its tendency to sideline the creative work of engaging with "biology" as a source of knowledge in its own right: as agential, vital, vibrant.[46] Given this pair of insights about *the politics of science and the possibilities of biology*, I endeavor to engage the apparatus of measurement and the "biological" behavior being measured in the lab in conjunction with one another. Here, I offer a reading of the behavioral test used to measure monogamy—the partner preference test—and the physiological explanations offered to account for both the experimental design and its outcomes. I argue that assumptions about sexuality embedded in the partner preference test naturalize the coupling that we know, but a closer look at what is being measured suggests that sexuality is an interpretive frame imposed on pair-bonding behaviors.

Although I had read most of the lab's published work over several years and dozens of popular press articles on the topic, I had somehow imagined voles in the "wild," in the style of a nature documentary or children's book—some living like Beatrix Potter's characters in loving families, others running about doing lord-knows-what, without jackets and mittens. Illustrations like the one in figure 2.2 from a National Science Foundation press release on Young's lab's research both reflect the pervasiveness of and perpetuate this kind of anthropomorphic imagery.[47] The image depicts two voles. The monogamous one, on the right, with the longer strand of microsatellite DNA, is shown "indoors" caring for his young. The vole with the shorter strand, on the left, is shown outdoors with his nose up ostensibly to catch the scent of potential sexual partners. This type of imagery obscures understandings of how translations between human and animal behavior are made.

The genetic findings represented in such images are the results of experiments based on the use of voles as animal models, as proxies for human differences. This means that animals who are held and, most often, bred in captivity are physically manipulated (e.g., by gene manipulation, drug injections, cutting out parts of their brains, breeding, rearing in isolation) in a way that causes them to exhibit a set of symptoms or behaviors that are associated with a human disease or disorder.[48] This means the animals may be administered

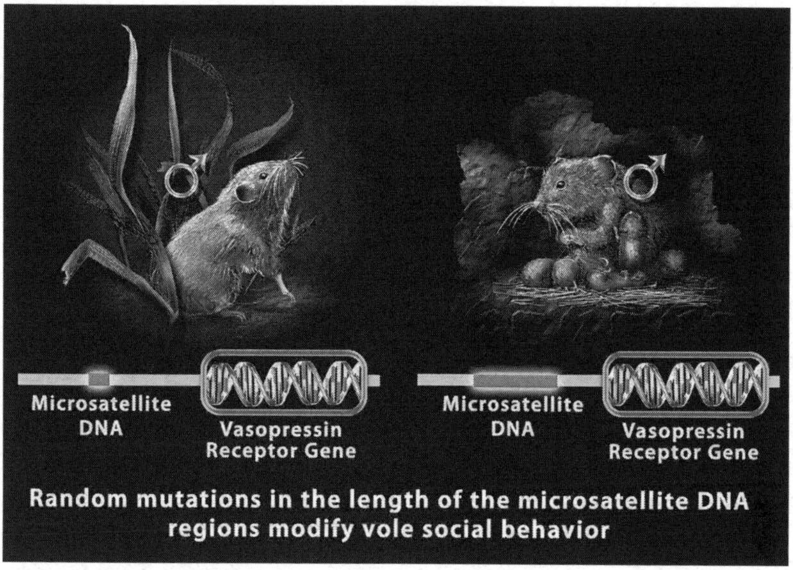

FIG 2.2 Representation of monogamous and promiscuous vole species. Nicolle Rager Fuller, National Science Foundation.

a drug or bred transgenically (with genetic material from another species) or otherwise altered in some way that causes them to behave in a manner that scientists observing them can recognize or interpret as similar to ways humans might behave in a given circumstance—the behavior of the animal serves as a proxy for the human behavior in question. Scientists then figure out how to standardize that effect and further manipulate the subjects to try to alter the behavior or "treat" the "symptom." This is how translational research works. In Young's lab, researchers use what they deem nonmonogamous or promiscuous behaviors as markers of "asocial" conditions like autism and drug addiction.[49] Pair bond formation is the desired, healthy change they aim to reproduce.[50]

The set of symptoms or behaviors that the scientists aim to change or achieve are identified by having the animals perform "tests" that can be quantified. The test for measuring monogamy is called a "partner preference test." Researchers place a male animal in a cage with a female animal, usually for eighteen to twenty-four hours.[51] In this time, they are expected to mate—that is to have "sex," which means here, as it does in most animal studies, penis-in-vagina intercourse.[52] This eighteen hours is important, because in the test, mating and pair bonding are causally linked. Mating is the stimulus said to cause the hormones oxytocin or vasopressin to be released. These hormones

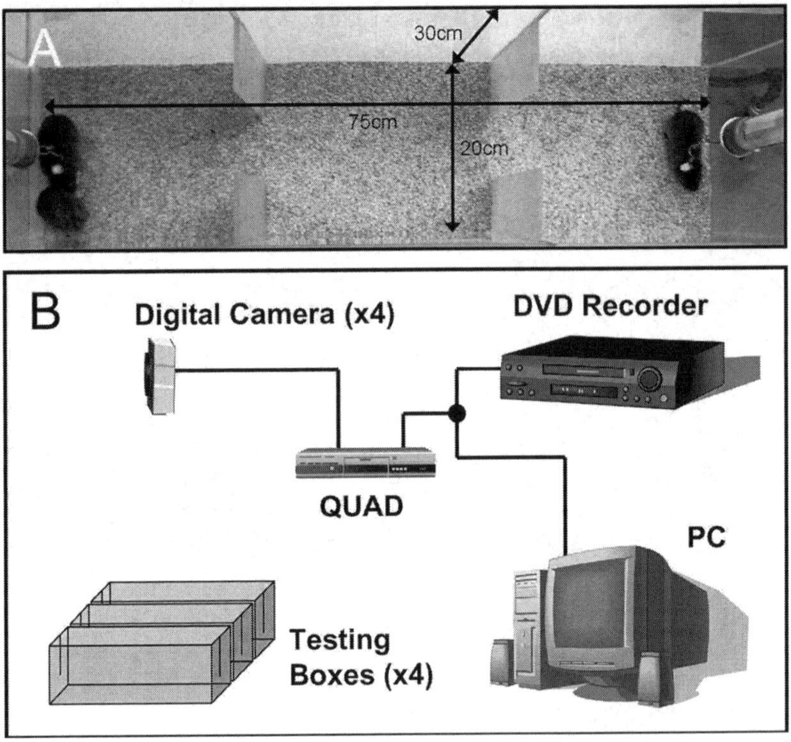

FIG 2.3 (a) Partner preference test cage setup. (b) Partner preference test recording setup. From Todd H. Ahern, Meera E. Modi, James P. Burkett, and Larry J. Young, "Evaluation of Two Automated Metrics for Analyzing Partner Preference Tests," *Journal of Neuroscience Methods* 182, no. 2 (September 15, 2009): 181.

will bind with receptors in the reward centers of the brains of the voles with the genetic variation associated with monogamy.[53] If they are genetically monogamous, the voles will form a pair bond after mating. If they are not, they will fail to form a pair bond.

After the original pair has presumably mated, a second unfamiliar female is placed in the cage, and the two females are separated by being "tethered" or tied to different sides of the cage. The female with whom the male is assumed to have mated is called the "partner," while the unfamiliar female is called the "stranger." The male is free to move throughout the three chambers of the cage (see fig. 2.3A). The activity in the cage is recorded both by software that tracks the movement of microchips in the "collars" of the three voles and by motion-sensing video cameras (see fig. 2.3B). Later, a researcher will check the software and/or watch the footage and count the number of minutes that the male animal spends with each female. If the male spends more than one-third of the time with the "familiar" female, then the animal is said to show a partner preference and thus to be "monogamous."

After an analogue of the pathologized behavior has been effectively reproduced in a test animal, the model is then used to find potential ways to treat the human disease or disorder by altering the animal with drugs or gene therapies and using the same tests to look for changes in symptoms or behaviors. Changing the genetic makeup of an animal can alter the neurochemical process. A drug interferes with that process to change the behavioral outcome. In the case of Young's lab, an animal who does not show a partner preference will be treated with a drug—usually oxytocin—and then put through the partner preference test once again. If an animal who did not show a partner preference initially does show a partner preference after treatment, the researchers conclude that whatever has altered the neurochemistry and thus led to the behavioral change has potential as a treatment for "asocial" human behaviors. The administration of oxytocin injections has been shown to increase partner preference in some voles. It is on this basis that oxytocin is being used in clinical trials to treat autism.[54]

I entered the lab in December 2007 with the general sense that biologizing explanations for sexual behavior were always necessarily reductive, unable to account for the complex nature of human sexuality. As for the monogamy gene research, I was concerned about the use of language—the projection of human categories onto animal behavior, such that assumptions about those categories would in a circular fashion be "proven" by science. Specifically, I questioned the application of the word "monogamy"—whose etymology links it to the legal institution of marriage—to describe the pairing off of animals. In truth, I did not question that the animals somehow coupled. As the type of amateur animal behavioralist that most human members of long-term interspecies relationships become, I knew that love was not uniquely human. (My dog loved me, and my mostly feral kitten loved the dog.) So in April 2008, when I was invited into the animal lab to observe the behavioral piece of this research, I fully expected that I would see what the researchers recorded having seen—something roughly translatable to "love."[55]

Early on the day I observed the partner preference test, I watched several minutes of video footage on a computer with Researcher A, who had invited me to observe in the animal lab. The animals appear in the software version of the mapping as blobs (see fig. 2.4). Two blobs are on one side; the other is

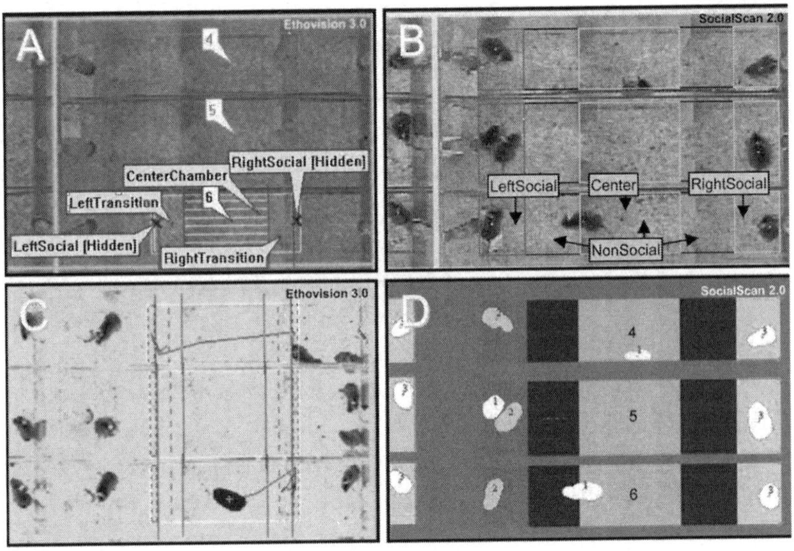

FIG 2.4 Partner preference test recorded images. From Todd H. Ahern, Meera E. Modi, James P. Burkett, and Larry J. Young, "Evaluation of Two Automated Metrics for Analyzing Partner Preference Tests," *Journal of Neuroscience Methods* 182, no. 2 (September 15, 2009): 182.

alone on the other side. Sometimes two blobs would become one bigger blob. In the video, taken from a bird's-eye view distant enough to capture a dozen cages, their actions were similarly obscured. The image in figure 2.4 is from an article that compares automated metrics in the partner preference test. In these images and elsewhere in the footage, the free vole appears occasionally to be on top of or touching one of the tethered voles, as on the left side chamber of the middle cage. To maintain neutrality in the reading of their behavior, the observer does not know which is the partner and which is the stranger vole (note the neutral labeling of "left" and "right" in images A and B). The experiment is about counting, plain and simple. Whom does the free vole spend more time with—the tethered vole on the right or on the left?

Animals with the genetic variation the press calls the monogamy gene were found on average to spend more time in the same section of the cage as the familiar animal—their "partner"—than those who lacked that genetic variation. This finding is the result of another process of mediation—statistical analysis in which the data on extreme outliers ("noise" in the data) is disposed of and then based on statistically significant group averages. This means that not all voles with the genetic variation spend more time with the familiar female and not all who lack it spend more time alone or with the "stranger."[56] Those genetically "monogamous" voles who actually spend more time with the stranger and those "promiscuous" ones who spend more time with their "partners" are not accounted for. What are reported are statistical results that highlight group averages and ignore individual variability.[57] This is one of the very powerful ways variation gets written out of science and "normal" becomes naturalized.

Neither the technological images nor my own analysis of the test results captured the profoundly social nature of vole behavior. What I observed in real time, in the actual lab, were twelve rectangular cages, each with a vole "tethered" at either end and a free one running back and forth. The collars are zip ties, closed tightly around their necks. They have to be tight, because a vole does not have much for a neck. The leashes with which they are tethered are short lightweight chains, resembling pieces of a cheap necklace. The leashes are attached to the cage well above the vole's head, providing very little leeway—if the vole takes more than one step it ends up on its hind legs. The free vole's head is fitted with a plastic shunt that is inserted through the top of the skull into the brain so that the drug that may or may not encourage bonding can easily be administered. The plastic has a hole in the top for a needle and sticks up about half an inch on the top of the vole's head, so that it appears to be wearing a strange little plastic top hat. The hat struck me as a darker rendition of the Beatrix Potter imagery that had secretly filled my head in the days I anticipated the experiment. In my notes, I referred to the voles as tethered and free, to the tie as a collar, and to the shunt as a hat.

Researcher A left me alone in the room with the cages, as none of the researchers chose to bear the tedium of watching the voles in real time. They make their observations instead from the video and software recordings, because they can be fast-forwarded and this allows the counting to happen much faster. Researcher A instructed me to stand very still so as not to trigger the motion-sensing video equipment as I prepared to watch twelve cages of three voles each—two tethered and one wearing a hat—play out the script I already knew well from the lab's publications. As she closed the door, I was certain I would be able to identify at least some pairs as "partners." I focused my concentration on trying to pair them, holding my notebook close, ready to jot down *L* or *R* to indicate my guess for which was the familiar animal next to the cage number in my crude map. I had problematized the lab's choice of "huddling," a word that rhymes with and means essentially "cuddling," to describe their closeness, and I wanted to see it for myself, to try to think of a more mundane, descriptive, less anthropomorphic way of describing their interactions.

Instead I found myself absolutely captivated, enchanted, as Jane Bennett has said, by another anthropomorphic reading. Bennett had not yet published her reclamation of the empathic and imaginative potential of anthropomorphizing in *Vibrant Matter*. She says: "Maybe it is worth running the risks associated with anthropomorphizing (superstition, the divinization of nature, romanticism) because it, oddly enough, works against anthropocentrism."[58] In this spirit of decentering the human, here in an experiment that quite literally operationalizes the lives of voles as models for human problems, I recount my observation of the test and how that watching/reading shaped my understanding of what was being measured.

As I watched, standing still, back to the wall, I saw free voles approaching tethered voles and chewing hard on their collars, pushing their paws against the other's face and pulling it with their teeth. I saw free voles climb on top of tethered voles and yank at the leash with their teeth, find the point of its attachment to the cage and shake it, pull it, bite it, or balance carefully on top of it, using it as a step to try to reach the top. I also saw tethered voles chew and pull on the hats of free voles, seemingly trying to remove them. Sometimes a free vole would sit alone scratching at its head, trying to reach the hat. In the forty-five minutes that I watched the voles, none of them settled down enough for a "huddle." There was a great deal of movement back and forth. Some free voles might well have spent more time in the same chamber with one tethered vole than the other, but this was in no way clear from my observations of any of the cages. In my anthropomorphic reading, the voles were prisoners, restrained and tortured, frightened, and driven to be free of the cages and of the instruments of their suffering. They were systematic, determined, and creative toward this end. And if any among them was *promiscuous* (as opposed to monogamous), they certainly were not *asocial*.

After this part of the experiment, and before these same voles were to be killed, Researcher A came to get me, and I asked her if the voles were trying to escape. "Oh yeah," she said, "and they're really smart" (June 12, 2008). It seemed the lab had spent a lot of money on cage design and newer, taller, more secure cages to keep the voles in. I had heard this perennial problem discussed at one of the weekly lab meetings but had not registered the implications. They do succeed in getting out from time to time, Researcher A explained, but they don't get far. I asked her if she thought they were scared. She replied that they probably were, since they do bite. Perhaps sensing my concern, she assured me that you get over thinking they are cute really quickly, because of the biting and because most people are actually allergic to them. Not everyone is allergic to the voles, but many, like Young himself, have strong allergic reactions to them, which makes the handling of voles different from the handling of rats and mice, which tends to be more intimate and evoke pet-human interactions for researchers.[59] Suffering rodent bites and suiting up or getting sick mediated the relationship between researchers and voles, fostering a sense of antagonism that allowed for distance.[60]

I observed aloud to Researcher A that the voles seemed to be trying to help each other take off the collars and the plastic thing, the little hat—the shunt, she informed me. This, she told me, is true—they are indeed aggravated by "foreign objects." In nature, they would help each other groom and try to remove anything stuck in their fur or trapping them. This idea of solidarity against experimenters—in the form of cooperative escape and removal of the foreign objects of experimentation—might well be thematized as evidence of some form of social bond, but the link to coupling was unclear to me. The projection of gendered sexual-romantic connotations onto this cooperative effort that, if asymmetrical in terms of time spent with familiar and unfamiliar when the females were tethered apart, was certainly not in any of the cases exclusive felt woefully inadequate. As Jennifer Terry surmised in her influential analysis of the scientific fascination with queer animal behavior, "assuming gender typicality is the same across species allows researchers to ignore or misunderstand variance among individual animals and across species."[61] Indeed, it was not that *too much* had been made of vole behavior but rather that *not enough* attention had been paid to the fantastically cooperative nature of their interactions.

Again, the partner preference test is the quantifiable measure of monogamy. Monogamy/love/pair bonding—coupling—is supposed to be the model for healthy social attachment. After observing the test, I wondered how the lab distinguishes between coupling and social bonding in general and how the social relationships the voles formed were being interpreted as monogamy. The answer lies not in "love" but rather in another aspect of compulsory monogamy: sex. A monogamous relationship may not be *sexually exclusive*, but it *is* always *sexual*. What makes voles who show a partner preference "monogamous" rather than "social"—capable of or adept at recognizing and responding to familiar faces and smells—is that they are presumed to have mated.

Mating is what researchers claim sets off the neurochemical chain of events that leads to coupling in animals with the right genetic variation—that is, in monogamous individuals and species. If my observations of the test raise questions about this distinction, researchers' explanations of the heterosexual assumptions embedded in the partner preference proxy render it even more curious. I asked each of my interviewees whether or not two females or two males could form pair bonds. Researcher A said that in theory any two animals could, and that bonding is not necessarily about sex per se. Although presumed vagino-cervical stimulation is the marker they use, it is certainly not the only thing that causes oxytocin to be released. This response makes sense, as Researcher A's project was at the time the only one in the lab specifically focused on autism, and social interaction in general is not linked to sex. The translation to autism suggests that a person should also recognize people he or she has not had sex with. If someone is more likely to form an attachment to a mate, he or she is *also* more likely to have "normal" social interactions, because oxytocin acts on the reward centers in the brain in both cases. But, then, why monogamy? Why not study sociality and asociality in voles without the monogamous/promiscuous proxy? Among the questions I asked the Young lab researchers, this proved a "difficult" one.

Difficult Biology

One of the researchers I interviewed explained to me that while I was right to question the causal link between mating and pair-bonding behavior, the lab uses mating to determine which dyads are "pair bonds" because "without sex the link to human biology becomes difficult to understand." In other words, while what researchers call pair bonding is in actuality not necessarily sexual, it has to be imagined through the lens of reproduction (the kind of sex that might make babies) in order to tell a story about its relationship to the brain (reward). The first time we talked, Researcher B explained to me that same-sex pair bonds do not exist, because two males or two females cannot have sex. When we talked a few months later in a more formal interview setting, her reply was a bit more nuanced:

> So it gets a little bit tricky when you start thinking about it, but basically what you're asking is if they have a preference for another individual. There are a multitude of ways to get a preference. One, long-term cohabitation; one, mating (we think of as speeding up the process); one, to get drugs like [Researcher A] is doing (speeding up the natural process of things). There has not been a lot of work done on it. There is no reason

> not to look at it. It gets a little bit difficult because you're making claims about same-sex partner preference and *if there's no mating involved then the link to human biology becomes difficult to understand*. Are they friends? Are they partners? This is how a journalist would probably approach it. (June 12, 2008; emphasis mine)

Researcher B's explanation points to a larger assumption in biomedical research on monogamy: bonding can be triggered by cohabitation, but mating is the proxy because *mating provides the link to human biology!* Scientists understand the role of mating in human biology on the basis of the assumption that humans function with the aim of reproducing our own genetic material, motivating us on a molecular level. That is, despite compelling accounts of the queerness of the nonhuman world, the science of sexuality persistently understands human nature as most fundamentally reproductive.[62] The assumption that humans are essentially reproductive is the reason the lab uses mating as the proxy for bonding. They justify using it in turn by finding that mating is in fact the basis of pair bonding. If cohabitation or long-term contact were the proxy, then the importance of sex—at least the special role of sex—in pair bonding in particular and to understandings of social behavior in general would be unclear. According to Researcher B's analysis, the link between social behavior and human biology might be dangerously destabilized.

Researcher B's response is not anomalous but rather reflects foundational assumptions of the laboratory and of biomedical research on monogamy in general—coupling is always already sexual. If it is not, it is not coupling. This is reflected in Young's response to my queries about same-sex pair bonds:

> We haven't done it [tested for such bonds]. I believe we would not have male-male pair bonds, because they would fight. Female-female pair bonds, I think there is a paper out there that does, but questions then become: *is this really a pair bond*, and *how is a pair bond different from other kinds of relationships?* . . . If you put two females together, then test them, I think under certain conditions you would get that females prefer their familiar partner. *Then what kind of relationship is that?* Lesbian? Not necessarily lesbian. Doesn't have to have a sexual component. But think of a female-female relationship as a friend, *you would expect the same thing*. (April 22, 2008; emphasis mine)

Here Young hints at the different evolutionary explanations for male and female pair bonding. While scientists presume females want a mate to help protect their young, they presume males are motivated to couple because they are territorial, which makes them naturally aggressive toward other males.

The gendered hormone story of monogamy—where oxytocin makes us snuggle babies and vasopressin makes us mark our property—is the logic that makes the idea of a male-male pair bond unintelligible, evolutionarily speaking. In making this material accessible to a wider audience, Young's book *The Chemistry between Us: Love, Sex, and the Science of Attraction* (2012), co-authored with journalist Brian Alexander, renders the gendered logic fully transparent. The chapter on female monogamy is called "Be My Baby" and the chapter on male monogamy "Be My Territory."[63] While female-female bonds are not impossible to imagine, Young asserts, we would be amiss to think of them as pair bonds rather than friendships, because they would not be sexual in nature. Sex here is heterosexual, and hetero-sex makes it monogamy.

If we should expect the same sort of attachment to form between friends as between lovers of the same sex, the same it seems would be true of opposite-sex pairs. As I said, to establish the "familiarity" of the partnered voles, a male and female vole are placed alone together for eighteen to twenty-four hours. This gives them enough time to have mated, but it does not ensure that they *have* mated. Unlike the partner preference test "itself," where the triads of voles in three chambered cages are recorded in a variety of ways, researchers make no record of this eighteen- to twenty-four-hour part of the experiment. This cannot be read as a mere oversight. Despite how the scientific pair-bonding story goes, what the voles actually do while they are alone is not particularly important, because mating is not—in biological fact—required to create the bond that interests researchers. Still, if the test subject shows a preference for the familiar "partner" over the stranger, we do not need to ask "what kind of bond is that?" The confusion that troubles attempts to imagine how we might conceptualize same-sex bonds in no way upsets researchers' representations of opposite-sex bonds as always already sexual. The assumption that the animals are in fact male and female precipitates the assumption that they have likely mated, which, in a circuitous fashion, serves as the ground for identifying them as a pair-bonded couple.

The two-sex model, in all its fragility, is vital to this research, as vole sex assignment plays a role not only in determining that pair bonds exist, but in distinguishing monogamous prairie voles from promiscuous vole species. As with humans, sex assignment of voles is binary and privileges some aspects of "sex" over others.[64] Voles are typically sexed by measuring the space between their tails and their indistinguishable external genitalia. The voles live in sex-segregated cages and sometimes one will have pups, in which case researchers resex the voles. The description of vole "sex determination and sex chromosome evolution" in "White Paper Proposal for Sequencing the Genome of the Prairie Vole (*Microtus ochrogaster*)" refers to a variety of sex "oddities," *more common in promiscuous species than in the prairie vole*. The monogamous species, modeling desirable, healthy behavior, is the most sexually dimorphic among vole species. Sexual dimorphism is, as I discussed in the introduction, long associated with racial evolutionary superiority: the more sexually differentiated the male and female, by a wide array of shifting measures, the higher on the evolutionary ladder. Hence the insight that racism is implicated in the deep cultural valuation of gender normativity.[65] The section on vole sex in the proposal ends with the assertion that "a full genome sequence of the prairie vole will provide an exciting starting point for detailed sequence analysis of the bizarre sex chromosome systems of voles."[66] Understanding the most normal/dimorphic of vole sex systems, though not *statistically normal*, will provide the ground for understanding other sex systems as strange variations. Words like "bizarre" and "odd" here suggest the complexity of vole sex and the inadequacy of binary models for representing it, much as analogous complexities captured under the umbrella of intersex suggest the conceptual inadequacy of sex/gender in humans.[67] The history of intersex is the history of both gender and race,[68] and monogamy depends on sexual dimorphism for its intelligibility and indeed, measurability. Without two complementary sexes there is no mating, and without mating there is no monogamy, at least not one we can imagine mattering.

Despite evidence that the voles learned to cooperate—which I have argued served as evidence of their pair bond—without having sex, the Young laboratory's publications, and reporting on them, are characterized by a common insistence on the innateness of sexuality and its centrality to human nature.[69] Despite the fact that voles' sex systems are complex, scientists read their behaviors through the lens of binary gender. The "dogged pursuit" of explanations for human behavior that naturalize monogamy is shaped not only by a romantic ideal of heterosexual coupling, but by the idea of sexual instinct.[70] Despite evidence that sex is inessential to the formation of pair bonds, it remains central to the definition of monogamy. And monogamy remains categorically important, because it is sexual, and sex provides "the link to human biology." The scientific naturalization of monogamy in this laboratory reinforces not only the "twoness" requirement for relationships but also the idea that the human is fundamentally sexual.

The naturalization of monogamy depends not only on the specter of sexual excess but also on the policing of sexual lack.[71] The special status of coupling depends on distinguishing it not only from casual or uncoupled sex but also from friendship, comradeship, and situational solidarity. Breaking down barriers between these naturalized categories has the potential to radically reshape how we understand the importance of sex to human nature. It calls us to rethink the pervasive cultural privileging of sexual relationships over other types of connections. It begs that we rethink the relationship of "falling in love" and "getting attached" to sex. Further, my analysis illustrates the dissonance between "science" and "the body." It suggests the vital importance of embedding our curiosity about embodiment within a critical approach to science.

3 MAKING OUR POLY NATURE

Monogamy's Inversion and the Reproduction of Difference

> For psychologists and evolutionary biologists, polyamory is a rare opportunity to see, out in the open, what happens when people stop suppressing their desire for multiple partners and embrace nonmonogamy.
>
> **—Annalee Newitz, "Love Unlimited: The Polyamorists" (2006)**

> Urgent questions remain about how current efforts to re-biologize sexual orientation might reflect or influence existing cultural anxieties and discourses about racialized bodies.
>
> **—Siobhan B. Somerville, *Queering the Color Line* (2000)**

> Violence, especially the liberal varieties, is often most easily perpetuated in the spaces and places where its possibility is unequivocally denounced. . . . It is easy, albeit painful, to point to the conservative elements of any political formation; it is less easy, and perhaps much more painful, to point to ourselves as accomplices of certain normativizing violences.
>
> **—Jasbir K. Puar, *Terrorist Assemblages* (2007)**

If the scientific naturalization of monogamy is heir to a history that produced sexuality as the truth of the self, so too is the naturalizing rhetoric surrounding polyamory, as my first epigraph suggests. While its truth claims are marginalized by comparison, the naturalization of nonmonogamy in poly discourse mirrors the scientific naturalization of monogamy in that it also relies on the kind of evolutionary logic I described in chapter 1. If Young's lab posits that we have evolved to monogamy, poly literature romanticizes an image of a pre-monogamy state of evolutionary and cultural development as more natural, or, at times, celebrates polyamory as a more advanced form of traditional monogamy. In this chapter I concern myself with these counter-discourses to show how they work with naturalizing stories about monogamy to reproduce sexuality as the truth of the self and coupling as a normative value in ways that renaturalize racial difference, as Somerville calls us to consider. I extend my analysis of the politics of science to these counter-narratives, foregrounding a capacious understanding of "science": one that includes claims about nature grounded in the language and theoretical frames of scientific ways of knowing and enjoying the status of scientific authority, in whatever context it does. Some might call some of these discourses scient*istic*, rather than scien*tific*.[1] I have argued elsewhere, with my coauthor Banu Subramaniam, that this distinction is a slippery and ultimately dangerous one in its consolidation of authority and recapitulation of proper disciplinary objects.[2] As the boundaries of disciplines become increasingly porous and we engage in collective cross-disciplinary struggle to think natureculturally about our worlds, policing what counts as science has become increasingly problematic.[3]

The texts I analyze here are not the publications of a multimillion-dollar laboratory. They range from the more recognizably scientific work of a younger, feminist neuroscience laboratory to ethnographic accounts of polyamorous existence and to fictional explications of poly relationships that are deeply engaged with naturalizing discourses. Cumulatively, this poly literature might be said to represent something of a "silly archive": a set of texts largely considered culturally unimportant but which offer insight not accessible via more widely respected sites of knowledge.[4] Nonmonogamy stories certainly do not enjoy the same cultural currency as those that naturalize monogamy, and the queer and feminist among them are marginal even within poly literature.[5] I focus my attention on these poly stories precisely because of their marginal status vis-à-vis the naturalization of monogamy. They begin from a rejection of the premises I have critiqued: that monogamy is natural and desirable, especially for women. In so doing, they mark the terrain of my own resistance to monogamy's nature, a site where complicity with normativizing violence, as Puar puts it, is undertheorized. This complicity is integral to polyamory's nature and thus an important site of intervention in queer feminist challenges to compulsory monogamy and projects of imagining alternative economies of social belonging. I argue here that contesting monogamy by arguing for the naturalness of its mirror image, in polyamory, is not the answer to the problem of "monogamy's law."

In the introduction I discussed Elizabeth Emens's groundbreaking "Monogamy's Law: Compulsory Monogamy and Polyamorous Existence." Here I return to it not to further explicate monogamy's compulsory status but to initiate an examination of "polyamorous existence" as an evidentiary challenge to monogamy's nature. In Emens's account of compulsory monogamy, scientific naturalizing discourse plays a part in shaping "monogamy's law," while polyamory serves as a field of resistance to that naturalization. Her argument has two major components. First, she offers an account of monogamy's compulsory status as evidenced by laws. This account includes a brief review of romantic and scientific stories that naturalize coupling. Emens breaks compulsory monogamy down into two sets of ideals that she calls "super monogamy," the ideal of having one partner for life, and "simple monogamy," the ideal of sexual exclusivity within a given relationship. Second, she posits "polyamorous existence," and the variety of practices of consensual nonmonogamy it entails, as an antidote to the problem of compulsory monogamy.[6] She suggests that while the use of minoritizing rhetoric may be the best strategy to facilitate *legal recognition* of nondyadic relationships, universalizing rhetoric around polyamory powerfully destabilizes monogamy because "it challenges people to admit their own transgressions and violations of the law of monogamy."[7] This universalizing rhetoric cites the ubiquity of adultery and divorce as evidence of the unnaturalness of simple and super monogamy, respectively.[8] In so doing, universalizing poly rhetoric suggests that everyone is "really" nonmonogamous, a claim that inverts the naturalizing claims of scientific discourse on monogamy, effectively naturalizing nonmonogamy.

Emens is certainly not alone in understanding the legal power *minoritizing* stories could hold for poly folks *or* in recognizing the more transformative potential of *universalizing* claims about polyamory to challenge compulsory monogamy. I engage her essay in some detail not to diminish the powerful work it does in exposing the ruse of naturalized monogamy but rather to open a space for a slightly different argument, which I pursue in the remaining chapters. That is, that monogamy and nonmonogamy are not biologically distinct conceptual or behavioral phenomena and that a naturecultural approach to their embodied reality opens space for new imaginings that nonmonogamy's naturalization does not. To be sure, I agree with Emens that scientific discourse plays an important role in naturalizing monogamy and rendering alternatives invisible, and this book is written from the perspective that this scientific naturalization of monogamy has still been undertheorized. I also agree with Emens that the visibility of the wide range of relationship formations grouped under the rubric of "polyamory" opens up possibilities for "choice" that are often foreclosed by the ubiquity of assumptions about the naturalness of monogamy. Similarly, I concur with feminist thinkers who have suggested that challenging the naturalized ideal of the couple opens up possibilities for structuring relationships in ways that can transform our worlds by decentering the domain of the nuclear family form.

If feminists have critiqued monogamy as a set of individualizing norms and values that alienate women and queers from one another and reinforce various aspects of patriarchal and heteronormative culture, including compulsory sexuality, I argue that polyamory discourse offers a challenge to monogamous forms of *sexual relating*. I want to challenge the epistemic status accorded the natural and, more specifically, recourse to a nature imagined as something categorically distinct from culture—either its determinative origin or the object of its betrayal. While feminists have critiqued monogamy in myriad ways, their attempts to challenge its compulsory status have often done so in ways that replicate the same naturalizing logics on which scientific claims that naturalize monogamy are founded: the human is fundamentally sexual, and sexuality is a naturally privileged organizing principle of relationships. Here, neo-Darwinian evolution continues to serve as an implicit explanatory frame for human sexuality. While I share the queer feminist desire to challenge compulsory monogamy, polyamory as sexuality, haunted by the history of monogamy's scientization in early twentieth-century sexology, offers limited and limiting resources for that project.

Polyamory as Sexuality

After a long history of only marginal academic attention, in the last decade or so polyamory has emerged as a vital object of inquiry within the purview of interdisciplinary sexuality studies. A growing body of scholarship on polyamory across disciplines includes a *Sexualities* special issue on polyamory (December 2006) and the edited collection *Understanding Non-monogamies* (2009). In 2005 the Kenneth R. Haslam Collection on Polyamory was established at Indiana University's Kinsey Institute. The archive—containing published and unpublished poly research and a wealth of materials on poly communities and polyamory in the media—suggests the maturation of the topic as an important one for the Kinsey Institute's mission of "advancing sexual knowledge." An active "poly researchers" listserv has been going strong since August 2006, and the third annual International Conference on the

Future of Monogamy and Nonmonogamy was held at Berkeley in February 2014.[9] This academic conference distinguishes itself from a sea of conferences, workshops, and weekends for poly communities, broaching as it does a wide range of conceptual concerns that reflect the status of consensual nonmonogamy as a multidisciplinary object of knowledge rather than a lifestyle or practice.[10]

In June 2012 I spent a week at the Haslam Collection reading correspondence among poly activists and researchers, sorting through conference programs and flyers for workshops, and watching VHS recordings of appearances by poly practitioners and experts—like longtime poly scholar-activist Deborah Anapol—on talk shows throughout the 1980s, 1990s, and early 2000s. What emerged loud and clear from these materials was that the naturalization of polyamory has been an important one in poly (and protopoly) discourse for the last four decades and has simultaneously taken both minoritizing and universalizing forms, sometimes, paradoxically, within the same utterance. Minoritizing forms follow the model of liberal pluralism, advocating the individual rights of the polyamorous. In these formulations, polyamory and monogamy are *analogous* forms. Universalizing forms have tended to challenge monogamy's law and cultural pervasiveness and are often articulated through critique of its devastating effects—for example, broken families, social isolation, and ecological costs of both nuclear family living and the cutting off of nonnuclear affective attachments. These universalizing stories tend to cast polyamory as the opposite of monogamy.

Polyamory, nearly every treatment of the topic explains, means "many loves." It is often defined not only—or even primarily—in contrast to monogamy but rather as distinctly unlike promiscuity and often polygamy.[11] The term "polyfidelity"—a sort of group marriage, where members are sexually exclusive within the group—is credited to the twenty-year-running Kerista Commune (1971–1991) based in the Haight-Ashbury district of San Francisco, whose papers are held in the Haslam Collection. "Polyamory" was coined more recently, in the early 1990s.[12] It comes from the Greek "poly," meaning "many"—similar to polygamy, polygyny, and polyandry (meaning many marriages, wives, and husbands, respectively). Polyamory distinguishes itself from these various marriage/relationship forms with its suffix from the Latin *amor*, or love. Likewise, the word "monoamory" has been coined as a "lovestyle" that separates sexual preference (for one partner) from sociosexual institutionalization (marriage to one person).[13] As in Havelock Ellis's attention to the fine distinction between natural and institutionalized marriage forms, polyamory is imagined as representing a kind of organicism through its focus on "love." While Kerista's model was one of intentional and politicized communal living, albeit strongly inflected with discourses of sexual liberation and freedom, polyamory emerges in contradistinction to monogamy as somehow innocent of culture, as the prediscursive before on which various forms impose their will: as *sexuality*.

The 2014 Berkeley conference description offers a window into the framework through which monogamy's intelligibility as a scholarly object is being collectively imagined. The one-page description that frames the call for papers and describes the conference in the "About" section of the conference's website begins thus: "One set of assumptions that has recently begun to be called into question has been that of the inevitability and desirability of monogamy in marriages and sexual relationships. Contemporary western psychotherapists have until recently insisted that monogamous relationships are the *only* kind that are natural, normal, and healthy. However, now a small but increasing number have begun to question such assumptions."[14] These opening lines establish the field as having been opened up by the questioning of prevailing assumptions about monogamy's naturalness. They also define the project of challenging that naturalness as one of exploring alternative possible configurations *within* "marriages and other sexual relationships."

The growing, yet still marginal, group of questioners finds evidence for their claims about other "natural, normal, and healthy" possibilities in an archive that collapses temporal and geographic alterity to tell an evolutionary story that decenters monogamy's claims to human nature. The then/them of ostensibly nonmonogamous times/cultures becomes a resource for imagining "our" nature "now" *differently*. The next paragraph of the conference description reads: "Numerous anthropological surveys have demonstrated that monogamous marriage is required in only a very small minority of societies. Other researchers have recently pointed out that polyandry, once considered to have been extremely rare, is far more common than previously assumed. The surprising frequency of polyandry among hunting and gathering people suggests it may have been even more common in very ancient times, and even among prehuman ancestors."[15] Having reimagined the terrain of possibility for sexual/romantic relating through this body of evidence, the conference organizers envision a new scientific project at the heart of the field. The conference description closes with these lines: "Is monogamy actually the natural, 'pre-programmed,' or instinctual pattern of the human species? And if not, then what is? What is the history and evolution of monogamous relationships, and what changes are likely in the near-term and long-term future? The conference does not take a position on whether nonmonogamy is desirable or practical, nor on the issue of whether any particular expression of nonmonogamy is healthy. We merely attempt to engage in an objective investigation of the subject." The echoes of Ellis's ushering in of sexological approaches to monogamy nearly a century ago resonate powerfully here. Whereas monogamy is imagined as a Christian and/or capitalist political project, the sexual love it perverts for conservative ends is imagined as a natural and politically neutral object.

A growing body of literature has begun the work of producing critical theories of polysexuality.[16] In this chapter the ways the racially gendered production of sexuality as such shape minoritizing and universalizing poly stories take center stage. My concern here is not with demographics in poly communities,[17] but rather with the links between race, gender, and sexuality in scientific and otherwise naturalizing polyamory rhetoric. This matters because the rebiologization of sexuality always has implications for how we understand difference more generally and specific "differences" in particular. Naturalizing poly rhetoric draws implicitly on either the idea that polyamory is like monogamy and therefore natural or is more natural than monogamy and to be recovered from our evolutionary past. My reading of these two types of naturalizing poly discourse is indebted to what Michel Foucault calls a "pessimistic" reading practice, one aimed at self-reflexive consideration of the embeddedness of liberatory rhetorics in the operations of power they resist. I draw here on Foucauldian approaches to the operationalization of race in science that read new stories about and approaches to the nature of difference not as scientific progress or political bias but as always embedded in the contested terrain of the racial and gendered politics of the moment.[18]

Through their shared reliance on the idea of an original sexuality—wild and either dangerously untamed or gloriously unencumbered by "civilizing" influences—psychoanalytic and evolutionary statements are implicated in both the minoritizing and universalizing naturalization of nonmonogamy in polyamory literature. The minoritizing comparison of polyamory to monogamy makes monogamy natural by claiming for it the sexual normativity of whiteness. The claim—often made in poly literature—that a place or persons are "primitive," offering access to a less mediated nature, more explicitly evokes the Great Chain of Being, which, with European whiteness at its apex, places people on a continuum beginning with primates.[19] While minoritizing rhetoric appropriates the normal, valorization or romanticization of a state of simpler or more childlike (polymorphous) sexuality inverts the value accorded sexual expressions that are already coded as civilized and uncivilized, adult and immature, healthy and unhealthy. Both are always already racialized.

Minoritizing Polyamory Discourse

In the literature on the practice of open and polyamorous relationships, "a monogamouslike emotional exclusivity or bondedness remains by and large naturalized and privileged as the highest experience of human relationships. As such, the traditional ideology of coupledom . . . is not being fundamentally challenged in either theory or social practice but continually reinstated in the very alternatives being celebrated."[20] This monogamouslike bond, Heather Worth, Alison Reid, and Karen McMillan argue, is similarly reproduced in discourses of gay male nonmonogamy.[21] Mark Finn and Helen Malson analyze this seemingly ironic reification of coupledom in the literature and in the personal narratives of the nonmonogamous participants in their research on relationships as symptomatic of an uninterrogated ontological commitment to "realness" as "essence." Serena Petrella, too, names the figure of a self-governing, self-actualizing fully autonomous liberal individual as the responsible citizen-subject of polyamory self-help literature.[22] According to both Finn and Malson and Petrella, the legitimacy of alternative relationship models depends on establishing their benefit to the permanent, stable, and authentic self. This self is nurtured and protected within the imagined safe haven of "home." The metaphoric discourse of home in these narratives operates as a strategy of what Finn and Malson call "dyadic containment."[23] Dyadic containment makes polyamory knowable in a liberal humanist epistemic economy that presumes both the subject's autonomy and a chaotic "outside" that threatens its stability and well-being.

It is not altogether surprising, given this frame of intelligibility, that when polyamory emerges as a scientific category it is often with reference to its *likeness* to monogamy. In a series of groundbreaking studies that eschew what I have argued are foundational assumptions of the monogamy research of Larry Young's laboratory, feminist neuroendocrinologist Sari van Anders and colleagues have brought polyamory explicitly into the neuroscience of social bonding.[24] They directly take on assumptions about pair bonding both as essentially heterosexual and as exclusive, arguing instead that humans are "obviously" a species where individuals of the same "sex/gender" form pair bonds and, further, that the exclusive "two point" nature of pair bonds has been

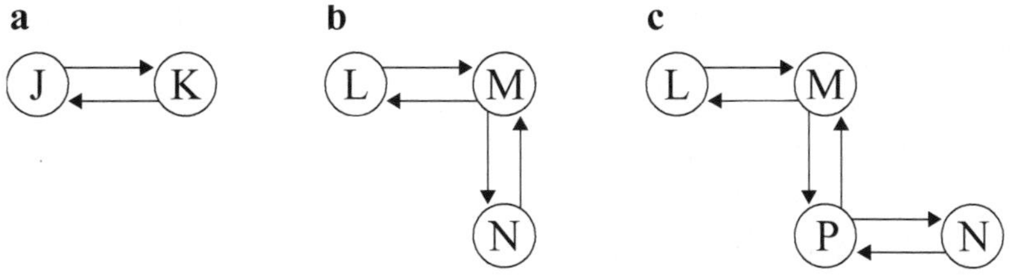

Figure 1. Examples of pair bonds in multiple configurations: (a) 'two-point', as is typically conceptualized, where each individual is in only one pair-bond; (b) 'embedded two-point' for L and N, where L and N are in only one pair-bond each, but their partner is not exclusively bonded to them; 'multi-point' for M, where M has two pair-bonds, and each of these pair bond partners is only pair-bonded with M; and (c) 'embedded two-point' for L and N; 'embedded multi-point' for M and P, where M and P have two pair bonds each, which include a mixture of partners exclusively bonded with them and bonded with others. Letters represent separate individuals, and arrows represent the direction of the bond. An example of (b) is polygyny or polyandry; and of (c) is polyamory for individuals M and P (and potentially L and N, depending on definitions).

FIG 3.1 Polyamory as multipoint pair bonds. From Sari M. Van Anders, Katherine L. Goldey, and Patty X. Kuo, "The Steroid/Peptide Theory of Social Bonds: Integrating Testosterone and Peptide Responses for Classifying Social Behavioral Contexts," *Psychoneuroendocrinology* 36, no. 9 (October 2011): 1267.

taken for granted and thereby understudied.[25] The significance of bonding research that refuses naturalized hetero-monogamy as its point of departure should not be understated! Given the dominant models of "monogamous" and "promiscuous," the representation of other relationship configurations suggests the vastness of a terrain we thought we knew well. In redefining the terms of the study of pair bonding, this research reveals its inherent limitations as well.

Figure 3.1, from van Anders's research, describes a new model, one that takes individual pair bonds as the building block for multiple possible relationship configurations.[26] Polyamory, according to the figure's original caption, is an example of the kind of configuration represented by image c in figure 3.1. This multipoint bond is polyamory for the two multiply pair-bonded individuals and, potentially, "depending upon definitions," for each of the four connected individuals, including those only in two-point bonds, L and N. This parenthetical consideration points to the contested nature of understandings of polyamory. Depending on how an individual defines the concept, partners' multipoint bonds may or may not lead them to identify as polyamorous or to describe their relationship as a polyamorous one. These competing definitions, which lend themselves to different readings of relationship status, largely hinge on whether the ends of an individual multipoint bond (M and N, for example, in image b) see their relationships to one another and to their mutual partner (here, M) as in some way exceeding the definition of monogamy. If N, who is not, as M is in image c, part of another pair bond, is not interested in pairing with anyone other than P and regards that disinterest as an *orientation* toward monogamy, N would not be polyamorous by virtue of N's partner's polyamory. Van Anders and colleagues develop this distinction between "relationship orientation" and "relationship status" elsewhere.[27]

Defining polyamory as a practice of multiple-point pair bonds (see fig. 3.1), or "plural monogamy," extends its conceptual use for science beyond a dyadic model that places the "liberated couple" at the center of analysis, recognizing as it does the "realness" of each bond.[28] In this sense, the model has potentially radical implications for how we think about "family" in evolutionary terms. Despite the potential for denaturalizing nuclearity, the conceptualization of polyamory within the discourse of pair bonding reifies the pair bond as the primary social/biological unit. More to the point, it illustrates for us the limits of challenging the *exclusivity* of pair bonding, the limits of polyamory as it were. That is to say, while the unit's size may grow, the intimate bonds of a presumptively sexual "home" remain the privileged site for understanding human relating and biology, thus naturalizing the inside/outside, domestic/public, affective/nonaffective dualisms that have tended to structure understandings of human evolution. The implications for the legal status of polyamory are vast. That polyamory should be considered a sexual orientation, and that the poly unit should be considered a natural family, contains, like gay marriage, would-be challenges to the privatization of wealth and care in the middle-class home.[29] To the extent that polyamory is conceptualized as *like* monogamy, its capacity to answer queer feminist critiques of coupled forms of social belonging is foreclosed.

Oxytocin connects monogamy to polyamory as an object of bioscientific inquiry as the peptide/hormone associated with attachment, exclusive or otherwise. Its slipperiness captures the implicit interconnectedness of the biological conceptions of belonging and exclusion that underlie both relationship models. Not only is oxytocin important to pair bonds, single and multipoint, it has also been touted for its more general effects on feelings of belonging. Oxytocin is what makes the maternal brain, it is the love hormone, the trust hormone, and the "moral molecule" that makes us do right by others.[30] Indeed oxytocin is among the most vital and versatile (and, importantly, subject to other influences—see chapter 5 on plasticity) variables in human behavior.[31]

Some reports have referred to it as a *mystery* hormone and as "the new dopamine," for its status as the new buzzword in an industry that sells better living through chemistry.[32] Recent studies and popular reports have explored what they have called oxytocin's "dark side."[33] These scientific stories have been focused on the larger implications of oxytocin-induced attachment—be it a partnership or some other in-group affiliation. These stories suggest that the flip side of attachment is disdain for outsiders. They have referred to oxytocin as "the ethnocentrism hormone," arguing that it promotes racial bias and xenophobic attitudes and facilitates dishonesty and disinterest in fairness when they benefit the in-group.[34] These findings are often reported in a rather crass naturalization of racism, which seems more a symptom itself than a diagnosis, but opens up some important conceptual space to interrogate the notion of attachment on which the biologization of both monogamy and polyamory depends.

The formulation of attachment vis-à-vis its outside, the flip side of "preference," offers a different perspective on the neurobiology of non/monogamy: one that helps make visible naturecultural connections between racism and pair bonding. As I demonstrated in my analysis of the partner preference test in chapter 2, a pair bond is typically evidenced by a statistically registerable—though not exclusive—*preference* for spending time in closer proximity to a familiar. The leap from preference for "familiarity" to loyalty to members of one's race or nation expressed in reports on oxytocin as the "ethnocentrism hormone" is an enormous one but should not necessarily be dismissed out of hand. Familiarity is in fact *intimate* and not categorical. It is established through proximity. A correlation between familiarity and racial or ethnic identification is not unlikely, however, in contexts of racial and ethnic segregation. Familiarity and similarity are not the same thing. But in a racist and race-stratified society, where familiarity and race are likely to correlate, what does it mean to celebrate the naturalized "home" as the core of human nature and thus the ground for poly acceptance? The naturalization of familial love is deeply enmeshed with the naturalization of capitalist forms. Families are not just neutral social or biological entities but are also economic ones, which serve as the vehicle for passing along wealth (or not). In other words, in the name of looking out for the welfare of our families many breaches of social justice principles seem justified, and inequities reproduce themselves thus.[35] The minoritizing naturalization of polyamory, recentering love as the basis of social belonging, is ill equipped to intervene in the violence of a monogamy-centric culture that hinges on forsaking all others. Universalizing poly discourse, in contrast, frames monogamy and its attendant rules of engagement as an *imposition* on our true nature.

Universalizing Polyamory Discourse

In this section I turn my attention to the naturalization of nonmonogamy in universalizing polyamory discourse. While literature on ethical nonmonogamy in the West has taken mostly heteronormative forms, I chose sites of deployment of polyamorous counter-narratives in specifically feminist/antimasculinist and especially queer/anti-heterocentric feminist stories about monogamy. I offer readings of selections from two such poly readers, examining the evidence they use to support their claims about our poly nature, to illustrate the racial underpinnings of universalizing poly discourse. I read *Plural Loves: Designs for Bi and Poly Living*, edited by feminist scholar and poly activist Serena Anderlini-D'Onofrio, and *The Lesbian Polyamory Reader*, edited by Marcia Munson and Judith Stelboum, also published as a special issue of the *Journal of Lesbian Studies* in 1999.[36] After analyzing these readers, I end the section with a discussion of *Gaia and the New Politics of Love*, Anderlini-D'Onofrio's ecofeminist manifesto on the urgency of embracing the bi and poly lovestyles introduced in *Plural Loves*.[37] Distinguishing themselves from a vast archive of universalizing poly literature, these three texts are both more explicitly feminist and more theoretical than many of their counterparts. That is to say, they are attentive to sexism in poly discourse and intentionally not of the self-help/how-to genre. They are also at pains to redress the heterosexual orientation of most poly literature. As explicit challenges to the naturalness of monogamy grounded in queer and feminist stakes, these arguments function in the interstices where I see myself engaging in a productive reimagining of monogamy-centric culture.[38] In order to make its claims, each of these texts encodes an explicit set of assumptions about the naturalness of nonmonogamy. The naturalizing rhetoric they deploy evokes a racial economy grounded in neo-Darwinian evolutionary theory with powerful resonances in *this* historical moment.

I begin with *The Lesbian Polyamory Reader* (1999) to discuss an array of types of naturalizing claims made in the text, as well as its structure and use of images. Many feminist poly author/activists casually suggest or reference the naturalness of nonmonogamy in familiar expressions about the naturally nonmonogamous nature of particular groups or the universal desirability of nonmonogamy, for everyone. Nannette Gartrell explains how she and her partner came to the decision to become polyamorous: "It seemed unlikely that we would be more successful at suppressing inopportune lust than countless other lesbians who had tried and failed to do so."[39] Here, lesbians, like men, are simply too amorous to realistically succeed at monogamy. In "Lesbians as Luvbeins" JoAnn Loulan similarly asserts that "the basic principle [underlying polyamory] is that sexual feelings are part of our lives from birth to death."[40] The centrality of sexual drive discourse in these poly stories focuses on reclaiming sexual agency for women at the expense of sustained incorporation of critiques of compulsory sexuality and the privileging of sexual-romantic connections. Kate Millet's classic critique of Friedrich Engels's explanation for women's willingness to submit to monogamy against their own best interests is an excellent example of how discourses of sexual liberation are invoked to challenge entrenched gendered monogamy stories. She takes on Engels's argument that women find sexuality burdensome by offering as counter-evidence an account of the scientific arguments suggesting that "the female possesses, biologically and inherently, a far greater capacity for sexuality than the male."[41]

Claims about the naturalness of nonmonogamy in terms of drives or, more generally, as an inherently and universally desirable way of relating, being, or living reinforce the notion of sexuality as natural, inevitable, and vitally important. In her contribution to *The Lesbian Polyamory Reader*, in a section titled "Intimacy," Anne Dal Vera makes both types of claims. Her use of a quote from Terry Tempest Williams is useful for understanding how: "What kind of impoverishment is this to withhold emotion, *to restrain our passionate nature in the face of a generous life just to appease our fears*? A man or woman whose mind reins in the heart when the body sings desperately for connection can only expect more *isolation and ecological disease*. Our lack of intimacy with each other is in direct proportion to our lack of intimacy with the land. We have taken our love inside and *abandoned the wild*."[42] In this account, not only does the body naturally "sing out," it does so in its own best interests. To suppress or deny desire is to be untrue to one's self. It is true that "critics of monogamy often found their arguments on the assumption of the power of underlying sexual drives, which people repress only to their detriment, or even which they are unable to repress at all."[43] However, repressing those drives is not, for Dal Vera, only to one's own detriment but also to that of "the land." In this formulation, we have a moral responsibility, psychic *and* ecological, to return to the passionate nature we have abandoned by fearfully taking refuge in monogamy. This legacy of romanticizing a naturalized connection between eros and ecology is a common struggle for antiracist queer feminisms in and beyond poly literature.[44] I will thus return to ecological polyamory again at the end of this chapter.

While ostensibly race neutral, this type of evidence about the naturalness of nonmonogamy evokes a racial economy that was foundational to turn-of-the-century sexology and is alive and well in contemporary science and culture.[45] Two photographs from the *Lesbian Polyamory Reader* offer examples of how this return to "wild connections" between women is figured. The way this pair of photographs is presented in the text and the framing of the individual photographs both rely on this economy to naturalize nonmonogamy. These two photos are printed in the same section, titled "Living the Dream." This section is the only place in the book where photographs of black women appear. The two photographs, entitled "Festival Showers" and "May Day Celebration," are of large groups of nude and seminude women, outdoors. They are perfect examples of the racialized aesthetic Carla Williams describes as "the National Geographic aesthetic" in that both appear to have been taken by an outside observer and rely on an ethnographic model for their effect.[46] That aesthetic is used here in the service of illustrating a "dream" of sexual freedom that relies on an idealized notion of a simple, pure, and sexually uninhibited primitivism to impart its meaning: that nonmonogamy is natural.

The two photos in the section titled "Friends and Lovers"—"the three of cups" and "healing hands"—present a very different sort of narrative. These photos of women massaging each other and posing in a garden have the appearance of intimacy and represent a domesticity that contrasts sharply with the tone of the earlier pair of photos. While the first set are wild and natural (outside of home and key contextual markers), the second depends on politicized lesbian feminist challenges to the logic of the sexual family (which I discuss more in the next chapter). While the first pair highlights ritual and sexual freedom, the second draws on the stability and comfort of the promise of intimate friendship. The use of black bodies and a racialized aesthetic *as evidence* of the naturalness of nonmonogamy in these passages signals the naturalizing of poly discourse as a site of tensions around race in ways that I will elaborate in my reading of *Plural Loves*.

Plural Loves announces the advent of a new polyamory that promises to be more attentive to gender and "sexual orientation" than many of its predecessors. In the introduction Anderlini-D'Onofrio states that this sort of polyamorous thinking has, since the 1980s, shared with bisexuality "an interest for pre-modern and 'primitive' social organizations where the homo/hetero divide is not enforced." She goes on to argue that in primitive societies "erotic love is often part of a pantheistic concept of the sacred which calls for a gentler, contemplative, more 'feminine' relationship with nature."[47] Not only do these passages mark the text as a feminist undertaking, they link its gender awareness explicitly to the notion of a utopian *before*. Before patriarchy, monotheism, modernization, and in the case of Deborah Anapol's essay in the same volume, colonization, so the story goes, there was a simpler world, one in which sexuality was not fraught with the restrictions that limit "us," here and now. I use the language of "us" and "them" to draw attention to a narrative formulation evoked in the passages I read, one that while using the Other to make claims about the naturalness of nonmonogamy, continually situates the presumed poly reader as implicitly white and Anglo-American.[48]

The mythic them, there, and then, before or outside compulsory monogamy, is a favorite trope of poly fiction and nonfiction alike. It is of course very powerful to point out that values like monogamy are culturally and historically contingent. The specific power of this strategy often rests at least in part on the racial resonances of this truth claim. In a white supremacist culture where racism is deeply sexualized, it is not difficult for "us" to buy that, for example, precolonial Hawaii (Anapol) and "Africa" (Anderlini-D'Onofrio) were and are sexually more "free" than "we" imagine ourselves to be. Saying that "we" want to be more like "them" (and/or "then" as the case may be) further legitimates highly contested scientific and anthropological constructions of otherness that posit the popular notions of primitive sexuality with which we have become familiar. Whether we look with feelings of disgust or longing, if we are reading these racial constructions as unproblematically "true," something is wrong. When we rearticulate it as utopian, it has the same racial resonances.

Merl Storr's analysis of universalizing claims around bisexuality helps to illustrate this point.[49] Because the ground of an enlightened bisexuality is the place where *Plural Loves* opens, Storr's critique of universalizing discourse on bisexuality warrants review here. Storr argues that claims about the naturalness of bisexuality, as we now understand it—as desire for both men and women—reflect and reinforce the historic racialization of bodies. Storr makes her argument by tracing a genealogy of bisexuality's meanings.[50] Sexologists explained bisexuality as the existence of characteristics of "both sexes" in one body, usually in terms of secondary sex characteristics. Bisexual bodies—what we would now call intersex bodies—were thus not wholly or acceptably male or female. As sexual differentiation was widely understood to correlate with evolutionary development, as I have discussed, "bisexuals" were less fully evolved, more "primitive" as it were. Claims of bisexuality as universally natural today (i.e., "everyone is 'really' bisexual"), Storr explains, necessarily play on this notion of a primitive sexuality.[51] They "make sense" in part because of the racialized imaginary of primitive sexuality that is so familiar in Anglo-American science and culture.[52]

Having been seen historically as an immature, transitional, or underdeveloped sexuality or as a primitive, less evolved state of being, "bisexuality"—and here its relation to claims about polyamory—carries the baggage of a fraught history in the biosocial science of human variation.[53] As Anderlini-D'Onofrio's introduction suggests, polyamory has its own distinct investments in "primitive" cultures and sexualities as well. I will explore these in more detail, with the assumption that wherever the idea of primitive sexuality is evoked, it carries racial resonances. I will look closely at one nonfiction essay and one short story from *Plural Loves* to illustrate my concerns. While much can certainly be said of the value of these works, I am reading here for the racial resonances of their evidentiary apparatuses and will confine my analysis to those themes that are illustrative of the discourses I have described. I will begin with Deborah Taj Anapol's short piece "A Glimpse of Harmony" and then discuss Taliesin the Bard's fictional work "Just Like a Hollywood Movie."

Psychologist, activist, ethnographer, and longtime expert spokesperson for poly women, Anapol is widely read, and her arguments for the naturalness of polyamory are well known. It is worth noting here that my archival encounter with Anapol at the Kinsey Institute revealed a shift from more overtly politicized critiques of monogamy in the 1980s and early 1990s to more naturalizing discourses on polyamory later in the 1990s and into the 2000s.[54] This later and better known era of her work is well represented by "A Glimpse of Harmony." The piece posits precolonial Hawaii as a poly utopia of sorts. On the basis of her research, she asserts that the language, child-rearing practices, and variety of accepted relationship formations in pre-European-contact Hawaii all suggest a harmoniously "sex-positive" culture. She contrasts this culture with the "sex negative" culture of the United States, which she argues mandates monogamy, ignores or punishes the sexuality of children, and is generally repressive. At first glance, much of her characterization of U.S. culture seems fair enough, and her description of particular practices, like the existence of a Hawaiian word—*punalua*—to describe one's relationship to one's partner's exes, seem to offer an exciting alternative model of kinship. I want to address two problems with her argument—first, her deployment of the concept of "culture," and second, the role of "the Feminine" in her analysis.

First, I want to suggest that enough context is missing from her portrait of "old Hawaii" to make her romantic conclusions about its sexual harmony suspect. The out-of-context retrieval of particular concepts or practices is an exoticizing move that makes her point at the expense of a nuanced understanding of a culture that we might fairly assume was complex: that is, not monolithic but rather full of internal contradiction, like any culture.[55] Questioning the deployment of the notion of "culture" here, good and bad, sex-positive and sex-negative cultures as it were, pushes us to ask not only what Hawaii is Anapol talking about, but what United States? The norms she describes as characteristic of sex-negative U.S. culture are coded in terms of race and class. For example, cooperative child-rearing and valued intergenerational relationships are not uncommon in U.S. families outside the white middle class.[56] Lesbian kinship in the United States has also been read as a model of adopting exes into one's family that challenges heteronormative patterns of relating.[57] Notably, the existence of practices that Anapol considers "sex-positive" in the United States has not made bisexuality *or* polyamory harmoniously mundane. As for the loving grooming of children for adult sexuality that she describes—like genital massage and rituals acknowledging changes in adolescent bodies—it is unclear from her writing when and where and by whom these rites were practiced or what they might have meant to their practitioners. It is also unclear how they might be interpreted as challenging heterosexual or monogamous expectations for adult sexuality.

The premise on which Anapol's explanation for the culture of old Hawaii relies is my second major concern, though it is perhaps better read as a symptom of the first. The reason for the radical openness of old Hawaii, she argues, is the Feminine, for which the Hawaiian Islands are apparently well known. The Feminine is both geographical and cultural in her argument, and the link between them is important. Geographically speaking, all the features of the climate "combine their power with the land, to create a sensual, even erotic atmosphere. An atmosphere favoring relaxation and play over ambition and linear thought." Culturally speaking, this Feminine, the essence of which is *connection*, was honored in Hawaii through the worship of female deities. While the "practices" on which this honor is evidenced are no longer a part of Hawaiian culture, according to Anapol's research, the Feminine remains strong there: it is "the bridge between past and present." Masculinity does not seem to exist there—in fact, Anapol's own need for "internal male support" was unmet "amidst all the softness!"[58] I will leave aside any critique of her use of masculinity and femininity to categorize various traits. Instead I concern myself with two effects of her account, effects that co-constitute polyamory's naturalization.

First, in her description of Hawaii she has painted a portrait of a world where violence, racism, economic exploitation, sexism, and homophobia seem not to exist, a world where people seem more concerned with sensuality than rent. Not surprisingly, on the beach, where she encounters people on vacation, Anapol senses a powerful "transcendence" of "ambition and linear thought."[59] The lives of real residents of Hawaii, old and new, seem to have informed her analysis only marginally, which in no way curtails her claims to represent a world unmarred by culture. She misses the contested nature of culture—that power dynamics in a political geographical space play a role in determining what counts as culture.[60]

Second, the lack of gender differentiation Anapol perceives in Hawaii, and which she situates as both evidence and cause of a purer, less polluted sexual culture, is discursively dangerous in its particular invocation of evolutionary theory. As I explained in the introduction, the analogous relationship posited between race and gender played a major role in scientific theorizing about human variation throughout the nineteenth and twentieth centuries. Notions of racial and gender difference were used by scientists to explain one another on many counts, one of the most enduring of which is the notion that less sexually differentiated bodies are evidence of racial and evolutionary inferiority.[61] The universal femininity of Hawaii feminizes Hawaiian men, thus evoking a lack of sexual differentiation historically associated with "lesser races." Further, sexual "promiscuity," spun rather as openness, lack of taboo or inhibition, when described appreciatively, is of course a hallmark of "primitive" sexuality. In other words, the discourses of reviled colonial corruption and celebrated civilizing missions refer to the same historic moments. The implication either way is that the intruded-on "culture" was waiting in a state of nature, sexually freer and innately simpler than our own.

Fictional narratives about polyamory no less than nonfiction have challenged compulsory monogamy through recourse to naturalizing discourse. The premise of Taliesin the Bard's "Just Like a Hollywood Movie" is a triadic sexual-romantic relationship whose three members, who work together in the adult film industry, decide to make a movie—the first feature-length film about polyamory. The fictional film is called *The Compersion Effect*.[62] The characters discuss establishing the credibility of the film's central premise—that polyamory is natural and therefore good—throughout the story. They hire a cultural anthropologist and an evolutionary biologist as "expert advisors" on the film in order to make sure they accurately represent "the facts." The facts, as such, serve as a catalogue of examples of nonmonogamy in *nature*. According to the experts, whose knowledge the protagonists share with the public at press conferences about the film, "aboriginal cultures existing today," "early humans," and "bonobos" all share similar patterns of sexual relating.[63] They have no concept of paternity and therefore have no need to exercise ownership of women through monogamy in order to establish it. Several things happen in this story within a story, perhaps the most interesting of which for my purposes is that evolutionary theory is deployed directly to legitimate nonmonogamy, in ways that make it apparent that the theory's more subtle invocations elsewhere in the book are operating as the epistemic ground of claims about our poly nature.

The assumption that early humans were like nonhuman primates alive today and that there exist groups of people who are now largely untouched by the evolutionary and cultural changes that have affected most human primates is a very fragile premise for many reasons, but here, I am more interested in what it *does* than why it is not "true." The argument that humans are like nonhuman primates, and particularly that some humans are closer to them than others, directly evokes the Great Chain of Being, wherein a line from nonhuman primates to the European male was effectively established as an explanatory regime for social inequities. Arguments about the naturalness of non/monogamy based on this logic are powerful because evolutionary explanations are powerful. The classification of humans into these groupings makes sense in part because racism does.

In this fictional account of polyamory's nature, the characters critique scientific naturalizing discourse on monogamy as science through "religious filters."[64] They assume that evolutionary arguments about nonmonogamy are, however, an unmediated, apolitical representation of the natural world. What about science through white supremacist filters? As Sandra Harding asks in *Science and Social Inequality: Feminist and Postcolonial Issues*: "Under what conditions could it occur that a society with widespread and powerful forms of structural racism—a race segregated social structure—could produce sciences that did *not* participate in justifying and maintaining such white supremacy?"[65] What kinds of scientific proclamations might resist the idea of types of people more or less human than others?[66] The assumption that science is the Truth and the privileging of culturally entrenched facts about primitive sexuality as scientific evidence are what function to undermine monogamy in the story. In order to make the film work to "advocate polyamory," the characters determine that they will need "unbiased science"; that people will see the light of polyamory if the film's presentation of scientific evidence achieves "transcendence" of political, social, and religious beliefs. Despite the potential for *engagement* rather than transcendence, in attempts to paint polyamory in a positive light, nature so often remains the basket into which all of our proverbial eggs are placed. Before, underneath, and, if our dreams come true, *after* the smokescreen of culture, so the story goes, is the truth of how "humans were intended to live, polyamorously, polysexually."[67]

When feminists narrate recouping "the body" as an *alternative* approach to *critiquing* science, rather than an integrated process in service of making sense of the naturecultural world, we authorize the romanticization of nature "itself" as somehow outside time, space, and/or politics, which entails considerable risk. This is easier to see, perhaps, in the invocation of neo-Darwinian evolutionary time through stories of primitives and bonobos but is not confined to such "dated" scientific evidence. In her most recent book, Anderlini-D'Onofrio has bridged minoritizing and universalizing rhetorics in an argument that draws heavily on the science of neuroplasticity. She posits that what she has called "bi and poly lovestyles"—forms of relating that encourage "loving more," rather than confining affection to one sexual-romantic connection—encourage the release of oxytocin, which makes us happier and thus more compassionate. Polyamory, in this way, her argument goes, can change our brains and thus the world: "The nonviolent, consensual forms of intimacy that oxytocin promotes tend to lead to states of tantric ecstasy and enchanted elation similar to the ones that characterized the first phase of modernity, with its openness to joy, pleasure, surprise, wonder, and amazement."[68] The projection of feelings of "enchanted elation" onto an imagined geo/temporal Other in the historically indeterminate "first phase of modernity" does the work of scientizing both nonmonogamy and racial difference through a casual invocation of neo-Darwinian evolutionism. The introduction of contingency, the hallmark of "new" understandings of evolutionary time that represent nature as always *in formation*, does nothing in itself to disrupt old stories about monogamy's nature. In fact, the new story depends for its intelligibility on these figures. Whether it is the sexual openness of an abstract "before," the sacred Femininity of Hawaii, or the enlightening proclivities of "early man," these universalizing stories present a racialized sexual Other who, like the bonobo, can purportedly teach us something about ourselves. They are made to stand, populations and individuals, as representatives of our "natural" sexual selves. And it is this evidentiary schema that enables the moral reversal enacted by universalizing poly narratives.

Minoritizing naturalizing stories about nonmonogamy are easily contained within pluralist models of sexual difference and do little to challenge a culture of compulsory monogamy that privileges sexual-romantic connection over other forms of social belonging. While universalizing claims challenge monogamy as a culture, making it *right* to resist the socialization that naturalizes monogamy, they do so at significant cost. The logic problematically privileges scientific explanations over other critiques of monogamy—producing the mandate to be sexually exclusive as more important than any other aspect of monogamy-centric or mononormative culture. It also relies on a racial typography that reinscribes historic assumptions about what race is and the relationship of race to sexuality. If our aim is to destabilize monogamy-centric culture, we do not need more scientific evidence that nonmonogamy is natural. We need more nuanced analyses of the naturecultural production of monogamy, in which scientific pronouncements are often implicated. In addition to critiques of naturalizing poly discourse, we need alternatives to this mirroring effect: another way of seeing monogamy.

4 RETHINKING MONOGAMY'S NATURE

From the Truth of Non/Monogamy to a Dyke Ethics of "Antimonogamy"

> A way of life can be shared among individuals of different age, status, and social activity. It can yield intense relations not resembling those that are institutionalized. It seems to me that a way of life can yield a culture and an ethics.
>
> **—Michel Foucault, "Friendship as a Way of Life" (1997)**

> Being sexually non-exclusive is not enough to change society. . . . It is anti-monogamy . . . which aims to break down this very system that dictates how we should conduct our relationships.
>
> **—Becky Rosa, "Anti-monogamy: A Radical Challenge to Compulsory Heterosexuality?" (1994)**

> At first, I admit, what attracted me about lesbianism was the sex. . . . While I stood on the sidelines gaping with awe, it became clear to me that sex was merely the tip of the lesbian iceberg.
>
> **—Alison Bechdel, *Dykes and Sundry Other Carbon-Based Life-Forms to Watch Out For* (1992)**

In scientific naturalizing stories about both monogamy and nonmonogamy, the natural remains an epistemically privileged site, leaving historically entrenched assumptions about both nature and sexuality fully intact and unquestioned. In the tradition of reflexivity in feminist theory, I have come to this reading of the normalizing imperatives of the monogamy gene and polyamory discourse through struggle—intellectual, emotional, and always political. I share with many of the poly women writers whose work I critique a hope for new forms of relationships not built on the primacy of the couple, economically and otherwise. I also share with them a feminist political desire for something more than instability. I have heard this desire echoed in new work on materiality in feminist theory and affectivity in queer theory over the last decade or so. These new strands of attention to materiality and affect have moved in many directions and opened new doors for thinking bodily. We have witnessed an invitation to experiment with what it might mean to re-envision the world onto-epistemologically, from the perspective that knowing and being are inextricably bound, such that what once was "merely culture" can be seen to incite new becomings.[1] Which makes cultural texts important resources for understanding the nature of non/monogamy.

Guides to and stories about polyamory offer us some models, but as they gain popularity in our (queer) communities, recipes for poly living are increasingly prescriptive and often couple-centric. As I argued in chapter 3, in different ways both the minoritizing and universalizing naturalization of nonmonogamy in poly discourse reinvoke notions of race and difference out of which monogamy's nature emerged. I find Rosa's distinction between "nonmonogamy" and "antimonogamy" useful here. Despite its linguistic formulation, antimonogamy for Rosa is not the opposite of monogamy. It is not an alternate sexual subjectivity but rather "a way of life" oriented to *undoing* monogamy. As Foucault says in the lines following those in this chapter's first epigraph, "to be 'gay,' I think, is not to identify with the psychological traits and the visible masks of the homosexual but to try to define and develop a way of life."[2] Antimonogamy is not a set of psychological traits at all but is rather aspirational. Its ambitions stem from a rejection of certain tenets that would proscribe our relationships and define our desire in reductive ways: it suggests an ethics of destabilization. If non/monogamies have achieved their intelligibility through processes of racialization and antimonogamy makes that schema itself the object of critical resistance, antimonogamy resists the renaturalization of racial difference. In so doing, it opens space for thinking about power within and in relation to different structures and systems of belonging. Rosa's destabilizing "antimonogamy" is a deferral of the question of monogamy's nature, of the science of monogamy as it were.

To defer engagement with questions science has posed about monogamy (are we or are we not wired for it?) is to open space for creativity. Rosa asks feminists to consider how the nuclear family undermines friendship, why we associate "falling in love" with sex, and how "compulsory sexuality" functions to make sex a central organizing principle of our relationships. These questions do not foreclose scientific ones; they rather defer them, suggesting that "monogamy" needs to be far more rigorously interrogated. Monogamy becomes "monogamy" in this process of destabilization: no longer an a priori given. Rosa asks us to recognize and resist the "pressure on lesbians to be as 'normal' as possible" and instead to "invent our own relationships," individually and collectively.[3] This call to invention cannot be read as disengaging materiality in favor of discourse. It begins from an embodied subject position—that of "lesbians." To think against the logic of monogamy's nature is to foray into another conceptual terrain for thinking about bodies, and specifically for thinking about bodies in context.

In her articulation of lesbianism's scope, Alison Bechdel offers us a self-consciously performative reclamation of sexological "lesbianism" as a *way of life* that makes possible a culture not premised on the logic of the couple, without prescribing and renaturalizing alternatives.[4] Writing against the risk of simply adding to the "program of proposals," I want to consider the "instruments for polymorphic, varied, and individually modulated relationships" made available to us in the fictional world of Bechdel's lesbian comic strip *Dykes to Watch Out For* (*DTWOF*), which ran from 1983 to 2008.[5] In "Friendship as a Way of Life" Foucault argued that "something well-considered like a magazine"—or a comic strip, I contend—"ought to make possible a homosexual culture," offering these "instruments" without creating a "program of proposals" that "become law." Bechdel's comic strip is just such a resource for a dyke antimonogamy.

Especially since the publication of her celebrated graphic memoir *Fun Home: A Family Tragicomic* in 2006, Bechdel has received accolades for her contributions to lesbian and queer cultures.[6] Bechdel's work, reviewers seem to agree, "provides a welcome alternative to public discourses about LGBTQ politics that are increasingly homonormative and dedicated to family values."[7] Part of *DTWOF*'s anti-"homonormative" ethos, I argue, is a destabilizing, antimonogamy sensibility. That is to say, it offers a sense that monogamy is a feminist issue and an ideal that should not be taken for granted, but without offering easy or prescriptive answers or suggesting that its strictures are mere social impositions from which the availability of legal or moral alternatives might liberate our desire. This dyke ethics of "antimonogamy," through its grounding in notions of friendship, community, and social justice, decenters the sexual dyad in a way that polyamory does not. In so doing it offers first a way of rethinking the story of monogamy's nature as a naturecultural tale about mononormative desire and further places that desire in a field of relationality that renders its significance as a feature of humanness and an object of scientific inquiry newly strange.

Toward a Dyke Ethics

Like Lynne Huffer in *Are the Lips a Grave?*, I'm convinced that "bringing the term *lesbian* back into the picture" is vital to theorizing a queer feminist ethics of sex and social belonging.[8] The embodied lesbian, fictional or not, forces us to question stories that tell us what feminist and queer desires look like, and circumscribe what a feminist or queer take on monogamy might be. Unsurprisingly, given the richness of Huffer's archive and the iconic status of *DTWOF* as a uniquely and distinctly lesbian text, she draws on Bechdel's autobiographical account of her own coming out to frame the case for reclaiming lesbian.[9] Bechdel's journey, depicted in "Coming Out Story," begins one "fateful day" at her college's co-op bookstore and is filled, in classic Bechdelian fashion, with written texts. In between scenes at the co-op and at the library of the gay student union she finally joins, readers are treated to an iconic *DTWOF* scene of a woman alone in bed with books. Huffer argues that "Bechdel helps us think about queer feminist subjectivity by figuring it visually as the one-handed reading of the masturbating dyke." In her reading of these frames of Bechdel in bed with her books, Huffer eloquently interprets that dyke figure: "Her quest is both erotic and epistemological: 'an insatiable hunger' for 'knowledge' that is at once literary, corporeal, and female."[10] Jane Tolmie offers a similar reading of the effect of Bechdel's masturbating dyke: "A small frame of the narrator masturbating while reading Anaïs Nin titillatingly reminds the reader of the multiple intersections of text and body, constructed identity and experience, art and life."[11] While Huffer tracks a "genealogy of masturbatory queer dyke-love" through which she theorizes "mutuality, reciprocity, and respect for difference" as the ground for a new ethics to inspiring effect, I am most interested here in the "at once" textual and material figuration of the dyke.

I use "dyke" here for its lesbian-feminist signifying power and for its nature-cultural valence. "Feminist" is a deeply denaturalized category, and is in fact often characterized as a philosophy and worldview operating from a foundational myth of willful denial about nature itself.[12] And "lesbian" is historically a scientific category. It described the female whose purportedly masculine tastes and/or sexual proclivities toward women evidenced her inversion, whether congenital or acquired. Acquired inversion evokes the specter of feminism, as its history is inextricably bound with anxieties about gender roles.[13] At the heart of lesbian-feminism are questions about the contested nature of difference and desire. As Kim Emery so concisely put it: "The question of whether lesbians are born or made may seem new . . . but it is hardly news to lesbians; versions of this debate—from late nineteenth-century distinctions between 'congenital' and 'acquired' inversion to late twentieth-century disagreements over the difference between sexual 'orientation' and sexual 'preference'—have animated popular as well as professional representations of lesbian possibility from the very beginning. Indeed, the crystallization of this structuring division might be said to mark the beginning of what we now understand as 'lesbian.'"[14] Here Emery evokes a genealogy of *lesbian* as a category of analysis not simply caught in a nature/nurture debate, but effectively materialized out of it. In other words, ostensibly "essentialist" and "constructivist" accounts of lesbianism coproduce its meanings. Birch Moonwomon-Baird reaches a similar conclusion that leads her to reject both queer and feminist dismissals of essentialism as "innatest" and ahistorical, arguing that her lesbian research subjects deployed "essentialism" in ways that allow for "both agency and mutability."[15] If lesbianism seems to embody the debate, calling its constituents' positions to the fore, "dyke," as a slang term for lesbian, marks a subtle epistemological reorientation.

The question of where lesbianism comes from is decentered in the ardent and powerful claiming of it embodied in the term "dyke." It takes on an ontological status, that is to say a "realness," that is decidedly naturecultural. Dykes might be born unassimilable within the heteropatriarchally gendered order of things or recruited by the lure of feminist propaganda. The moniker does not lend itself to such speculation. Dyke signifies a real *and* situated difference. It is at once specific and fantastically capacious—bull dyke, femme dyke, bi dyke (or byke), trans dyke, tryke.[16] As a reclaimed slur, dyke is an explicitly politicized category that lends itself differently from "lesbian" to this kind of capaciousness. It emerges out of and evokes histories of sexism/homophobia/transphobia that cannot be parsed. This history both evokes and eschews conceptions of lesbianism that would describe it in reductively anatomical or psychoanalytic terms. My reading of "dyke" is not that it enables us to transcend the epistemological in favor of the ontological but rather that its deployment offers a lens through which to see history and embodiment, community and desire, the *literary* and the *corporeal* in the same frame. In other words, a dyke ethics might be understood in part as a naturecultural shift away from the nature/culture debate and toward an embodied politics wherein the inextricability of desire from context is taken for granted.

Indeed much of the humor of *DTWOF* lies in its simultaneous marking of deeply embodied desire and the contexts that enable its materialization. The comic's humor is a deeply self-reflexive one. Laughing at ourselves and our communities can function as a practice of feminist political accountability.[17] This accountability is not to a moralism that presumes to know right from wrong but is rather an ethos that recognizes our complicity with power as inevitable, and that "dangerous," to paraphrase Foucault, doesn't necessarily mean "bad." Without doubt, Bechdel's comics are drawn from love, but not the new relationship energy kind of love that renders the lovers' flaws imperceptible. Bechdel's insider-love of lesbians is a complex one that depends on reflexivity for its humor. Bechdel's proliferation of dyke stereotypes invites us to see what is at stake in the debates that constitute our imagined communities.[18] The characters allow more than an outlet for reflecting on the fucked-up outside world and our struggles to navigate it; they also allow for reflections on our *humanness*, in a frame that never allows us to image that humanness outside of context.[19]

In the comic's early years that context is a Reagan-era sex-wars lesbian-feminism embodied in the juxtaposition of hilariously puritanical feminist moralist Mo and her sexually libertine best friend, Lois, who work together at the feminist bookstore.[20] Over the years the comic's primary preoccupations shift toward engaging debates taking place in queer studies.[21] With this shift, the comic's focus on a dyke "way of life" distinguishes itself from the project of representing lesbian lives from which it emerged. Bechdel describes the origins of her love affair with lesbianism thus: "What lurked beneath [sex with women] was a worldview, an entire logical system in which homophobia was inextricably linked to sexism and racism and militarism and classism and imperialism. And a few other things. And the beauty of it was this: that in order to address any one of these problems, we needed to address them all. It was a compelling schema, and if in my excitement I confused the personal with the political, well, that was part of the idea."[22] This dyke way of life was one oriented to social justice and invested in a conception of power in which matters considered personal are in fact always already political. Bechdel marks the queering of this way of life in the introduction to her *Dykes and Sundry Other Carbon-Based Life-Forms to Watch Out For* (2003), where she explains how she came to realize that you did not have to be a lesbian, at least "in the technical sense," to care about the things that lesbians care about.[23] And in the introduction to her 2008 retrospective *The Essential Dykes to Watch Out For*, she reflects comically on the breakdown of the romantic version of "lesbians" that saw her through the 1980s. Here Bechdel concedes that not all women who sleep with women share in her dyke worldview, nor are all of those who do share in this worldview lesbians per se.

In the strip this queering is constituted by a gradual but systematic diversification of the cast to include, among others, three trans characters, Janis, Jerry, and Jillian; major character Toni's gay male best friend, Carlos; bi dyke Sparrow's straight cis male life partner, Stu; and perhaps most prominently, Mo's primary partner, Sydney, a cynical and consumerist professor of gender and queer studies.[24] In her insistence on the literary and cultural importance of DTWOF, a legacy often overshadowed by the critical success of Bechdel's *Fun Home*, Judith Gardiner reads depictions of Sydney's "coming out" about her massive consumer debt and secret shopping as an example of how an "ethic of full disclosure" operates as a central feature of the comic's ethical universe.[25] She goes on to say that this ethic similarly applies to monogamy in the text.

Without doubt, monogamy is one of the themes that bridges the comic's eras. It is clearly an important issue in the world of DTWOF. I too see the comic as a resource for thinking about a queer feminist ethical relationship to monogamy, but I read its treatment of the topic as far richer and more complex than an ethic of disclosure suggests. Rather than a world in which characters may breach norms of sexual monogamy as long as they are honest with partners, I argue that Bechdel offers us a world in which monogamy is visible as a powerful social rule, a compelling cultural story, and a set of deeply embodied desires. In this world, dykes practice a way of life in which alternatives to monogamous coupling are considered as a matter of course and in which affective ties and networks of social support are not organized primarily around sex. While various versions of nonmonogamy and polyamory play a part in this lesbian culture, they are not the opposite of monogamy or the antidote to feminist critiques of it. In this sense, the strip embodies Rosa's insight that replacing monogamy with nonmonogamy circumscribes possibility in ways a queer feminism should resist. Through deft feminist humor and artful storytelling, dyke antimonogamy emerges in DTWOF as a Foucauldian way of life.

Mononormativity and Embodiment

The reconfiguration of naturalized monogamy as mononormative embodiment creates space for thinking critically about monogamy without hinging new futures on the proposition that it is unnatural. "Mononormative" allows us to talk about monogamy as a normativized characteristic of culture and desire. "Embodiment" is attentive to the materiality of desire. Within the epistemic framework of a dyke ethics, *monogamy's nature* is deferred and *mononor-*

mative embodiment becomes visible, funny, and an object of critical reflection. The term "mononormativity" was coined by Marianne Pieper and Robin Bauer in the call for papers for the first academic conference on non/monogamy, held in Hamburg, Germany, in November 2005.[26] With this perspectival shift, the International Conference on Polyamory and Mononormativity brought into use a term analogous to "heteronormativity," one that made it possible to examine the values and assumptions that render monogamy-centric culture invisible, thus making monogamy itself an object of critical concern.[27] As I have said, I think a dyke ethics is also one that both seeks to destabilize norms and respects embodiment. By respect for embodiment, I do not mean the disclosure or acceptance of the truth of the self. I mean attention to bodies as important loci of meaning in our political lives.

I trace the contours of Bechdel's comic articulation of mononormative embodiment through the pages of her graphic novella *Serial Monogamy*, which was published as part of her fourth collection of DTWOF comics in 1992. She uses humor here to guide us through the protagonist's inner struggle between a lesbian-feminist politics critical of monogamy and a desire for "the picket fence."[28] The novella does three things: (1) it articulates a feminist critique of monogamy that comically illustrates its importance as a feature of dyke ethics, (2) it renders aspects of compulsory monogamy other than the mandate to sexual exclusivity visible through cultural critique, and (3) it refuses a finite resolution. By refusing a resolution I mean to say that this tension between monogamous desire and critiques of monogamy is set up as context, not as a problem to be solved once and for all. I discuss the novella in three parts. First, I read the narrative produced by the three frames that show the protagonist at different ages as an outline of the problem of mononormative embodiment through the lens of a dyke ethics. Second, I read the middle passage wherein the protagonist considers alternatives to pursuit of the cultural holy grail of super monogamy (the ever after) as critical commentary on the myriad features of compulsory monogamy that we might variously (or simultaneously) desire and resist. Finally, I consider the self-effacing humor of the unresolved concluding frames as an acceptance of the naturecultural fact of mononormative embodiment as part of the ethical world in which we live.

Frames showing the protagonist at ages twenty-one, eleven, and thirty-one are interspersed throughout the narrative as documentary-style self-reflection. Reminiscent of Bechdel's own "Coming Out Story," the first frame shows the protagonist in her dormitory bedroom at twenty-one. She is reading feminist theory, listening to lesbian music, and sporting a new short haircut. Part of this lesbian becoming meant, as the copy suggests, having learned that "monogamy and romantic love were just male-supremacist constructs designed to keep women in their place." While naturalizing poly rhetoric redresses this feminist critique of monogamy by celebrating nonmonogamy, Bechdel's story opens up the critique without presuming that these cultural mandates are reducible to the naturalization of sexual exclusivity. Monogamy here is a couple-focused lifestyle, not defined primarily in sexual terms. Knowing that coupledom is a powerful social rule, and seeing it in action in the lives of her parents and other unhappily coupled people, the protagonist contemplates why she still longs to find the love of her life and to "live happily ever after." In a comic reflection on the role of popular culture in perpetuating monogamy's compulsory status, she blames *The Brady Bunch*. Depicted in this frame as a child sitting close to the television screen, a decade before she became a lesbian, the protagonist is being indoctrinated into the patriarchal, monogamy-centric culture of family values. Bechdel's evocation of the power and pervasiveness of these values in culture effectively complicates the idea that the deep and embodied desire the protagonist experiences to "pair off" is a prediscursive fact of human nature. No less real for this revelation, its painful persistence preoccupies her as an adult.

In the frame depicting her at thirty-one, she has read in the paper about an intergenerational sex scandal in the cast of *The Brady Bunch* and thereby become finally convinced that the promise of monogamous bliss is indeed mythological. All grown up—her maturity comically marked by the absence of the television of her youth and the drugs of her early twenties, the protagonist contemplates her situation: why is she so "hellbent on pairing off?" she asks herself. She sits with her scrapbook of exes and contemplates her patterns: "Fall in love, process, break-up; fall in love, fight, get dumped; fall in love, get bored, fall out of love."[29] Humor here allows the angst, the therapy-talk, the "work" of self-awareness to emerge as the affectionate object of dyke reflexivity that makes visible the protagonists' complicity with discourses of coupled bliss and longevity that she finds troubling. This is not a naturalistic invocation of desire as an excuse to do what one will, nor the moralistic call to trump embodiment with reason. It is the refusal to cede moral authority to either narrative that makes a naturecultural reading of mononormative embodiment here possible.

In the middle section of the novella, the self-indulgent preoccupations of one neurotic lesbian become a call to rethink, through laughter, the stories we often hear about monogamy, stories that tend to either pathologize or celebrate alternatives or become subsumed within the definition of monogamy itself. Dating, for example, is the protagonist's first considered alternative. As she pictures herself attempting to casually date, we see her asking someone to dinner while she imagines herself on one knee proposing. Named as an alternative to both monogamy and nonmonogamy (the next alternative), casually dating is not inevitably about the pursuit of the ever after, though for the protagonist, afflicted by a fierce drive toward mononormativity, it is. She dismisses the possibility of committed nonmonogamy as something she can't imagine having energy for, in a frame that depicts her forgetting which of her lovers is under the covers. Celibacy, perhaps, is the solution: "No intimacy issues! No codependence! No getting dumped!" Or maybe sex without emotional commitments: Lover (over a handshake): "Hey, thanks for the orgasms!" Protagonist: "Sure thing! You really stimulated my nervous system!" Each of these represents a potential alternative to the serial pursuit of wedded-style bliss in which the protagonist has been engaged. In every frame depicting this aspirational lesbian cohabitation, someone is crying, scowling, or "if [they're] lucky" quietly nurturing a "gnawing sense of resentment" as they think "not once has she ever written me a sonnet!"[30] The idea of monogamic bliss is comically represented here as unrealistic and bound to disappoint.

After recounting scenes from a series of failed relationship stories, the protagonist revisits the idea of failure, reflecting that she is "proud to say that some of [her] best friends are ex-lovers!"[31] In these frames she captures the most famous feature of dyke antimonogamy: lesbian kinship. Or what queer feminist musician, writer, and performance artist Lynnee Breedlove calls "extended family." "Don't wanna have a baby?," Breedlove says in his "One Freak Show," "that's alright, just wait 'til one of your exes pops one out."[32] While the protagonist in *Serial Monogamy* embraces this facet of dyke life in a decidedly antimonogamy valuation of friendship and community, she wants "more out of life than an extended family of ex-lovers!" In a hilarious fit of expression of deeply embodied mononormative desire, she articulates that "more" in terms that render it simultaneously absurd and sympathetic (see fig. 4.1). Bechdel's rendering of the protagonist's flustered disposition, as well as the comedic mixing of phrases, like "rose-covered checking account," illustrate the irrational embodiment of her desires. After this comic outburst, she is back on the floor, doing yoga alongside her cat in the hopes of becoming less controlling, more "at peace with the universe," in the service of improving her chances of finding success in love. As she moves through a series of postures, in each one she raises another question about how to readjust so that she might attain

FIG 4.1 Embodying mononormativity. From Alison Bechdel, "Serial Monogamy: A Documentary," in *Dykes to Watch Out For: The Sequel: Added Attraction! "Serial Monogamy": A Documentary* (Ithaca, NY: Firebrand Books, 1992), 127.

that rose-covered checking account. For instance: How many of your needs can you "reasonably expect [one person] to meet?" In how many ways can you hope to be compatible with another person? "What does it mean to trust someone?" How do you know when to break up with someone and when to keep trying?[33]

These are familiar questions in our monogamy-centric culture. They are *versions* of questions we might encounter in any women's magazine and about which feminist critics of monogamy have raised questions. They are framed in such a way that we realize the speaker is speaking from within the ethical purview of an antimonogamy way of life. She is versed in queer feminist critiques of the institution of monogamy and doesn't take it for granted as desirable or inevitable. She does not ask how she can get her needs met otherwise; she asks how many needs she can expect to have met within the context of a coupled relationship. Here the idea that overinvesting in one relationship is "bad" for women and for feminism leads the protagonist not to pursue multiple sexual or romantic relationships but to try to determine what modifications her expectations of "true love" require. In the second question, she asks what it means to "trust someone." She does not ask what it means to trust in general or to feel safe in the world—in this question the "someone" is a lover. Trust here is the foundation of a lasting romantic relationship and thus fundamental to the ideal of super monogamy, rather than an important part of relating in general. This privileging of presumably sexual romantic relationships over other types of relating is foundational to monogamy's compulsory status, and part of the humor lies in the fact that the protagonist knows this. It is made visible as such as part of her desperate attempts to hold onto the ideal of monogamic bliss that was embodied for her in *The Brady Bunch*. The final question she asks, about how you know when to break up with someone, also makes the ideal of super monogamy (the ever after) comically visible. The protagonist wants to know how you decide that the person to whom you are attached is not "the one." In more pragmatic terms, she wants "to be available when the love of [her] life comes along."[34]

At the end of the novella, we cycle back through the ethical stakes of dyke antimonogamy and embodied mononormativity once more, disrupting once and for all any teleological arc from monogamy to liberation or from dyke ideals to an ultimately inevitable monogamy. Up off the floor, the protagonist again questions the questions themselves: "But isn't that precisely the essence and glory of the lesbian experience? To question, to strive, to transcend outmoded paradigms of behavior? How fortunate I am to be part of this great experiment. How thrilling to be free of the suffocating constraints, the shackles and trammels of thousands of years of heterosexual dogma and convention!"[35] In these frames we are laughing self-reflexively at both our "striving" and our "failures"—both at monogamy and at letting it go. Alas, we are only human.[36] Our desires are not biologically determined, but neither are they imminently malleable. Despite common assessments of cultural critique as inattentive to embodiment, many insist that

> to say that our "natures" are constructed is not to say that we have the freedom to become anything we like. Neither individualism nor subjectiv-

> ism are going to be able to take root in the soil of theories concerning the social construction of subjectivity. Again, this illusion arises from paying insufficient attention to the embodiedness of this nature. Our embodied history cannot be thrown off as if it were a coat that one has donned only involuntarily in the first place. Whether we like it or not, in so far as our values and our "ways of being" are embodied they cannot be wished away or dismissed by a pure act of will.[37]

We are not in fact free of the "shackles" of compulsory monogamy—that is precisely what is funny. We cannot get outside it. Embodied desire runs deep. Still, we cannot take it for granted. "Lesbianism" is marked here as more than a preference for sex with women: it is a cultural "experiment," a "way of life." An essential part of that "way of life" is *invention*. As the novella's protagonist says of her scrapbook of exes in the final frames, "these weren't failed ventures at all, but successful reconnaissance missions in the vast uncharted terrain of human relationship potential! . . . Still, the picket fence would be nice . . ." This inventing takes place in a world with a history, one in which resistance is possible. We cannot simply erase this history by rewriting it as a story about the repression of nonmonogamy. Still we can resist its prescriptions, by naming them and making them the object of humor. A dyke may or may not long for the picket fence, but either way she has the resources to reinterpret what our monogamy-centric culture considers failure. She has friends and an extended family of exes with whom she shares various aspects of her life and on whom she relies for the companionship and support usually relegated exclusively to the locus of the couple.

A Decade of Dyke Relationships

Serial Monogamy offers an entrée into this dyke way of life, a sampling of the vast world of relating we encounter in *DTWOF*. While mononormative desire is embodied in often comically visible ways, its longings do not translate into a world where coupledom reigns. Over the course of twenty-five years of the comic, Bechdel gives us unlikely, long-term, intergenerational friendships (between Samia and Cynthia and Lois and Janis), multiadult households of various configurations, and coparenting and cohomeownership among adults who are not coupled. These configurations of relationships offer versions of resistance to compulsory monogamy that decenter sex as the central organizing principle structuring relationship networks. The fact that several of the friendships that connect the characters to one another have lasted so long—and have in fact long outlasted many coupled relationships—makes friendship visible as the central structuring element in this world. That many of these long-term friendships began as sexual or romantic relationships—Mo and Clarice dated in college, and Lois and Sparrow had a brief affair that began when they met at a protest—blurs the line between friendship and "love" that is so central to the scientific naturalization of monogamy discussed in chapter 2. Further, the romance of both love and friendship are elided, as many of the comics' most intimate relationships are premised on a kind of solidarity characterized more by commitment to community than by what we might characterize as affective attachment. The comic adds an expressly political dimension to relationality that exceeds the explanatory potential of monogamous pathways and bi and poly lovestyles. A comic timeline of *DTWOF* highlights from 1987 and 1997 illustrates these themes well.[38]

In the "Condensed Dykes to Watch Out For" timeline, Bechdel tells us in five concurrent lines what is happening in the world and in each of the four main plotlines over the course of a decade (1987–1997). The decade of dykes begins with the Iran-Contra Affair and the National March on Washington for Gay and Lesbian Rights in 1987 and George H. W. Bush's election in 1988; spans the War on Drugs, U.S. invasions in Latin America, and the first Gulf War; and is punctuated by major events such as the Montreal Massacre,[39] the *Exxon Valdez* oil spill in 1989, Nelson Mandela's release in 1990, Clarence Thomas's confirmation in 1991, the Los Angeles riots in 1992, the Bosnian rape trials in 1993, the passage of the Contract for America in 1994, the O.J. Simpson trial in 1995, the passage of the Defense of Marriage Act in 1996, and Ellen Degeneres's televised coming out in 1997. The effect of combining U.S. foreign and domestic policy with cultural shifts in U.S. queer life is that we are forced to think them together. Queers become a niche market and an object of apparently redemptive scientific interest (the gay gene in 1991 and lesbian mathematical superiority in 1993), all while, as fictive feminist bookstore intern, poet, and student Anjali puts it in 1997: "Global capitalism is colonizing humanity as well as the planet in an ever-expanding and increasingly brutal quest to feed a handful of bloated multinationals."[40] It is through a lens critically alert to the intertwined and often racialized local and transnational processes of normalization and violence as well as the ironies of queer resistance that we are invited to laugh at a decade of daily dyke living. These dyke lives are represented in distinct plotlines whose taxonomy represents different configurations of relationships that all have their own logics within this larger context. Because these relationships are represented as stories populated by many bodies, rather than abstractions that seek to represent "the body," the politics of monogamy cannot be imagined as race neutral.

The four plotlines chronicle a decade in the lives of four entities: Mo (the main character); Clarice and Toni (the couple); Sparrow, Ginger, and Lois (housemates/queer family); and Madwimmin Books (the larger dyke community).[41] Mo, like the protagonist of *Serial Monogamy*, is serially monogamous and embodies a struggle between impassioned resistance to "assimilation" and complicity on the one hand and "normal" desires around both work and love on the other. Toni and Clarice are DTWOF's perennial couple and as such serve as a canvas for sketching tensions around the desirability of nuclear family life. Sparrow, Ginger, and Lois are housemates and friends; their home is the most consistent set in DTWOF over the years and a key node in a variety of interpersonal networks. Other characters move, and Madwimmin eventually closes, but Sparrow, Ginger, and Lois's home is there for the entire duration of the comic. The Madwimmin Books timeline represents Jezanna, the store's owner, and the larger lesbian feminist community, with a revolving cast of customers, employees, writers, and interns. Its struggle to stay afloat as "Bunns and Noodle" (Barnes and Noble) and "Medusa Books" (Amazon.com) take over the market represents the struggle of lesbian communities and cultures to survive as distinct.[42] The stories interconnect in many ways, but the logic of separating them thus illustrates something important about the world of DTWOF. Neither couple-centric nor individualist, the relational units that emerge as significant over the course of a decade of dykes reflect a decidedly antimonogamy way of life. Collectively, these narrative threads suggest myriad shifting and interconnected relational possibilities, none more natural than the other, none outside time and place.

EX-TENDED FAMILY

Mo's timeline highlights include mention of a series of love interests, beginning with meeting Harriet in 1987 and ending with the start of her second long-term relationship, with Sydney, in 1997. In between, there are lots of therapists and dead-end dates. The comic form of the timeline allows us to see the humor in the compelling momentum of the monogamous script by showing retrospectively that the turn from bad to worse in Mo and Harriet's tumultuous relationship directly preceded their decision to cohabitate. While the serial pursuit of coupled bliss is at the center of this solo dyke's story line, her single life is not a lonely one marked by lack. Besides her long-term relationship with two cats, Vanessa and Veronica, Mo has an extended family of friends and exes.

The forging of Harriet and Mo's ex-tended family relationship is marked as a major event in 1995, just as meeting new lovers is marked. Harriet and Mo remain close, and Mo supports Harriet through her pregnancy years later. Although Sydney is her new paramour, Harriet and Mo have a strong intimate bond that exceeds their earlier bond as partners. As the protagonist of *Serial Monogamy* so deftly described the intimacy between exes: "Weird as it can be, there's nothing quite like that bond. No matter who you get involved with subsequently, your ex will always have known you longer."[43] Mo's intimate familial friendships with ex-lovers, most importantly Clarice and Harriet, work against the monogamy-centric logic of regarding past sexual-romantic relationships as either mistakes or stepping stones to "the one." Clarice and Mo's friendship, born out of a college romance, is the longest relationship in *DTWOF* and is often what connects the larger world of *DTWOF* to the nuclear existence of Clarice and Toni's relationship, especially once they move out to the suburbs.

The intimate interface of Clarice and Toni's homonormativity and Mo's judgment of it is one of the sites where the racial politics of monogamy are visible in the comic. Again, because they are connected to bodies, the decisions each character makes about sexual-romantic relationships bring different aspects of monogamy's meanings into relief. Mo's (downwardly mobile) middle-class whiteness is comically visible as she interfaces with her parents and yuppy golfing brother. Her embodied desire to reproduce the stability of her own white middle-class childhood, even as she waxes on against it, is part of humor. Clarice is black and Toni is Latina. Toni's devoutly Catholic family and Clarice's white-male-dominated law career provide a backdrop for thinking about the importance of the racially gendered politics of respectability to how we understand monogamy. Mo's endless processing is funny in part because of the privileged space of whiteness and a familial safety net from which she chooses how to negotiate her own political conflicts. The comic rendering of the white middle-class particularity of this sometimes-universalized dyke archetype reveals a broad range of dyke investments in various notions of family, always complexly mediated by race and class. No relationship formation in *DTWOF* enjoys the status of political innocence: all are situated within broader operations of power.

DENATURALIZING THE COUPLE

Toni and Clarice's twenty-plus-year relationship is a *DTWOF* institution. Their timeline begins with Clarice in her first year of law school, joking with Mo about selling out and becoming a corporate tax lawyer and getting a microwave and a Volvo station wagon.[44] Again, the form of the timeline does some comic work, because we know that in 1993, after discovering that Toni's insemination has been successful, Clarice will buy that Volvo station wagon and take on a high-pressure (though virtuously underpaid) job. The self-reflexive humor makes room for complexity in ways that resist individualizing our personal choices as apolitical.

We (fans) love Toni and Clarice, but not because their coupledom is idealized—it most certainly is not. Their timeline marks the events of a successful life course of two professional middle-class lesbians (Toni is a tax accountant): five-year anniversary (1987); commitment ceremony (1990); Clarice's graduation from law school (1991); insemination (1992); acquisition of Volvo, acceptance of job, and birth of Raffi (1993); second-parent adoption (1996); move to the suburbs, Raffi's start of school, and Toni's return to work (1997). In between, they each have affairs—Clarice with Ginger (1988) and Toni with her close friend and fellow right-to-marry activist Gloria (1995). Their relationship comically represents the normative family model we are all supposed to want, and the strife internal to it reveals the inherent instability of the ideals of both super and simple monogamy.[45]

Throughout the years Toni and Clarice's relationship has destabilized the ideal of monogamy by rendering it visible, not only through its internal processes but also as an occasion for discussion by other characters. An early strip, "Getting Respectable" (1987), shows both. The strip follows Clarice through a day that begins with a call from Mo, as Toni leaves the scene of domestic bliss for work. Clarice tries to tell Mo that she's never been so happy, but Mo is absorbed in her own self-pity about being single and isn't listening. Later, on campus (Clarice is in law school), someone Clarice hasn't seen for months asks if she and Toni are still together, belying assumptions about the short lives of lesbian relationships. Later that afternoon, over coffee, Lois tells Clarice about tension with her two girlfriends: "My other girlfriend Angela is kind of uptight about me seeing Naomi. Angela is a real linear thinker. She can't seem to transcend the monogamous mindset." Clarice's growing frustration is marked by her expression in each of these frames. In the second half of the strip, she's back home with Toni, venting about her day, leading with "I was afraid since this morning you decided monogamy was too linear and so you transcended it" and going on to lament the lack of support for long-term relationships among dykes. Toni listens for a couple of frames and then asks, with a teasing expression, "So now we need a support group for happy couples?"

In this strip, Mo's longing for the monogamic bliss that Toni and Clarice share and Lois's "transcendence" of it denaturalize it by making it visible as a cultural ideal. We are invited here to laugh at all of it: Lois's "transcendence," Mo's romanticization, and Clarice's bemoaning the lack of support lesbian relationships receive. There was undoubtedly a grain of truth in Clarice's gripe: lesbian coupledom (at least as of the 1980s) had never been as bolstered by social support as straight marriages were. Toni is the voice of dyke reason here who reminds us, lest we get caught up in Clarice's self-pity, that the proposition that happy couples are marginalized is, well, funny. Ultimately, Clarice and Toni's romance makes visible the social pressures and rewards associated with couple-centric living, even as it offers up depictions of its joys. Monogamy is destabilized without being entirely displaced: nuclear family life is represented as particular and at the same time no more or less inherently fulfilling, healthy, or un/natural than other paths.

REFIGURING HOME

Sparrow, Ginger, and Lois are housemates. Sparrow, like Mo, is vegetarian. She is a new-agey spiritualist and works at a women's shelter. Ginger is a dissertation-writing grad student for more than a decade and then a women's studies professor at the fictional Buffalo Lake State. Her primary affective ties are without doubt with her dog of many years, Digger, whose death is a major event in the comic, the community, and Ginger's life. Lois is the playboy of the comic, defying lesbian stereotypes with the high priority sex plays in her daily life. Lois works at Madwimmin Books and is a Lesbian Avenger and drag king.[46] Their collective timeline begins with a protest to get the "US out of El Salvador" and Lois in bed with secondary character Naomi, who works at the lesbian-owned vegetarian café and at the food co-op in 1987. It ends with Ginger finishing her dissertation, Lois getting on antidepressants that help, and Sparrow getting a bit of a makeover in 1997. In between are many trysts—from Lois bringing home one of Ginger's students(!) to commitment-phobe Ginger's try at long distance with one of her seemingly habitual conference flings and to Sparrow's trip to couples therapy three months into a relationship with June (her only lover that decade). In their timeline's very last frame, the three find out that their landlord is putting their house on the market. Their household is too important to let dissolve. Bechdel acknowledges that "the real-life likelihood of three lesbians who aren't involved with each other remaining at the same address that long is about one in a septillion,"[47] but they work well together.

Indeed, their household works, and its unrealistic longevity gives us a glimpse of another world, a world made possible by a dyke ethics of antimonogamy. This lesbian housing co-op is not a sexy utopian fantasy of a world beyond power. Indeed the characters are constantly talking about racism, education, gender normativity, and so on. They hold one another accountable to the ideals that they share and air conflicting perspectives, which is the source of much of the comic tension in their triad. It is also not a liberatory queer narrative in which the children/home/and so on are abandoned for the now. Neither is this the sealed and sacred home of the nuclear family. Theirs is a dyke refiguring of home as a simultaneously intimate and politicized space. While cooperative living is often represented as utopian—either in celebration or in order to dismiss it as fantasy—it is represented in *DTWOF* as neither romantic nor an impossible dream. It emerges as a form out of both economic circumstance and queer feminist desire. This capacious and decidedly unromantic approach to the nature of new forms is at the heart of a dyke ethics of antimonogamy.

Ginger and Sparrow decide to buy the house after renting it together with Lois for many years.[48] Sparrow's partner, Stu, moves in after they buy the place and realize a fourth to help with the mortgage would make sense. Stu is a lefty, sensitive cis man, whose lesbionic tendencies are a source of much humor in the strip. Stu and Sparrow are the only coupled members of the household. While these four are the house's official residents, they are not the only characters who people the household. Jasmine, who briefly dated Ginger before getting nonexclusively romantically involved with Lois, is also often there (from 2001 on) with her daughter Janis (still Jonas in early strips depicting the reallocation of households). In a strip titled "Mamma Mia" (2002), Ginger comes home on the last day of classes ready to relax, only to discover a full house and everyone weighing in on what in other worlds might be a very private matter, Sparrow's pregnancy.

This depiction of dyke antimonogamy at home places the ostensibly heteronormative unplanned pregnancy at the center of a drama that queerly includes all of the adults who would be in the hypothetical child's daily life and, feminist-ly, places the pregnant person's body (and not the couple's privacy) at the center. In this moment of high emotion, they all say the wrong things: Stu whines that he wants to be a father, Jasmine says how glad she is she has Jonas, Lois reminds Sparrow that she knew this could happen when she started having sex with Stu. They are funny because they are scripts that these characters (and Bechdel's readers) know are problematic—they capture real tensions between the embodiment of stories we grew up with (on different temporal scales) and feminist political desires to "live elsewhere," to use Avery Gordon's turn of phrase. Stu's faltering articulations of desire for a baby are funny because of his anxiety in knowing as well as the houseful of dykes he's living with that the decision about what happens next is Sparrow's. Yet that does not stop him from resorting in the moment to a classic tactic of antichoice unwanted pregnancy "support" in comparing the unborn fetus to a living child: "Look at Jonas!" Nor does it keep Lois from dropping a snarky, ill-timed, and decidedly misogynist comment about Sparrow's decision to begin a sexual relationship with a man (a long, drawn-out, and difficult decision for Sparrow and a difficult transition for the household). Their queer choices are not the result of being more highly evolved, nor are they choices made against the best interest of repressed drives toward nuclearity. Without reducing "desire" to text, *DTWOF* denaturalizes the work of home-making. Importantly, the embodiment of sometimes violently normative feeling does not foreclose the possibility of living otherwise, as in the familiar schema where the naturalization of desire stands in for an ethics of living.

Sparrow does decide to have the baby—Jiao Raizel—and they all stay living there together for some years, actively sharing in coparenting. After nearly two decades, Ginger moves out to move in with her girlfriend, Samia. This is a move into another kind of multiadult household, less intentional and more circumstantial, yet equally queer. The household includes Samia's husband, from whom she is separated but with whom she remains family, and Cynthia, a neoconservative undergraduate whom Samia has taken under her wing and befriended. And Clarice, after her separation from Toni, moves in with Lois and Sparrow temporarily, which puts their now teenage son Raffi there some of the time as well. Meanwhile, Mo and Sydney's path to cohabitation has been sped up by Mo's insistence that Sydney get on a budget and start paying off her outrageous consumer debt.

All three newly constructed households are depicted in the strip "From the Subprime to the Ridiculous" (2008). Notably, the intimate networks out of which these households formed and *into* which they reorganized are not primarily sexual. The ideal of friendship on which they are premised is also quite expansive. Cynthia is Ginger's ex-student, and Samia tutors her in Arabic.

They are not "friends" in a traditional sense. When Cynthia comes out to her conservative family and they will no longer support her, Samia invites Cynthia to stay with her. This ethic of investing emotionally and otherwise in community directly and materially challenges the privatization of resources within the couple and is foundational to this antimonogamy way of life. In the second half of this strip, we see Clarice and Jasmine, both with teenage children, interacting in the communal home Clarice now shares with Lois, Sparrow, Stu, Jiao Raizel, and sometimes Jasmine and Janis. While the decidedly unromantic chaos of these strange collectivities looms large, the last frame of the strip reminds us that the well-worn path of coupledom is *also* ridiculous, as we watch Mo and Sydney on their own practicing good liberal citizenship as they enjoy their tax rebate in the form of a box of new sex toys. In characteristic Bechdelian fashion, the newspaper headlines and television news sound bites in the background of these frames never allow us the luxury of imaging sexual subjectivity or desire outside of the political and economic contexts in which they are embodied and enacted.

Provincializing Polyamory

In addition to multiadult households and complex kinship networks decentering the domain of the couple, there is plenty of nonmonogamy and polyamory in the world of *DTWOF*. Polyamory is part of the world of dyke antimonogamy but is never represented as monogamy's opposite. Rather, like mononormative embodiment, polyamorous desires are figured in context, as the naturecultural fruits of a world we have to laugh about. They are the object of the same sort of self-reflexive humor that makes our longing for the "picket cottage" a comic window onto another ethical worldview. Over the years we see Lois in a variety of relationship formations—"fuck buddies" (with Yoshi and Jerry), multiple nonhierarchical romances (with Naomi and Angela), and as a secondary partner (to Dorothy). Mo is a committed serial monogamist hungry for the picket fence until she ends up with Sydney, who talks her into exploring polyamory. Their first conversation about it happens in "Economy of Scale" (1999), over lattes at Bounders Books, where Sydney takes advantage of Mo's distraction by her new niece to introduce the topic.[49] Making purchases at a corporate bookstore chain is something Mo would not normally do, which evidences her distraction. Polyamory becomes an interesting comic object in the strip, because it is both a shiny retail object, like the Jane Austen books on sale in the background and the latte Mo uncharacteristically consumes,

FIG 4.2 Consuming polyamory. From Alison Bechdel, "Economy of Scale," in *The Essential Dykes to Watch Out For* (Boston: Houghton Mifflin Harcourt, 2008), 234.

and proposed/marketed as an oppositional consciousness in line with Mo's politics (see fig. 4.2).

Sydney's deft academic critique of the reification of monogamy-centric culture in a political climate where forces like the Human Rights Campaign want to present an image of queer culture as more conservative than that of the right-wingers themselves—or than that of infamous puritan Cotton Mather—is powerful, but there is, as Mo intuits, something wrong with Sydney's easy fix. While critiquing monogamy and always showing its fissures, Bechdel never romanticizes alternatives to it. She shows them as also embedded in culture and in structures of power. In this antimonogamy way of life, both monogamy and polyamory are denaturalized. Sydney's desire for multiple partners is as much the object of self-reflexive humor as Mo's investments in mononormativity (see fig. 4.3). In these frames from "Holiday on Ice" (1999) Sydney's pronouncement of her desire to be "normal" and buy Christmas gifts is followed immediately by one of her not infrequent monologues on the radical potential of polyamory. Here, both monogamy and consumerism are marked as symptoms of a larger cultural machinery that we should resist because it harms people. Martha Stewart's crafting magazines and polyamory are comically marked as *part* of that machinery. They do not offer us a way outside its logic: they mirror it in their opposition. Sydney's comfort with corporate lattes and sweatshop textiles is constantly juxtaposed to her impassioned political pleas for rejecting monogamy. Sydney's privileging of

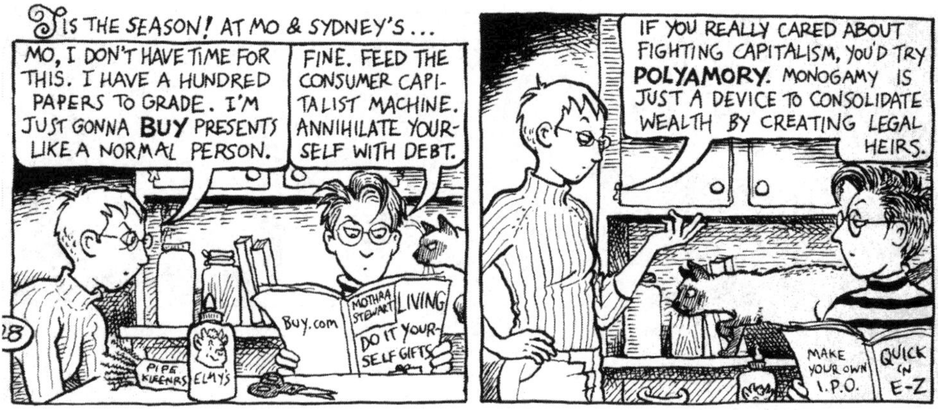

FIG 4.3 Consuming polyamory, continued. From Alison Bechdel, "Holiday on Ice," in *The Essential Dykes to Watch Out For* (Boston: Houghton Mifflin Harcourt, 2008), 235.

sexuality as a locus of resistance to capitalism (and patriarchy) is also part of the joke.

Lest we read this joking as wholesale dismissal of polyamorous possibility, by *DTWOF*'s sabbatical in 2006 we see Mo and Sydney settled into a stable primary partnership, each with an ongoing secondary partnership. Mo is dating a paramour from library school and Sydney an old flame from graduate school. In a frame that captures the poly-lesbionic equilibrium they have reached, they are sitting at the veterinary clinic, each with a cat on her lap, and when Vanessa and Veronica are called into the examination room, each ends a cell phone call with her lover.

In the final months of their marriage, Clarice and Toni talk about opening up their relationship, too. Notably, they explore polyamory as a solution to their relationship problems, as a way of sustaining the couple at a point where its fragility is most apparent. These frames show them discussing feeling suffocated in their marriage and their crushes on other women with their couples therapist, who responds to their concerns with a variety of ideas for improving their situation, ideas about how they could both "continue to grow." Part of the humor, captured in their eagerness juxtaposed with the therapist's bewildered expression, is that these options are not equally compelling to these protagonists—they are both far more interested in polyamory at this moment than reflecting on their career paths or planning a trip (see fig. 4.4). Although Clarice and Toni do not want to end their relationship, they both have crushes

FIG 4.4 The compatibility of couple-centrism and polyamory. From Alison Bechdel, "Flow State," in *Post-Dykes to Watch Out For* (Ithaca, NY: Firebrand Books, 2000), 112.

on other women. The tension between the frame of relationship work and the deeply embodied desire they feel to explore their connections with other women is funny. It is funny in part because this desire runs counter to the logic of mononormative commitment. It is also funny because polyamory is in this formulation made assimilable *within the logic* of mononormativity, and because therapy in general and couples therapy in particular is part of that normative logic.

A scene at the feminist bookstore in "Booked" (2000) brings stories about monogamy and polyamory—in the form of texts on the shelves—into contact with embodiment in ways that further undo non/monogamy. Toni and Clarice are perusing Dossie Easton and Catherine Liszt's *The Ethical Slut* (known by some as "the polyamory bible") and Deborah Anapol's *Polyamory: The New Love without Limits.*[50] Encountering these texts (which I engaged in chapter 3) in the relationship section of the local feminist bookstore reveals their quest as, in Huffer's words, simultaneously epistemological and corporeal. Polyamory, too, is naturecultural, not a drive repressed by the dictates of mononormativity.

Lest we read Toni and Clarice's extradyadic desires as a victorious reorientation from a suffocating monogamy to liberatory polyamory or reoxygenated marital bliss, the next frames invite us to laugh at the embodied conflicts with which our heroines struggle. They run into Gloria—Toni's crush—in the last frames of the strip. She mentions being desperate for some grown-up reading after months of reading Harry Potter to her daughter, Stella. Clarice picks up and coolly hands Gloria a book titled *Monogamy: A Precious Flower*, commenting that it was a terrific read that changed her life. The pair's mixed feelings are unremarkable on their own, a common trope of self-discovery and coming out.

It is the *texts* sitting side by side the way they do that problematizes the truth of non/monogamy, that is, the true/false question about monogamy's nature. There are two stories here; they might literally *buy* either one. The two books on polyamory are real books, written by feminists. *Monogamy: A Precious Flower* is a fictional text that stands in, hilariously, for the innumerable self-help books designed to help couples improve their communication, keep their sexual relationships exciting, and stay together forever. The monogamy "everybook" marks the dominant discourse in its generality. Monogamy-centric culture is thus made visible. Even as we understand polyamory's marginalization vis-à-vis the dominant story of coupledom, however, the texts represent a certain parallelism, side by side on the shelf, both resources for our unhappy couple. Polyamory is provincialized here, caught up with monogamy in intertwined narratives about the vital import of sexual-romantic love to health and happiness in a consumer culture.

Bechdel brings these monogamy stories into the same frame and invites us to laugh at them. This laughter belies a dyke ethics that understands non/monogamies in context. In this ethical world, longevity is not the province of sexual romantic love. From ex-tended families to intergenerational friendships to cohousing (not to mention pets!), the world of *DTWOF* is a world of proliferating intimate networks founded on friendship and commitment to imagined community. No one form is relegated to the status of essential or represented as uniquely qualified to deliver fulfillment or stability. By offering us a world in which each connection is but one model and but one relationship in the lives of each of these characters, and where sex is consequently decentered, this ethics offers instruments for invention. Among those instruments is a refiguring of monogamy's nature that embeds it, always, in culture. If the embodiment of non/monogamous desires is a naturecultural reality that both reflects and impacts aspects of the worlds we inhabit, how might we rethink the science of monogamy? If knowledge and desire, the textual and the corporeal, are always enmeshed, this antimonogamy ethics, it would seem, has the potential to reorient our desires. And those queer feminist political desires, feminist science studies would suggest, have the potential to reorient our knowledges.

5 BIOPOSSIBILITY

Molecular Monogamy and Audre Lorde's Erotic

> That deep and irreplaceable knowledge of my capacity for joy comes to demand from all of my life that it be lived within the knowledge that such satisfaction is possible, and does not have to be called marriage, nor god, nor an afterlife.
>
> **—Audre Lorde, "Uses of the Erotic" (1978)**

> To suspend the future, radically, may be to enter a kind of freedom that we do not readily know or even *want* to know in these cultures of phallicized whiteness. . . . It means to be involved in experiences and pleasures that offer no return to the closed economies of societal meaning, driven by utility and the mandate of concise, clear endpoints. It means to queer our worlds. And to queer is not to respond to the law of desire or its illusion of scarcity: it is to have no fixed idea of who or what you are or might become, and to find this an extraordinary pleasure.
>
> **—Shannon Winnubst, *Queering Freedom* (2006)**

In this final chapter, my project shifts to more experimental terrain. If the science of sex and love lends itself to naturalizing stories about both monogamy and polyamory and a dyke ethics provincializes both within an economy of belonging that values friendship and community, how do we think about the nature of monogamy? Throughout chapters 1–3 of this book I was engaged with the politics of scientific stories while gesturing to the space between "Science" and "the body" that I highlighted in the introduction. In chapter 4 I proposed an ethical disposition toward the question of monogamy's nature that both respects the embodied nature of desire and appreciates the politics in which it is embroiled. Within the purview of that dyke ethics, affectivity and commitment exceed the monogamy/nonmonogamy schema in ways that call us to query monogamy's special status as a bioscientific object. This chapter's aim is to mobilize this critical insight not to dismiss monogamy science's potential to tell us anything meaningful but, on the contrary, to guide a return to it in order to raise and meditate on some questions about those processes being named and measured—to think about the *possibilities of biology* as it were.

I stage this return as a queer feminist materialist science studies project, that is, one oriented toward possibility, toward making imaginable new naturecultural forms of being and belonging. I chose the epigraphs that introduce this chapter for the different ways "possibility" figures prominently in each. In the first, Audre Lorde intervenes in the conventional naming of that deeply embodied capacity that we recognize in ourselves and that has served as evidence for so many regimes of truth. She accepts that deep knowledge of *possibility* as *real*, without buying into its status as *proof*. That it has been and might yet be called many things does not lend itself to the conclusion that it is, in itself, anything more (or less) than potential. Shannon Winnubst asks us to think not about the *possibility of joy* that Lorde celebrates as an enabling force but about the *joy of possibility* as the crux of queer freedom.

Freedom in this formulation is not the freedom to marry one or more partners, nor to be otherwise recognized for the humanness of our myriad sexual-romantic proclivities. Queer freedom in Winnubst's formulation is to think against the logics of phallicized whiteness in which we find the comfort of the familiar, and to aspire to release assumptions about what we are and might become, in the service of imagination. To paraphrase the ethical impetus of Foucault's "Friendship as a Way of Life" echoed here: we cannot afford to accept that what exists is all that is possible. Winnubst is interested not only in a projected future *becoming* that might refuse allegiance to the "closed economies" of meaning that would delimit its possibilities, but an openness about what we *are* in the same spirit. Indeed new conceptions of what we are hold the possibility of begetting new logics of belonging, ones that render strange those that seem so natural. I would like to accept Winnubst's premise that despite our knowledge-inheritances, in the haunting words of performance artist and musician Laurie Anderson, "we don't know where we come from / we don't know what we are."[1] In this refusal to accept proffered definitions of the self/human/life, we necessarily reopen claims about the character of that ostensibly known ontological object. In committing thus to contingent ontologies we accept an invitation to the *extraordinary pleasure* of queer freedom as a practice of "worlding," to borrow Haraway's appropriation of the term to describe the material-discursive bringing into being of new naturecultural forms.[2]

The experimental suspension of futurity is perhaps paradoxically key to this politicized queer worlding. Winnubst's antifuturity is not the kind of presentism that conflates futurity with a caricature of moralistic feminism or with homonormativity, in so doing sidestepping questions of ethical accountability.[3] It is, rather, a kind of ethical disposition that acknowledges what Nicole Seymour speculates is perhaps "the most delicious, and queerest irony of all . . . that it might be, say, the childless or unmarried person, or the queer who lives 'in the now,' or the person whose body is constructed through 'unnatural technology'—in short, the person who has everything to lose and nothing to gain—who cares most for the future well-being of non-human and human others."[4] The imaginary advanced by Seymour's *queer empathy* is one in which our subject positions are inevitably invested with power in ways that compromise our ethical relationships to human and nonhuman others. The less we have invested in what Winnubst calls cultures of phallicized whiteness, the greater our freedom to participate in the bringing into being of different futures. Seymour's ethical worldview binds us to what Lynne Huffer calls that "certain burden" so often elided by queer celebrations of new forms of sociality, that is, "the ethical burden to examine the conditions of possibility of the discursive structures through which our own inscription in a social practice can even be thought at all." Possibility itself, she argues, is at stake in how we regard this burden: "This self-critical 'ethical work' constitutes an obligation of thought, because this is what allows thought to remain open to diffuse 'otherness,' that sense of newness, invention, and difference so dear to Foucault."[5] This type of self-critical ethical work, I have argued, is at the heart of a dyke ethics and its invention of new forms of belonging.

To take on this obligation of thought and remain open to the possibilities that we have yet to think is to acknowledge our own agency, as Deboleena Roy describes, in science as a practice of worlding: "What has made me laugh as a feminist scientist, and what has allowed me to bring humor to my political project, has been the realization that each and every biological experiment I conducted in the lab was in fact an experiment in uncertainty, an experiment in transforming uncertainty into materiality. There is much room for feminist philosophies of subjectivity and theories of embodiment to guide these transformations from uncertainty to materiality. To do this, however, we must turn to the actual molecular matters of biology with desires for social justice."[6] So it is with desire for "social justice"—for freedom from the racist and sexist logics that undergird the naturalization of monogamy and from the impact of the naturalized privatization of wealth and care—that I turn in this chapter to the molecular, and to the materialization of monogamy. This chapter is a speculative exploration of the uses of a materialism grounded in the epistemological interventions of feminist and postcolonial science studies and queer historizations of sexuality. It is also, in its way, a hopeful meditation, from a critical science studies perspective, on the promises and pitfalls of the materialist turn in feminist theory. That is to say, this chapter seeks to offer a curious and creative approach to the materiality of embodiment that is critically alert to the ways in which certain disciplinary ways of knowing ("Science" with a capital *S*) have been constructed as less mediated access to that materiality than others (humanistic approaches to corporeality and embodiment). So rather than turning to a materialist genealogy that relies on "Science" to ground an ontological politics that might reshape our worlds, I turn to a genealogy grounded in a queer, feminist, and antiracist vision of the vital body as a source of knowledge and resistance. Specifically, I turn to a reading of Audre Lorde's "Uses of the Erotic: The Erotic as Power" to develop a theory of "biopossibility," a concept I hope will enable a queer feminist critical-materialist account of monogamy.

It is my contention that a queer feminist critical-materialist approach should ask: How do we engage the molecular with queer feminist desires for new biocultural stories and forms? As we create new approaches to science's proper objects, how do we ground them in queer and feminist critiques of the stability of those very objects—hormones, muscles, chromosomes, and brains, for example?[7] How do we passionately challenge a view of biology as flat and predictable without locating our salvation in it through a framing that romanticizes nature's agency, contingency, self-organization, or plasticity?[8] That is to say, such an approach should begin by querying the contexts that inform the intelligibility of our understandings of nature, deterministic or otherwise. I develop biopossibility as a conceptual resource for our collective toolbox, one that might aid in the project of holding the material-discursive conditions of scientific knowledge production and the materialization of bodies in the same frame.

I define biopossibility as a species- and context-specific capacity to embody socially meaningful traits or desires. I use "biopossibilities" rather than "biological possibilities" in an express effort to problematize the presumed locus of the "-logical." The study of bios in the natural sciences—in biology as it were—has certainly been no more successful than the body theory of the humanities at illuminating the nature of embodiment. Biopossibility seeks to capture conceptually that our creaturely capacities depend on the constraints of both intelligibility and matter, concepts whose comediation has been described most capaciously by Donna Haraway's concept of the naturecultural. I intend biopossibility as a tool for naturecultural thinking. A capacity to embody is always naturecultural, such that new biopossibilities emerge through "entangled" processes of bio/political becoming.[9] In this naturecultural world, nothing is "merely textual" and everything matters. That is to say, the *intelligibility* of a biopossibility and our capacity to *actually embody* it are interconnected in nonlinear ways. A theory of biopossibility does not require that we map or otherwise simplify those processes in order to name them; indeed it actively resists the division between the pretheoretical realms of nature/biology and culture/language (the proper objects of the sciences and humanities, respectively). In so doing, it resists service to evidentiary schemas in support of "fixed ideas of what we are and might become."[10]

In the first section of this chapter, I read Audre Lorde as part of a genealogy of feminist approaches to the materiality of embodiment, and as a resource for thinking about *biopossibility* as a conceptual alternative to *biology* in naturecultural research on sexuality. In the second section, I introduce stories of gene-brain-behavior connections in current neuroscientific research using voles to understand monogamy and affiliative behavior, research that my reading of Lorde has opened up conceptual space to revisit from what I call a critical queer feminist materialist perspective. In the third and final section before I reach my conclusions, I ask what it might look like to "eroticize" the complex processes that social neuroscience has called monogamy's "dark matter," from the perspective of Lorde's biopossibility of the erotic.

Lorde's Materialism: Toward a Theory of Erotic Biopossibility

Audre Lorde is an important figure for a feminist genealogy of materialist thought. Here I focus on a reading of her "Uses of the Erotic: The Erotic as Power," one of the most famous works of one of the most influential feminist thinkers of the twentieth century. Deeply committed to both embodiment and politics in her writing, Lorde is among those whose work has been variously claimed as both essentialist and antiessentialist. As such a border figure, she has allowed us to hold the agentive force of both bodies and politics, without placing them in hierarchical relation as causal elements in the making of experience. Lorde's erotic, like her anger, provides resources for holding our analyses of embodiment accountable to our critical engagements with "culture," and vice versa.

For Lorde, bodies are not simply oppressed by or drawn into the service of power; they are also a critical site of resistance. The political potential of connection between individuals is one of the defining features of Lorde's erotic, and one that has inspired much thinking about the importance of relationships to social change. She says: "The erotic functions for me in several ways, and the first is in providing the power which comes from sharing deeply any pursuit with another person. The sharing of joy, *whether physical, emotional, psychic, or intellectual*, forms a bridge between the sharers which can be the basis for understanding much of what is not shared between them, and lessens the threat of their difference."[11] I would like to draw our attention to Lorde's care in interrupting a reading that would reduce the "sharing" she speaks of to sexual-romantic exchanges. The "physical" is far broader than the sexual, and the "emotional" far more so than the romantic. The sexual and the romantic become both dislodged from one another and subsumed within two of four larger categories, shrinking them down to size in the schema of human connection potential. These other less celebrated forms of human connection become larger when they stand parallel to physical and emotional sharing. The range of sharing that might be imagined to cultivate the formation of this bridge of understanding opens up our vision of types of interactions that benefit us by providing this power. In the lingo of popular neuro-metaphors, it helps us to think more creatively about what we are "wired" for, and indeed about hardwiring metaphors for biology themselves.

And the displacement of sexual-romantic love, which I will discuss in more detail, is not the only function of the erotic: "Another important way in which the erotic connection functions is the open and fearless underlining of my capacity for joy, in the way my body stretches to music and opens into response, harkening to its deepest rhythms so every level upon which I sense also opens to the erotically satisfying experience whether it is dancing, building a bookcase, writing a poem, or examining an idea."[12] For Lorde, the erotic *openly* and *fearlessly* underlines our capacity for joy. This "underlining" marks a kind of knowing. This body-knowledge begins not from activities categorized in advance but rather from its own capacious aptitudes. It opens us, at every level, to what Lorde calls "the erotically satisfying experience," whatever it may be.

Dancing, listening, building, writing, examining, and sharing are all potential avenues to erotic fulfillment here.

But why refer to her theory of the erotic as a *biopossibility of the erotic*? Surely, we must read Lorde's words as in part an act of resistance to the scientization of sexuality and desire, which has certainly tended toward what Lorde critiques as the *pornographic*. I use "biopossibility" to refer to Lorde's theory of the erotic here in order to challenge the locus and authority of claims about the material body in the sciences, and to mark an alternative conceptual terrain. *Matter* is too often conflated with scientific ways of knowing it. Biology, the study of the body in the sciences, leaves little space for interdisciplinary feminist innovation. Like other feminist scholars trying to rethink the corporeal—notably Stacy Alaimo in *Bodily Natures*—I have found resources in Audre Lorde.[13] Lorde's words often capture viscerally a body that exceeds scientific and social reductionism. It is at once material and palpably situated. Most important, bodies for Lorde are a source of power, agential in that they resist annihilation. In other words, for Lorde, there is something in our embodiment that is oriented toward something that materialists like Elizabeth Grosz (using Darwin) or Samantha Frost (using Hobbes) might call "life."[14] Others have turned to aspects of Spinoza's monism or to Lucretius on that "something" in our breast that makes resisting outside force possible.[15] Terms like "liveliness" and "vibrancy" are often used to capture a quality of matter that exceeds or precedes its textual representation. Drawing on a Western philosophical tradition of trying to account for what "is" scientifically has been a powerfully authorizing resource for new materialisms, but alternate, underexplored—and feminist—genealogies are full of generative potential. Lorde's "joy"—an embodied sense of fulfillment that stems from what she calls erotic experience, for example, offers not only another account of that "vibrancy" in our nature, but an expressly and specifically grounded queer feminist account of its uses, both dangerous and enabling. Importantly, in Lorde this vital element is described as a quality of *embodiment* rather than of matter (or *nature "itself"*). There is no pretense to knowledge of a universal body, and bodies for Lorde are always bodies-in-context. In theorizing the effective similarity of seemingly disparate environmental and experiential stimuli, Lorde's account of this experiential capacity of bodies-in-context lends itself to an innovative theory of affective biopossibility, a biology irreducible to matter.

Lorde's erotic is at once difficult to pin down and richly elaborated with examples. She postulates that there is no qualitative difference between experiences of building a bookcase, thinking about an idea, making love to a woman, listening to music, and writing a poem. These are all potential experiential stimuli for the realization of this capacity she refers to as both "joy" and "fulfillment." Joy here is unlike *happiness*, that treasure whose pursuit is a protected American freedom. Joy as Lorde describes it is rather something fleeting, immediate, and visceral, that can be motivational in terms of behavior—"rewarding," in neurochemical lingo—and can thus inform orientation to certain practices, activities, and objects in everyday life. In Lorde, if we do not fear the erotic, and it is thus able to "open us" internally to the reward different experiential stimuli can bring, we will become accustomed to the feeling, and we will desire its repeated effects. This logic is typically explained in terms of stimulation of reward centers as the neurochemical support for habitual behavior, in ways that often lend themselves to reductive stories about gene-brain-behavior connections.[16]

In "Uses of the Erotic" Lorde offers an account of how and why the vital capacity for joy gets written out of our stories of human nature: "In order to perpetuate itself, every oppression must corrupt or distort those various sources of power within the culture of the oppressed that can provide energy for change. For women, this has meant a suppression of the erotic as a considered source of power and information within our lives." This is a very powerful statement about the place of the erotic in the nexus of power/knowledge. Knowledge of the erotic is dangerous, because its capacities are potentially transformative. We have been taught to suspect this "depth of feeling" and to believe that our strength lies in overcoming it. While the erotic can be a "replenishing and provocative" force in our lives, orienting them toward joy and change, it is often misappropriated.[17] Lorde makes a distinctly materialist claim on behalf of the import of a rich concept of "human need" as a key principle in the bringing into being of a world in which we would like to live, and that need, importantly, is neither prescriptive nor confining: it does not codify sex, bonding, or even sociality as its driving force. In fact, it has no essential demand. This need is rather for the freedom to realize a diffuse capacity for an embodied sense of fulfillment. And naming that capacity, for Lorde, paves the way for a decidedly naturecultural ethics. She says: "That deep and irreplaceable knowledge of my capacity for joy comes to demand from all of my life that it be lived within the knowledge that such satisfaction is possible." Lorde's biopossibility of the erotic offers an expressly politicized ontology of becoming that depends on an epistemic renegotiation. We must be willing to critique sexuality as we know it in order to understand this reontologization of the erotic body. If we understand ourselves as "erotic," rather than (self-evidently, or universally) "sexual," our creatureliness has a different valence, with implications for how we imagine success, adulthood, wellness, and so on. Possibility is at the heart of this conception of humanness. If "the erotic is a measure between our sense of self and the chaos of our strongest feelings . . . an internal sense of satisfaction to which, once we have experienced it, we know we can aspire," the idea that we are creatures motivated by an instinct that is sexual or reproductive—*or* strictly by social pressures to conform to such a script—seems inadequate. We are rather, in this formulation, always becoming, where bodily capacity for reward/fulfillment/joy constitutes a condition of possibility for those becomings.

Lorde's erotic lies on "a deeply female and spiritual plane."[18] Rather than narrating emphasis on the female as part of the essentialism/antiessentialism debates that characterize storytelling about feminism's "second wave," I read Lorde's lesbian feminist eros as a productive site for theorizing embodiment.[19] Lorde argues that "the erotic has often been misnamed by men and used against women. It has been made into the confused, the trivial, the psychotic, and plasticized sensation. For this reason, we have turned away from the exploration and consideration of the erotic as a source of power and information, confusing it with the pornographic."[20] This passage has often been read as outlining a "sex negative" distinction between "pornography" and "erotica."[21] The place of Lorde's erotic in debates over pornography specifically or feminism and sexuality more generally is not the focus of my analysis, but suffice it to say, something of value is being theorized here that has not been adequately engaged.[22] To read this passage as outlining a distinction between misogynist and feminist sex, or between queer freedom and feminist ethics, wherein the erotic stands in for good, feminist sex, is inadequate to the expansiveness of Lorde's theoretical and ethical/political project. In *The Erotic Life of Racism*, Sharon Holland describes this passage as "one of the most important feminist statements of the latter part of the twentieth century [because] it places the most visible branch of black feminist theory in direct opposition to an emerging sexuality studies."[23] Like Holland, I read Lorde's words here as a direct challenge to the notion that we have a shared stake in *liberating sexuality*.

Lorde's project suggests an alternate field of resistance to compulsory heterosexuality and otherwise normativizing stories about the naturalness and desirability of the nuclear family form. If we read "the pornographic" and "the erotic" figuratively, Lorde describes how one becomes a distorting shorthand for the other—the pornographic is reductionist, and in so reducing, it contains, erases, and redefines for its own purposes the meaning and content of the erotic. The breadth of her examples of potentially erotic experience suggests an understanding of sexuality as one expression of a more expansive set of capacities, something we do not have adequate conceptual resources to deal with, and something that "sexuality" renders problematically difficult to articulate. In other words, the pornographic is sexuality as the truth of the self. Displacing the pornographic paves the way for the suspension of foregone conclusions about what we are and might become, replacing those ontological assumptions not with reversals but with possibility. For this reason, I read Lorde's treatise on "the erotic" as a *biopossibility of the erotic* that directly challenges the necessary specialness of "sexuality," as such, as a biocultural fact of humanness.

We can read Lorde's biopossibility as a critique of "sexuality" as a mischaracterization of something we might call "the erotic," and one enabled by misogynist and racist fears of women's power. Read as an analysis of the biopolitical perpetuation of sexuality as a foundational myth, the project is indeed powerful. Still, Lorde's primary task is not to critique sexuality but rather to attend to the biological resources rendered unintelligible by its imposition as an explanatory frame. The erotic is from the root "eros," which Lorde defines as a broad and diffuse conception of something we might call "love." This love is something rather akin to Gayatri Spivak's "risky love."[24] Spivak argues that while "love" is always haunted by what she calls reproductive heteronormativity, it can still inform an orientation toward the world and its inhabitants that might inform political praxis.[25] Huffer, too, embraces the possibility of such reappropriation, suggesting that we might yet evoke and reclaim love in ways that challenge its "schmaltzified, narcissistic, possessive structures."[26] I read Lorde's eros as springing from such a queer feminist conception of love—both claimed and queered. As Cynthia Willet explains in *Soul of Justice*, "while Freudian and Post-Freudian writers portray love as the threat of immersion, black writers like Lorde and Walker present love as a force for the expansion of the human personality in relationship with others. [Lorde's] [e]ros is most decidedly a primary source for, and not a primitive threat to, subjectivity."[27] Eros is not the primordial sexual-romantic love of Freudian discourse. Rather, it names a capacity. Lorde's account of eros emerges in the struggle to articulate an account of embodied capacities in ways that acknowledge present forms (like sexuality) while challenging their prediscursive facticity. A biopossibility of the erotic, then, is an approach to embodied desire and behavior attuned to relationships between knowledge politics and materialization. Lorde's eros can help us to approach forms of embodiment that have calcified in narrative and in flesh as *biopossibilities*, neither reducible to text nor essential to human nature.

Revisiting the Matter of Monogamy

Lorde's biopossibility of the erotic has opened up conceptual space for me to reengage the "material" of monogamy gene research, research that underlies vast neuroscientific data not only on pair bonding and promiscuity, but on attachment, social processing disorders, and affiliative behavior in general.[28] Lorde provides resources for undoing the categories that structure the research without dismissing its findings or simply appropriating its data. As I discussed in chapter 2, Larry Young's laboratory at the Yerkes National Primate Research Center uses a "monogamous" vole species as a neural model for healthy attachment in humans. The laboratory's multimillion-dollar funding situates it at the cutting edge of neuroscientific research on affiliative behavior.[29] My interest in the contexts that make the laboratory's frames, models, and conclusions intelligible has been haunted, at moments enchanted, to call up Jane Bennett, by the materialist turn in the humanities in general and within feminist theory in particular. This haunting-enchantment lies in the specter of the extratextual realness of the objects of my analysis.

Over the years, many people have been curious about my research in Young's laboratory, and several have asked me some version of the question: "So . . . *is there* a monogamy gene?" As they say in the lab, there is always a "quick and dirty" answer. Mine to this question is that this depends on how you define both "gene" and "monogamy." I have been apt to argue that "the monogamy gene" is a misleading or useless formulation; simply put, it's the wrong question. By this do I mean to say that bodies do not matter in any way to our understanding of the reproduction of monogamy-centric culture? That "biology" is but another discourse drawn into the maintenance of the status quo, and nothing more? Not exactly. I think a dyke ethics requires more. Embodied desire is doubtlessly part of the naturecultural world in which we navigate the ethics of belonging. Rather than asking whether or not the human (or the prairie or meadow vole for that matter) is a "monogamous" or pair-bonding species (or conversely a promiscuous one), however, it may be fruitful to think about the capacity to form attachments to other human or nonhuman animals as a biopossibility that can inform our understandings of certain "becomings" without foreclosing as yet unrealized or unintelligible biopossibilities.

My fieldwork in the laboratory suggested that the "monogamy" that apparently characterizes human biology is not necessarily sexual, nor is it necessarily exclusive. I used these findings to call into question the will to distinguish "monogamy" not only from promiscuity or polygamy but also from friendship. If we agree to define monogamy as a behavioral responsiveness to a familiar individual in a scenario that is not necessarily sexual or exclusive (as this is what is actually measured), and if we understand that the expression of a "gene" depends on multiple, complexly mediated, and often ill-understood processes of transcription that allow for the articulation of correlative relationships between variations in DNA and complex social behaviors, it is possible to talk about monogamy's molecular substrates. That is to say, one condition of possibility for the behaviors associated with what we call "pair bonding" is *material*. *Attachment to other animals is thus a biopossibility among humans and prairie voles in a way that it is not for members of all species.*

Yet when we name "species" (or other biological types) monogamous and nonmonogamous, social and asocial, we obscure the contingency of those biopossibilities. Even as the categories themselves remain stable, the molecular *complexity* of the processes to which they refer has become the object of increasing attention. In 1999 Young's laboratory discovered a genetic variation between two species of voles: the prairie vole (*Microtus ochrogaster*) and the meadow vole (*Microtus pennsylvanicus*), considered behaviorally monogamous and promiscuous, respectively. Not all of the "monogamous voles" had the genetic variation, and not all who *did* have it showed a partner preference. However, the integrity of the categories themselves stayed intact and remains the primary descriptor of the two types, which serve as models for healthy and unhealthy social variation in humans. In 2004 the laboratory succeeded in genetically modifying a promiscuous vole to make it monogamous by measures of partner preference, the test used to measure monogamy by scoring an individual vole's preference for proximity to a familiar ("partner") over an unfamiliar ("stranger") vole.[30] With this gene story the laboratory became famous. By 2008, however, they explicitly acknowledged that this genetic variation did not fully account for the behavioral differences between species considered monogamous and promiscuous.[31] In 2009 they succeeded in attaining the resources (approval for vole genome mapping) to better understand the complex regulatory processes that produce behavioral differences among vole species. And this world of complexity, with its attention to epigenetic and other factors in making voles (and humans) monogamous, offers us a rich language surrounding "regulatory elements" and "transcription factors" that mediate what we call monogamy.[32] While the scope of their referents remains conceptually narrow, the naming of a category of important but unknown variables is ripe with potential for naturecultural thinking.

In light of Lorde's insights about the embodied likeness of experiences considered sexual and not, I turn to the known and unknown factors that mediate gene expression and in so doing bring into being certain biopossibilities. Social neuroscience seeks to understand what Tom Insel, director of the National Institute of Mental Health and forefather of monogamy gene research, calls "dark matter," those processes that link experiential "receptive" input to "expressive" behavioral output.[33] The dark matter metaphor directly analogizes the biosciences and physics, suggesting a system that is complicated but ultimately mapable.[34] Simple models that have treated "genes" as an on/off switch for behaviors or single hormones as "key" to human characteristics are indeed widely outmoded and regarded as too reductive to be of any use at all, despite their startling persistence in popular scientific and medical discourse.[35] Complex systems modeling, which is reshaping the biosciences, offers possibilities that Mendelian genetics discourse never could, including the provision of evidence to support the undoing of its own categories.

I do not mean to suggest that we have bad/simple science and good/complex science, the former to be critiqued and the latter to serve as a resource to queer (and) feminist theorizing. Aspects of complex approaches are influencing and being taken up in more traditional modeling, and "complexity" is being drawn into old epistemological agendas. Without doubt, emergent fields like social neuroscience are building a bridge that revives the dream of naturalizing complex social behaviors precisely by setting out to discover and map the content of the body's "dark matter." We must be willing to trade not only simplicity for complexity, but "essence" for "potential," as Jordan Young has argued.[36] It is the acknowledgment of naturecultural possibility that opens doors for imagining our worlds anew.

As we approach the evolving science of sexuality, in all of its emergent complexity, we must also remember that even when complexity serves our theories of contingency, we need to pay attention to the *politics* of science. Indeed epigenetic approaches to molecular monogamy have so far yielded the kinds of sociobiological insights that gave us evolutionary explanations for rape and racial disparities in IQ test scores, combined with a classic medicalization of difference, all with the temporal flexibility to incorporate elements of the culture-of-poverty thesis. In these emergent scientific stories, the inability to form pair bonds is considered pathologically asocial, but treatable, and is linked, epigenetically, to being raised without a father.[37] Of course plasticity is no more politically innocent than determinism, when we look at histories of science. Innatist theories about socially salient differences have certainly been the object of much feminist and antiracist critique of science, but entangled with histories of determinist theories of difference are histories of civilizing, treating, and otherwise exploiting the body's presumed plasticity. Colonization and clinical responses to homosexuality perhaps most vividly illustrate the power of this logic. The plasticity of monogamous and promiscuous pathways is not an inherently queer or feminist proposition. To approach that data through the lens of erotic biopossibility, we must be willing to query the categories themselves.

Eroticizing Monogamy's Dark Matter

I aim to eroticize representations of the dark matter of monogamous and nonmonogamous pathways, both drawing on and problematizing the story Tom Insel's review of the neuroscience of affiliative behavior tells in order to problematize the integrity of the categories themselves. Prairie voles and meadow voles, respectively, are used to represent "monogamous" and "promiscuous" affiliative "pathways" in this research. The former models healthy affiliative behavior, and the latter, as I have said, social processing disorders. The idea is that some genetic variation in the two species leads to different outcomes or "expressions" of the "receptive" experiential input of "copulation."[38] The research attempts to map and compare the processes that produce these pathways from copulation to pair bonding in "monogamous" prairie voles and from copulation to not pair bonding in "promiscuous" meadow voles. Researchers increasingly understand the factors that facilitate the transcription from "gene" to "behavior" as complex but continue to treat them as ultimately stable and measurable.

The genetic marker associated with monogamous species of voles is a microsatellite of the V1a receptor gene, which affects the distribution of arginine vasopressin receptors in the forebrain.[39] The story goes that a concentration of vasopressin receptors in reward centers of the brain is the precondition for as yet unmapped transcription factors to effect monogamous behavior in males. A concentration of oxytocin receptors in the same regions is associated with monogamous behaviors in females. Drug therapies and gene manipulations, reports on the research say, have turned "promiscuous mammals into stay at home dads."[40] The ability to turn the "promiscuous pathway" "monogamous" is precisely the point of this research. In clinical applications, the neurochemical capacity to form pair bonds in voles is the model for healthy affiliative behavior in humans, and conversely the inability to form pair bonds is the model for disordered affiliative behavior, like autism. The ability to turn a promiscuous vole monogamous (or, more accurately, to make a vole who is largely independent by measures of partner preference more responsive to other animals) suggests, then, the possibility of making an adult or child diagnosed with autism more responsive to familiars (parents or a partner, for example).[41]

Understanding a bit about the workings of these hormones and how they are administered in experimental and clinical settings can help to illuminate what is meant by monogamous and promiscuous pathways in ways that the data obscures. The story of monogamy hormones contains within it the idea that what we call monogamy is not monolithic. The story domesticates this insight within a familiar gendered schema, but still, I think, is instructive as a model of variance. The gendered story is undermined by the research itself. Still, the different processes by which the same receptive input (copulation) and expressive output (pair-bonding behavior) are represented as linked by wholly disparate processes in females and males opens the black box of monogamy's dark matter to readings that complicate its meanings. The use of these racialized metaphors to mark the unintelligible highlights the whiteness of the heteronormative lens through which we know monogamy. Here femininity is nurturant and masculinity protective. Oxytocin is the maternal hormone, associated with nurturance and gendered feminine; thus scientists understand pair-bonding behavior in females as both *like* a mother's bond with an infant and adaptive in the service of that bond. In other words, in this schema female monogamy is mediated by functional mechanisms that support the reproduction of the nuclear family through nurturance. In mating research, vasopressin is studied for its role in species-specific behaviors like territoriality and aggression and supports a different monogamy story. In this tale of complementary heterosexual mating strategies, male monogamy is mediated by functional mechanisms that support the reproduction of the nuclear family through mate-guarding—jealousy and protection.[42] Feminist science studies scholars have had a lot to say about the imposition of these types of racially gendered narratives onto biology and the ways they misrepresent and/or actually materialize the effects they purport to describe. These insights guide me here in my reading of monogamy's "dark matter."

While genetic markers for the distribution of oxytocin and vasopressin receptors in reward centers of the brain are usually represented as sexually dimorphic explanations for mammalian monogamy, oxytocin has been used to effect behavioral changes in both males and females. Oxytocin and vasopressin have a more fluid relationship than the monogamy gene frame suggests. In nonmammalian vertebrates they are considered one thing—a hormone known as vasotocin. In mammals, a certain amount of cross-receptivity among their receptors accounts for at least some of the apparent discrepancy between laboratory and clinical effects (gendered and not).[43] That is to say, oxytocin seems to be binding with vasopressin receptors, which suggests that despite lots of hetero-intuitive theorizing, we do not know what monogamy is, or, in another manner of speaking, what mechanisms enable pair-bonding behavior.

In addition to their high-affinity binding with one another, oxytocin and vasopressin systems are highly mediated by cortisol systems and testosterone and share some high-affinity binding sites with other hormones, like dopamine.[44] In controlled experiments, oxytocin was injected directly into vole forebrains in order to induce behavioral changes. But in human trials, oxytocin is not injected into the brain but rather administered intranasally. This means that a subject taking oxytocin to modify behavioral outputs will have high circulating levels of the hormone in the bloodstream, but the hormone may or may not cross the blood-brain barrier to allow binding with those receptors.[45] This points to the importance of binding sites outside the brain.[46] Sites of concentration of oxytocin and vasopressin receptors in other parts of the human body tend to be higher-affinity binding sites, both between oxytocin and vasopressin and with other hormones.[47] The cross-receptivity of various hormones with oxytocin and vasopressin receptors throughout human bodies suggests not only the fragility of the ideological commitment to understanding monogamy in gendered ways that shapes this research but also that the "dark matter" is best understood not as a "pathway" shrouded in shadow but rather as a collision of *indiscrete systems*.[48] The effect of "monogamy" is not the result of a linear chain of neurochemical events.

When we start to think natureculturally about the reality of the vast array of factors that contribute to variation in circulating levels of various hormones (diet, movement, interaction, and so on) in different stages of evolutionary time—hours, days, years, and generations[49]—the biology of monogamy starts to look very messy indeed. In their white paper bid to get the prairie vole genome sequenced, the laboratory references this complexity time and again. While the significance of the prairie voles' monogamous nature and its exemplary status as a model for human sociality are the main point of this white paper, the promise of unmasking what is *unknown* is at the heart of the case for genome mapping: "It should be noted that the simple presence or absence of this microsatellite is not associated with social organization in other *Microtus* species . . . suggesting that variation in other genes or regulatory elements also contribute to natural variation in social behavior. . . . Taking advantage of the genetic diversity in laboratory populations of prairie voles can lead to exciting insights into how variation in gene regulation affects behavior in rodents as well as in humans."[50] Here, the behavioral diversity that has been noted by critics, but largely ignored in the laboratory's research,[51] is explicitly named, and so, too, is the complexity of that diversity. Other genes and "regulatory elements" are acknowledged as important in the production of behaviors we call monogamous and promiscuous, social and asocial. The phrase "regulatory elements" seems to refer to a broad range of potential factors not internal to the animal and based on a static nature fairly fixed in slow evolutionary time: "The prairie vole brain is exquisitely sensitive to the influence of social experience which shapes the expression of behaviorally relevant genes. *The molecular mechanisms by which social experience alters brain gene expression and thereby behavior is unknown*."[52] The discrepancy between the plural "mechanisms" and singular "is" points to a tension in the text (and the field) between acknowledging the multiplicity of factors at play and at the same time wanting to retain the productive myth of singular knowability.

Importantly, those mechanisms by which "rates of molecular and chromosomal evolution in mammals" conspire to produce monogamous and nonmonogamous effects are *unknown*.[53] I depart from the ambitions of the white paper in my skepticism about their ultimate knowability. This suspension of knowledge opens up space for thinking critically about the intertwined processes of naming and becoming and makes space for raising ethical questions about pharmacology, storytelling, and other regulatory elements within our control. That is to say, it opens space for thinking about the complex field of ethical relations between epistemology and ontology, between what we know and what we are. Lorde's erotic suggests that part of this relationship is the exercise of power inherent in the naming of these possibilities, which itself forecloses potential materializations. "Biopossibility" provides a linguistic and conceptual resource for holding this onto-epistemological production of types in our view as we *choose how* to map matter.

Sexuality, affiliation, and partner bonding are without doubt complexly mediated biopossibilities for humans. So too are the vast range of increasingly coimplicated *erotic experiences*, like the exhilaration of creative expression, vigorous activity, and falling in love with one's work.[54] Oxytocin and vasopressin, the hormones and corresponding receptors credited with human and prairie vole monogamy and healthy sociality, are more than bonding hormones, and their receptors are themselves less monogamous than we once assumed. What the lens of Lorde's biopossibility makes legible is that the dark matter of monogamy, those processes by which copulation is transcribed into behavior we read as pair bonding, could be activated by any of a variety of environmental or experiential inputs. It also suggests that those individuals and species who are *not* expressing pair bonding—or healthy sociality—are not necessarily distinct biologically from those who do. For any variety of reasons, different "receptive" inputs could activate processes that make any variety of "expressive" behavioral outputs rewarding, through the exact same "pathways." Desire for close proximity to a familiar, a love of dance, and a passion for Legos, for example, might then all be read as different behavioral responses to the same neurochemistry, rather than as behavioral evidence of different genomes or brains.

Lorde's biopossibility of the erotic is a theory of a capacious aptitude for joy that can be realized in so many possible ways: touching, listening, thinking, talking, moving, building. In the verbs Lorde uses to characterize the experiences that reveal to us our erotic capacity, a world of biopossibility emerges. This biopossibility opens up space for thinking natureculturally not only about friendship, community, and/or our coevolution with nonhuman animals but also about human relationships to "things"—both abstract and material. To what, besides (or perhaps above or alongside) coupling and child-rearing, might our deepest desires be oriented? What might we be/come? If the factors that conspire to make some behaviors more rewarding than others vary for individual animals whose social contexts are vitally important regulatory elements on a variety of temporal evolutionary scales, we might begin to think of pairing off as an overdetermined biopossibility.

Biopossibility allows us to understand behaviors intelligible as non/monogamous and the processes we understand as their molecular substrates as one set of culturally and historically mediated expressions of our creaturely capacities in a naturecultural world. Demonstrating as it does the biopolitical intelligibility of this story, biopossibility serves as a tool for holding discourse and materialization within the same frame. As such, it can serve as a resource for fleshing out the insight that material variation among bodies is delimited (and enabled) by discourse.[55] In challenging the a priori biological distinction between both the sexual and nonsexual and the social and nonsocial, Lorde's biopossibility of the erotic upsets the idea that human nature is monogamous or nonmonogamous (or pluralistic with regard to non/monogamous "difference") and in so doing lends itself to a rethinking of the privileged status of science in the turn to materiality. Not because the natural sciences are without resources for feminisms, but because engagement with data cannot generate a "dis-organization" of the categories that organize our lives: here monogamous and promiscuous, social and asocial.[56] Data itself neither reveals nor engenders possibilities for materialities with which we can live. That requires queer feminist imaginations and the critical work of making intelligible.

EPILOGUE

DREAMS OF A DYKE SCIENCE

Throughout this book I have struggled to hold two important strands of what it means to me to do feminist scholarship within the same frame: the imperatives both to critique prevailing knowledges and to offer narrative resources for knowing otherwise. For my purposes, I named those strands "the politics of science" and "the possibilities of biology." In so doing, I sought to wrest science's proper objects—especially biological bodies—from collapse with disciplinary approaches to knowing them ("Science"). Storytelling practices that situate feminism and science as distinct, preformed projects that relate to one another either in antagonism or with sympathy, I have argued, obscure rich resources from feminist science studies. Recent feminist engagements with the methodological approaches and/or proper objects of the natural sciences have by and large been framed in this way, as engagements with science, rather than being situated within a genealogy of attempts to imagine the conditions of possibility for "feminist science." The idea of feminist science has been grounded in critiques of positivist epistemologies, critiques that recognize what passes as "Science," unqualified, as a culturally local and historically situated knowledge politics grounded in a myth of value neutrality and thereby unaccountable beyond the confines of its internal logics. Reclaiming that genealogy seems apropos to the project of imagining new ways of integrating insights about the imbrication of knowing and being—a project at the heart of my treatment of monogamy in this book.

An archival encounter with the "science" file at the Lesbian Herstory Archives in Brooklyn led me to (re)consider this genealogy as an underexplored dyke legacy for both science studies and queer feminisms. Let me offer a little background on the archive. It began in the early 1970s and has been housed in homes where the public could access it since its inception. Its statement of purpose reads:

> The Lesbian Herstory Archives exists to gather and preserve records of Lesbian lives and activities so that future generations will have ready access to materials relevant to their lives. The process of gathering this material will uncover and collect our herstory denied to us previously by patriarchal historians in the interests of the culture which they serve. We will be able to analyze and reevaluate the Lesbian experience; we also hope the existence of the Archives will encourage Lesbians to record their experiences in order to formulate our living herstory.
>
> We will collect and preserve any materials that are relevant to the lives and experiences of Lesbians: books, magazine, journals, news clippings (from establishment, Feminist or lesbian media), bibliographies, photos, historical information, tapes, films, diaries, oral histories, poetry and prose, biographies, autobiographies, notices of events, posters, graphics and other memorabilia.

The Lesbian Herstory Archives is an archive of the late twentieth-century lesbian feminist political movement out of which it emerged. It is a record of "lesbian lives," where, as Butlerian insights suggest, we can't presume to know exactly what that means. As Sandra Harding argued in *Whose Science? Whose Knowledge?*, "starting from lesbian lives" means challenging assumptions not only about heterosexuality, but about coupling, kinship, and social organization more generally. I have come to read this archive, this "herstory," as a resource for a genealogy of queer feminism that centers the figure of the lesbian. It is a repository for histories of dyke activism, for traces of a culture, a "way of life" that can inform our approaches to both science and its proper objects.

When I visited the Lesbian Herstory Archives for the first time, it was for their long list of holdings on "relationships," "marriage," and "non-monogamy." When I opened the long file drawer for *R* to retrieve a pile of "relationships" folders, I was surprised to see a slim file labeled "science" to its immediate right. I was surprised because despite my engagements in queer and feminist activist communities and my own training in the history of race, gender, and sexuality in the biosciences, I knew nothing of lesbian feminist science activism. The stack of typed documents, mostly fliers for talks and other events, included a manifesto called "I Dream of a Feminist Science." This ten-page typed document was a narrative by Carol Halpern about working in a laboratory and coming to think differently about scientific knowledge production through encounters with lesbian music, art, and political organizing.[1] It is a story of truth telling about the limitations of scientific agency, a story of loss in the decision to leave a science that could not be reconciled with a lesbian feminist political vision, and a story of imagination about another world in which another science—a science we really need—might be possible. Halpern speculates:

> Feminist science might be the study of how we can evolve with our universe, a way to figure out how we can live with each other to nourish ourselves at no others expense. . . . My strongest sense as I try to define (for myself) a feminist scientist is that she is aware of the way in which many personal and worldly problems are related, such as: disregard for wimmin's sense of value and her mind, forcing the point of view that men are superior in the important aspects of personality and thus that men have to be leaders, that chemical and radioactive waste dumping and accidents are inevitable, that there isn't enough food and resources to go around for everyone, that rape, hunger, poverty, and misery are unfortunate but cannot be avoided or realistically approached.
>
> The feminist scientists will redefine the scope of science to include us all the way.

Halpern's vision is neither dismissive of science nor poised to engage it strictly on its own terms. The feminist scientist will not only "be aware" of the interconnectedness of the personal and the political; that awareness will lead to a fundamental transformation of science's very definition. The dream is not for a better science, but for a different one.

Reading through these pages, I found the question of what science is and to whom the power to define it belongs loomed large. Science wasn't neutral, but wasn't necessarily the master's tools. The textures and contours of feminist discussions of science had unfamiliar affective valences. Dreams of another science were dreams of another world, of alternate systems of accountability. The possibility of feminist science depended not on bracketing critiques of its institutionalized forms but on realizing those critiques in new forms. Thumbing through these pages, I remembered labor organizer and musician Utah Phillips's line about the long memory (made famous to young feminists of my generation by his collaboration with folk singer Ani Difranco on the album *Fellow Workers*). He says: "The long memory is the most radical idea in this country. It is the loss of that long memory which deprives [us] of that connective flow of thoughts and events that clarifies our vision, not of where we're going, but where we want to go." Indeed. Part of what was lost in that forgetting—and the part that concerns me here—is a valuable resource for thinking about connections between critique and engagement: between studying the epistemologies, practices, and politics of science and the actual *doing* of science. The women-in-science question (which is also the question of *who knows*) is extracted almost entirely from critical feminist science studies through an implicit critique of essentialism: the question of who knows is one of equal access and rights, and critique is a matter of challenging the institution in which we seek inclusion *itself*. The assumption that difference as such makes a difference has long since been critiqued as naïve or as colluding ironically with antiwoman scientific tropes of gendered capacities for math and science. So it is that the question of what feminist scientists might do differently has been by and large sidelined in favor of other questions that leave intact existing criteria for what counts as science.

If we read the Lesbian Herstory Archives as offering a genealogy for queer feminism, its science holdings, however incomplete, offer up a unique archival object. One of the things that struck me about these holdings' contents was how integrated questions about who knows were with questions surrounding practices of knowledge production and larger questions of social and political accountability. And by integrated I mean not only that all of these types of feminist engagements turned up in the science file at the discretion of donator and/or archivist (in itself interesting, I think), but that some of the materials in the file brought these projects into simultaneous view as part of the legacy of this feminist history. For example, I was surprised to see the capaciousness of feminism and science panels. One symposium included feminists from environmental engineering, psychology, and human development alongside notoriously "antiscience" radical feminist thinkers, like Mary Daly (author of *(Gyn)Ecology*) and Susan Griffin (author of *Woman and Nature*), and panelists covering more recognizably critical science studies projects, like Beverly Smith on "experimentation on black and third world women" and Lynda Birke on "hormonal determinism in theories of lesbianism." What united all of them thematically seems to have been a shared sense of the importance of science to the making and remaking of our worlds and a political impetus toward transformation in the name of social justice. I won't speculate here about how they themselves imagined their shared projects.[2] This is not a tale of lost unity. Of interest for my purposes here is how reading them together suggests a genealogy for feminist science studies that disrupts some of the tidy storytelling schemas in which we imagine, now, where we want to go from here. For example, the temporalization according to which the concept of "women in science" came first and then gave way to feminist critiques of the production of gender that enables the exclusion of women from science, and these critiques in turn matured into feminist critiques of positivist epistemologies, which have finally been sidelined in the pursuit of more sophisticated engagements with "ontology" and matter. Another example is the sense captured on recent panels that we are only just now beginning to "queer" science studies. A long memory suggests that questions of knowing, being, and representation are coterminous and interconnected, and that queer concerns with both nature and politics have shaped conversations in feminist science studies for decades.

In this temporal disruption I see the flicker of an as yet unrealized dream of a dyke science: an approach to materiality that is ever self-reflexive, ever engaged with critique of science, and ever aware of its own situatedness as a knowledge project. Such an approach would recognize the importance of proliferating sciences (and not consolidating epistemic authority) to anti-imperial projects of worlding.

Why a *dyke* science? It's a placeholder of sorts. I choose it for now, for this epilogue, because in this book I've offered a dyke ethics of friendship and community valuation that decenters sex as an alternative to debating the naturalness and efficacy of monogamy and nonmonogamy. I've also argued for a reading of "dyke" as a term that captures the at-once-ness of the embodied/corporeal and political/historical nature of desire (see chapter 4). I mean for a dyke science to connote both of these meanings. A dyke science would be grounded in and accountable to the political critiques and insights of queer feminisms regarding marriage, family, the compulsory status of sexuality, and the unevenly distributed costs wrought by their naturalization. Recognizing the risks of reducing bodies to "nature" *or* "culture," a dyke science would also be naturecultural in its approaches.

I use "science" to refer to an intellectual project that would concern itself centrally with the proper objects of the natural sciences: bodies and the worlds (microscopic to cosmic) in and with which they are coevolving. I use the term "science" to refer to this project advisedly. My intention is not to exploit the epistemic cachet of "Science" as an imagined unitary project but rather to heed the postcolonial science studies insight that there are indeed worlds of sciences and that to claim as science those knowledge systems and projects that have been excluded from its definition is an act of protest to that exclusion. It is also to query the assumption that something called science "out there" needs reforming. Queer feminist activist, "ecosexual," and porn star Annie Sprinkle famously called feminists to make our own pornography. We can make our own sciences in the same spirit—they don't have to happen under the auspices of the same economic, epistemic, and institutional structures and logics that have tended to stand in as naturalized criteria for what "counts." The question of what types and degrees of departure from the scripts that constitute that criteria actually disrupt its status *as* science can and should remain open for debate. When we claim sciences, instead of "engaging" them, the terrain shifts from one of how un/friendly feminists are to Science to one of what a world of sciences has to offer, where so much is at stake.

NOTES

INTRODUCTION

Sections of the introduction were previously published as "Biopossibility: A Queer Feminist Materialist Science Studies Manifesto, with Special Reference to the Question of Monogamous Behavior," *Signs* 41, no. 3 (2016).

1 John Witte Jr., "Why Monogamy Is Natural," *Washington Post*, October 2, 2012.

2 Willey, "The Science of Love behind the Science of Rape."

3 The naturalization of reproductive heterosexuality is a remarkably flexible one. It is important to remember that the opposite of Akin's claim has a rich history in sociobiology. Because males are said to have the evolutionary aim of spreading their seed as far and wide as possible and because rape can result in the perpetuation of the rapist's genes, the claim has certainly been made that rape is natural. See Thornhill and Palmer, *A Natural History of Rape*.

4 Gordon, *Ghostly Matters*, 5.

5 See Subramaniam, *Ghost Stories for Darwin*, on the histories that haunt contemporary science.

6 Subramaniam, "And the Mirror Cracked!," 55.

7 Willey, "'Christian Nations,' 'Polygamic Races' and Women's Rights"; Iversen, *The Antipolygamy Controversy in U.S. Women's Movements, 1880–1925*. See Okin, *Is Multiculturalism Bad for Women?*, for an example of the kind of feminist rhetoric around polygamy that has tended to inform public debate (Narayan, *Dislocating Cultures*), and Honig, "My Culture Made Me Do It," for a response to Okin that directly addresses the assumption that monogamy is an inherently more desirable form of marriage than polygamy. See also Wing, "Polygamy in Black America."

8 Rich, "Compulsory Heterosexuality and Lesbian Existence."

9 Emens, "Monogamy's Law," 281.

10 Murray, "Forsaking All Others"; Ritchie and Barker, "Hot Bi Babes and Feminist Families"; Robinson, "My Baby Just Cares for Me," 145; Stelboum, "Patriarchal Monogamy," 43; Fleming and Washburne, *For Better, for Worse*, 301; Rosa, "Anti-monogamy," 110; Tibbetts, "Commitment in Monogamous and Polyamorous Relationships," 1–2.

11 Fleming and Washburne, *For Better, for Worse*, 270; Rust, "Monogamy and Polyamory," 132; Murray, "Forsaking All Others"; Rosa, "Anti-monogamy," 109–10; Jackson and Scott, "The Personal Is Still Political."

12 Science studies scholar and activist Kim TallBear gave an excellent talk likening interdisciplinarity to nonmonogamy in ways that complicate articulations of interdisciplinary endeavors as simply multidisciplinary or as somehow organically merged. In her formulation, our relationship to each discipline and interdisciplinary formation with which we engage is unique and complicated. TallBear, "Dear Indigenous Studies, It's Not Me, It's You."

13 Hemmings, *Why Stories Matter*.

14 Edelman, *No Future*; Klesse, "'How to Be a Happy Homosexual?!'"; Shernoff, "Negotiated Nonmonogamy and Male Couples."

15 Fleming and Washburne, *For Better, for Worse*; Emens, *Monogamy's Law*, 375.

16 Vera, "The Polyamory Quilt," 20.

17 Dilno, "Monogamy and Alternate Life-Styles," 56–57.

18 Murray, "Forsaking All Others," 296; Robinson, "My Baby Just Cares for Me," 145. Stelboum, "Patriarchal Monogamy," 43.

19 The use of paternity testing is an interesting example of how the law materializes monogamous and nonmonogamous subjects.

20 Goldman, *Anarchism and Other Essays*, 228; Murray, "Forsaking All Others," 296; Rosa, "Anti-monogamy," 111. See Olson, "Queer(y)ing Permanent Partnership," for a critique of how the homonationalist move toward immigration rights for queers in the form of "permanent partnership" reproduces such relationships of dependence.

21 Fleming and Washburne, *For Better, for Worse*, 301. See also Robinson, "My Baby Just Cares for Me," 145.

22 Quoted in Overall, "Monogamy, Nonmonogamy, and Identity," 3, emphasis mine.

23 Tibbetts, "Commitment in Monogamous and Polyamorous Relationships," 1–2; Murray, "Forsaking All Others," 297.

24 Dallos et al., *Couples, Sex and Power*, 139–41.

25 Brison, *Aftermath*; Lees, *Sugar and Spice*, 264–65.

26 Murray, "Forsaking All Others," 296.

27 Murray, "Forsaking All Others," 297.

28 Collins, *Black Feminist Thought*, 134; Ramazanoglu and Sharpe, *The Male in the Head*, 168; Lees, *Sugar and Spice*, 55.

29 Willey, "Constituting Compulsory Monogamy."

30 Rosa, "Anti-monogamy," 109; Robinson, "My Baby Just Cares for Me," 144.

31 Tsoulis, quoted in Robinson, "My Baby Just Cares for Me," 145, emphasis mine.
32 Robinson, "My Baby Just Cares for Me," 145.
33 Fleming and Washburne, *For Better, for Worse*, 270; Rosa, "Anti-monogamy," 110; Rust, "Monogamy and Polyamory," 132.
34 Overall, "Monogamy, Nonmonogamy, and Identity," 8.
35 Overall, "Monogamy, Nonmonogamy, and Identity," 9.
36 Overall's analysis sometimes conflates conscious and critical nonmonogamy with cheating and infidelity, resolving this only by pointing out that even when nonmonogamy is agreed to by *both* (always two) partners, jealousy and pain are present ("Monogamy, Nonmonogamy, and Identity," 2). The casual erasure of consent as an important factor in the structure of nonmonogamous relationships is a common and problematic move. This conflation of consensual and nonconsensual nonmonogamy ignores the potential of nonmonogamous arrangements to create conditions that challenge and transform jealousy. See Robinson, "My Baby Just Cares for Me," 148.
37 Rosa, "Anti-monogamy," 109.
38 Rosa, "Anti-monogamy," 110.
39 Scherrer, "What Asexuality Contributes to the Same-Sex Marriage Discussion."
40 Overall, "Monogamy, Nonmonogamy, and Identity," 14.
41 Rosa, "Anti-monogamy," 108.
42 Loulan, "Lesbians as Luvbeins," 36.
43 See Klesse, *The Spectre of Promiscuity*, on antigay promiscuity discourses.
44 Halpern, "If Love Is So Wonderful, What's So Scary about MORE?," 162; Murray, "Forsaking All Others," 301–3.
45 Halpern, "If Love Is So Wonderful, What's So Scary about MORE?," 158. "Love laws" is a phrase used by Arundhati Roy in *The God of Small Things* to refer to expectations and rules about "who should be loved. And how. And how much." Roy, *The God of Small Things*, 33.
46 Murray, "Forsaking All Others," 300.
47 Hemmings, *Bisexual Spaces*, 26.
48 Bisexual desire, many have made a point of explaining, need not manifest itself in a need for both female and male lovers (Halpern, "If Love Is So Wonderful, What's So Scary about MORE?," 162; Hemmings, *Bisexual Spaces*, 27), and "even bisexuals with multiple partners often have partners of only one sex" (Rust, *Bisexuality in the United States*, 414). Bi Academic Intervention, *The Bisexual Imaginary*, 203; Rust, *Bisexuality in the United States*, 421–22; Klesse, "Bisexual Women, Non-monogamy and Differentialist Anti-promiscuity Discourses"; Murray, "Forsaking All Others," 299–301.
49 Richards, "Trans and Non-monogamies."
50 DuCille, *The Coupling Convention*; Carter, *The Heart of Whiteness*; Cott, *Public Vows*.
51 Willey, "Constituting Compulsory Monogamy."
52 Puar, *Terrorist Assemblages*; Ferguson, *Aberrations in Black*; Holland, *The Erotic*

Life of Racism. See chapter 5 for a brief discussion of Holland's intervention in the appropriation of black feminist theory for the project of sexuality studies.

53 Ehlers, "Onerous Passions," 319; Roberts, "Sex, Race and 'Unnatural' Difference," 27.

54 Ehlers, "Onerous Passions," 324.

55 Magubane, "Spectacles and Scholarship."

56 Subramaniam, "Moored Metamorphoses."

57 Herlihy, "Biology and History."

58 Alcoff, "Justifying Feminist Social Science"; Nagel, *The View from Nowhere*; Haraway, *Simians, Cyborgs, and Women*.

59 Fisher, *Why We Love*; Nair and Young, "Vasopressin and Pair-Bond Formation."

60 Not all scientists make this claim; it depends on how monogamy is defined. See chapter 2.

61 These types of evolutionary arguments are grounded in single mother versus heterosexual nuclear family logic, where having more caregivers (two rather than one) is said to have evolved to provide more protection and/or food. In this formulation, cooperative child-rearing (with more than two caregivers) is not recognized as having potential benefits for species survival. Research on the evolution of cooperation (Roughgarden, *Evolution's Rainbow*) and the evolutionary importance of grandmothers and neighbors (Hrdy, *Mothers and Others*) directly challenges these stories.

62 See Martin, "The Egg and the Sperm." See also Irigaray, *Speculum of the Other Woman*, 15–16, for another approach to deconstructing the logic of active/passive sperm and egg.

63 Quirk, *It's Not You It's Biology*. See Quirk, *Sperm Are from Men, Eggs Are from Women*, for a fuller exposition of the logic of active and passive male and female sexuality and as an example of how this logic reenters public discourse as scientific.

64 Hubbard, *The Politics of Women's Biology*, 94.

65 See Lloyd, "Pre-theoretical Assumptions in Evolutionary Explanations of Female Sexuality," 145, for a detailed discussion of what she terms "the orgasm-intercourse discrepancy." This work is developed and updated in her book-length treatment of the topic, published decades later, Lloyd, *The Case of the Female Orgasm*. See Koedt, "The Myth of the Vaginal Orgasm," for a classic critique of how the assumptions underlying this discrepancy function in heterosexual relationships and Huffer, *Are the Lips a Grave?*, 123–24, for a discussion of the overlooked status of labia in feminist debates over the relative significance of the clitoris and vagina.

66 The most common scientific explanation for male monogamy is that it is linked to territoriality or jealousy. See, for example, Daly et al., "Male Sexual Jealousy." See also chapter 3 of Brizendine, *The Male Brain*, for a description of how "mate guarding" behavior causes men to commit to their mates. See Willey and

Giordano, "'Why Do Voles Fall in Love?,'" for an analysis of the pursuit of sexually dimorphic explanations for monogamy.

67 McWhorter, *Racism and Sexual Oppression in Anglo-America.*

68 Markowitz, "Pelvic Politics"; Schiebinger, *Nature's Body*; McWhorter, *Racism and Sexual Oppression in Anglo-America*; Stepan, "Race and Gender."

69 McWhorter, *Racism and Sexual Oppression in Anglo-America.*

70 Markowitz, "Pelvic Politics," 391.

71 Longino, "Subjects, Power, and Knowledge"; Schiebinger, *Nature's Body*; Birke, *Feminism and the Biological Body*; Harding, *Science and Social Inequality.*

72 Harding, "After the Neutrality Ideal"; Haraway, "Situated Knowledges"; Barad, "Agential Realism," 5; Barad, "Posthumanist Performativity"; Longino, "Can There Be a Feminist Science?"; Longino, *Science as Social Knowledge.*

73 Franklin, "Science as Culture, Cultures of Science." On similar aims, see, for example, Hird, "Feminist Matters."

74 Haraway, *Simians, Cyborgs, and Women*, 42.

75 Barad, "Agential Realism."

76 Barad, "Agential Realism," 6.

77 Longino, "Can There Be a Feminist Science?," 56.

78 Longino, "Can There Be a Feminist Science?," 61.

79 Kirby, "Initial Conditions," 204; Wilson, "Underbelly," 206–7.

80 Roy, "Somatic Matters."

81 See Mira Hird's seminal review essay on new materialism, "Feminist Matters." See also Davis, "New Materialism and Feminism's Anti-biologism"; Coole and Frost, *New Materialisms*. See Willey, "Biopossibility," for a detailed analysis of the separation of "critique" and "engagement."

82 Alaimo and Hekman, *Material Feminisms*; Ahmed, "Imaginary Prohibitions"; Barad, *Meeting the Universe Halfway*; Bennett, *Vibrant Matter*; Coole and Frost, *New Materialisms*; Hird, "Feminist Matters."

83 Alaimo and Hekman, *Material Feminisms*; Coole and Frost, *New Materialisms*; Grosz, *The Nick of Time*; Kirby, *Telling Flesh*; Wilson, *Psychosomatic.*

84 Ahmed, "Imaginary Prohibitions."

85 Ahmed, "Imaginary Prohibitions," 23–24.

86 Ahmed, "Imaginary Prohibitions," 24.

87 Davis, "New Materialism and Feminism's Anti-biologism."

88 Wilson, *Psychosomatic*, 13, emphasis mine. See Hemmings, "Telling Feminist Stories," for a discussion of the political ramifications of the stories we tell about feminist "waves" in general and of a reactionary 1970s in particular.

89 Roy and Subramaniam, "Matter in the Shadows."

90 Wilson, *Neural Geographies*, 14–15.

91 May, "Disciplinary Desires and Undisciplined Daughters."

92 Alaimo and Hekman, *Material Feminisms*, 5. For an alternative account, see Åsberg and Lykke, "Feminist Technoscience Studies."

93 Hemmings, *Why Stories Matter*.

94 Israel, *Radical Enlightenment*. Sarah Ellenzweig and Jack Zammito had the inspired foresight to organize readings for the first semester of the Rice University Humanities Research Center seminar "Materialism and New Materialism across the Disciplines" (2013–2014) around the citational practices of "new materialist" manifestos like Bennett, *Vibrant Matter*; Coole and Frost, *New Materialisms*; Grosz, "Matter, Life, and Other Variations." That reading list included, among others, Lucretius, Hobbes, Spinoza, Derrida, and Bergson. I owe thanks to the organizers and to my fellow fellows, with whom I had the distinct pleasure of debating the efficacy and limitations of this genealogy as well as exploring alternatives, feminist and otherwise.

95 Harding, *Science and Social Inequality*; Scott, *The Politics of the Veil*.

96 Alaimo, *Bodily Natures*, and Chen, *Animacies*, are two very different but both excellent examples of the kind of expansiveness I am imagining here. Their respective concepts of "trans-corporeality" and "animacy" are grounded in critical theory. They define concern with embodiment as always already queer, feminist, antiracist, and disability concerns, not as interventions within those critical traditions.

97 Kirby, *Telling Flesh*. Kirby's engagement with Butler has been rich, nuanced, and extensive. For two very different readings of nature in Butler, both in tension with Kirby's, see Barad, *Meeting the Universe Halfway*, and Huffer, "Foucault's Fossils."

98 Ehrenreich and English, *For Her Own Good*; Hubbard, *The Politics of Women's Biology*; Irigaray, *Speculum of the Other Woman*; Lewontin, Rose, and Kamin, *Not in Our Genes*.

99 I am thinking here of work in postcolonial science studies that has been attentive to both erasures and appropriations of knowledge systems that do not count as science. See, for example, Keating's critique of the "new" in "new materialism" in Keating, "Speculative Realism, Visionary Pragmatism, and Poet-Shamanic Aesthetics in Gloria Anzaldúa—and Beyond." See also Foster, *Critical Cultural Translation*.

100 Haraway, *Modest_Witness@Second_Millennium.FemaleMan©_Meets_ OncoMouse™*, 217.

101 Papoulias and Callard, "Biology's Gift."

102 Lorde, "Uses of the Erotic."

103 Roy, "Somatic Matters."

1. MONOGAMY'S NATURE

1 Katz, *The Invention of Heterosexuality*; Herrn, "On the History of Biological Theories of Homosexuality"; Storr, "The Sexual Reproduction of 'Race'"; Prosser, "Transsexuals and the Transexologists"; Dreger, *Hermaphrodites and the Medical Invention of Sex*; Frederickson, *The Ploy of Instinct*.

2 Foucault, *The History of Sexuality*, vol. 1.

3 Cott, *Public Vows*; Dowell, *They Two Shall Be One*; Witte, *From Sacrament to Contract*; Emens, *Monogamy's Law*.

4 Emens, *Monogamy's Law*, describes these two meanings of monogamy as separate ideals: that of super monogamy and simple monogamy, respectively. While we typically practice simple monogamy in the form of serial partnerships, we still hold super monogamy as an ideal, imagining that each new relationship will be the last.

5 Scott, *The Fantasy of Feminist History*.

6 That is, they *seem* right, on the basis not of evidence but of an affective response to a claim.

7 McClintock, *Imperial Leather*, 45.

8 See Leng, "Cultural Difference and Sexual 'Progress.'"

9 Yeng, "Foucault's Critique of the Science of Sexuality."

10 Rusert, "Delany's Comet."

11 Harding, *Science and Social Inequality*. In addition to a great breadth of work on scientific racism in the nineteenth and early twentieth centuries, great research has been done on deployments of biosciences of the period for antiracist ends. See, for example, Rusert, "The Science of Freedom"; Stepan and Gilman, "Appropriating the Idioms of Science."

12 For an elegant review of the "global texts and contexts" out of which nineteenth-century sciences produced different differences see Castañeda, "Developmentalism and the Child in Nineteenth-Century Science."

13 Castañeda, "Developmentalism and the Child in Nineteenth-Century Science."

14 Stepan, "Race and Gender."

15 See, for example, the primary and secondary source companion volumes Bland and Doan, *Sexology Uncensored*; Bland and Doan, *Sexology in Culture*.

16 Hemmings, *Why Stories Matter*.

17 See Lynne Huffer's eloquent explanation of Foucault's genealogy as an approach to history as "an archive of discourse" in *Are the Lips a Grave?*

18 Cryle and Forth, *Sexuality at the Fin de Siècle*; Bland and Doan, *Sexology in Culture*; Oosterhuis, *Stepchildren of Nature*.

19 See Grosfoguel and Mielants, "The Long-Durée Entanglement between Islamophobia and Racism in the Modern/Colonial Capitalist/Patriarchal World-System," for an excellent overview of Islamophobia as "the subalternization and inferiorization of Islam produced by the Christian-centric religious hierarchy of the world-system since the end of the fifteenth century," and the volume this essay introduces for more specific treatments of the subject in different periods.

20 Bravo López, "Towards a Definition of Islamophobia."

21 Parrinder, "Eugenics and Utopia."

22 Bauer, "Not a Translation but a Mutilation."

23 Bullough, *Science in the Bedroom*.

24 Ewing, "Naming Our Sexualities."

25 Burger and Kruger, *Queering the Middle Ages*; Puar, *Terrorist Assemblages*.

26 Krafft-Ebing, *Psychopathia Sexualis*, 4–5.

27 Willey, "'Christian Nations,' 'Polygamic Races' and Women's Rights."

28 Alloula, *The Colonial Harem*; Cott, *Public Vows*; Gottschalk and Greenberg, *Islamophobia*; Grosfoguel and Mielants, "The Long-Durée Entanglement between Islamophobia and Racism in the Modern/Colonial Capitalist/Patriarchal World-System"; Robinson-Dunn, *The Harem, Slavery and British Imperial Culture.*

29 Krafft-Ebing, *Psychopathia Sexualis*, 5. "Houri" here refers to a virgin woman promised to faithful Muslim men in the afterlife according to certain popularized readings of the Quran.

30 Kidd, *American Christians and Islam*; Nash, *From Empire to Orient.*

31 Kalmar, *Early Orientalism.*

32 See Shehabuddin, "Gender and the Figure of the 'Moderate Muslim,'" 105–11, for a concise history of discourse around Muslim women in colonial feminism.

33 See Grosfoguel and Mielants, "The Long-Durée Entanglement between Islamophobia and Racism in the Modern/Colonial Capitalist/Patriarchal World-System," for a discussion of Islamophobia and "epistemic racism."

34 Krafft-Ebing, *Psychopathia Sexualis*, 3–4.

35 Krafft-Ebing did support the decriminalization of male homosexuality by the end of his life, which sometimes puts him in the category of more "progressive" sexologists, like Ellis and Magnus Hirschfield.

36 See Rusert, "Disappointment in the Archives of Black Freedom," on "disappointment" with reference to her archival encounter with black women's friendship albums.

37 Ellis, *Sex in Relation to Society*, 491–92, 493–94.

38 On the widespread impact of the racialization of antipolygamy discourse in the nineteenth century see, for example, Burgett, "On the Mormon Question"; Denike, "The Racialization of White Man's Polygamy."

39 Ellis, *Sex in Relation to Society*, 421–22.

40 See Ellis's discussion of the findings of British anthropologist Ernest Crawley and American anatomist Edward Drinker Cope with regard to the nature of marriage (*Sex in Relation to Society*, 425).

41 *Sex in Relation to Society*, 425–26.

42 *Sex in Relation to Society*, 182–83.

43 *Sex in Relation to Society*, 134.

44 Schuller, "Taxonomies of Feeling," 287.

45 Ordover, *American Eugenics.*

46 Ellis, *Sex in Relation to Society*, 422–23.

47 Ellis, *Sex in Relation to Society*, 149–50.

48 Ludden, "Orientalist Empiricism," 250.

49 Steet, *Veils and Daggers.*

50 McWhorter, *Racism and Sexual Oppression in Anglo-America.*

51 The cementing of this linkage has been attributed to social Darwinism. Darwin

used the idea of "natural selection" to explain his theory that humans evolved slowly from animals. In Darwin, natural selection initially referred to the development of traits most likely to perpetuate survival. On the basis of these traits, evolutionists considered some species more "fit" for survival than others. When scientists and social commentators contemporaneously used the idea to explain mental and phenotypic variations among humans—and between racialized groups in particular—natural selection became linked to heredity (Stepan, *The Idea of Race in Science*, 55–56).

52 Ellis, *Sex in Relation to Society*, 186–87.

53 See Dudink, "Homosexuality, Race, and the Rhetoric of Nationalism," for a discussion of the usefulness of studying old nationalisms to understanding new ones.

54 Gordon and Radway, *Ghostly Matters*; Subramaniam, *Ghost Stories for Darwin*.

2. MAKING THE MONOGAMOUS HUMAN

1 Ballon, "To Have and to Vole"; Sample, "Love Is a Drug for Prairie Voles to Score"; Johnston, "How Geneticists Put the Romance Back into Mating."

2 Young and Wang, "The Neurobiology of Pair Bonding."

3 "The Young Lab," n.d., accessed October 12, 2015, https://younglab.yerkes.emory.edu.

4 "White Paper Proposal for Sequencing the Genome of the Prairie Vole (*Microtus ochrogaster*)."

5 Hubbard, *The Politics of Women's Biology*; Lloyd, *The Case of the Female Orgasm*.

6 There was no distinction between sexual and social monogamy in Darwin's catalogue of monogamous and polygamous species in Darwin, *The Descent of Man*, and until DNA testing, pairing to raise young with assumed sexual exclusivity seems to have remained more or less the referent for the term.

7 Barash and Lipton, *The Myth of Monogamy*.

8 Barash, "Deflating the Myth of Monogamy."

9 Fisher, *Why We Love*.

10 Young, "Being Human."

11 Ahern and Young, "The Impact of Early Life Family Structure on Adult Social Attachment, Alloparental Behavior, and the Neuropeptide Systems Regulating Affiliative Behaviors in the Monogamous Prairie Vole (*Microtus ochrogaster*)."

12 Donaldson and Young, "Oxytocin, Vasopressin, and the Neurogenetics of Sociality."

13 Anderson, *The Monogamy Gap*; Robinson, "My Baby Just Cares for Me," 151.

14 Willey and Giordano, "'Why Do Voles Fall in Love?"

15 See Lewenstein, "Science and the Media," for an analysis of the mutually beneficial relationship between science and the media, even when the science is reported less than accurately.

16 Harrison, "Novel Drug Modifies Core Autism Symptoms in Adults"; Kuan, "New

Study Indicates Oxytocin May Provide Treatment for Autism"; Price, "Will Oxytocin Nasal Spray Treatments for Autism Really Work?"

17 For discussions of the discourse of "sacrifice" in animal research, see Holmberg, "A Feeling for the Animal"; Roy, "Asking Different Questions"; and Birke and Arluke, *The Sacrifice*.

18 Stepan, "Race and Gender," 123.

19 See Insel, "Is Social Attachment an Addictive Disorder?" The vast majority of the laboratory's extensive budget comes from the National Institute of Mental Health, now directed by Thomas Insel, Young's mentor and the neuroscientist who began the vole research at Emory in the 1990s.

20 See, for example, the review essay by Ditzen et al., "Intranasal Oxytocin Increases Positive Communication and Reduces Cortisol Levels during Couple Conflict," and in the press, "'Love Drug' Oxytocin Could Be Used to Improve Marriage, Researchers Argue."

21 Young, "Being Human"; Insel, "Is Social Attachment an Addictive Disorder?"; Young et al., "Cellular Mechanisms of Social Attachment"; Insel, "The Challenge of Translation in Social Neuroscience."

22 Lim et al., "Enhanced Partner Preference in a Promiscuous Species by Manipulating the Expression of a Single Gene"; Donaldson and Young, "Oxytocin, Vasopressin, and the Neurogenetics of Sociality."

23 Willey et al., "The Mating Life of Geeks"; Willey and Subramaniam, "Inside the Social World of Asocials."

24 Willey et al., "The Mating Life of Geeks"; Baron-Cohen, *Essential Difference*.

25 Willey et al., "The Mating Life of Geeks."

26 See, for example, a vast relationship self-help literature in the vein of Gray, *Men Are from Mars, Women Are from Venus*, like Joe Quirk's *Sperm Are from Men, Eggs Are from Women*.

27 Silverman, *Understanding Autism*.

28 Ongoing clinical treatment trials with adults with autism at the Mount Sinai School of Medicine based on this model cite Young's lab's work extensively (Hollander, "Oxytocin Infusion Reduces Repetitive Behaviors in Adults with Autistic and Asperger's Disorders"; Bartz and Hollander, "The Neuroscience of Affiliation"; Hollander et al., "Oxytocin Increases Retention of Social Cognition in Autism"). See C. J. Liu et al., "Are We There Yet?," for a review of proliferating clinical trials using intranasal oxytocin. Two of my collaborations with other feminist science studies scholars have described this shift in scientific and popular understandings of autism (Willey et al., "The Mating Life of Geeks") and in the rise of the geek scientist through the television series *The Big Bang Theory* (Willey and Subramaniam, "Inside the Social World of Asocials").

29 Hammock and Young, "Microsatellite Instability Generates Diversity in Brain and Sociobehavioral Traits." What is now usually referred to as microsatellite DNA was once and is still sometimes called "junk" DNA, because before it was thought to

potentially mark genetic variability, it was dismissed as meaningless because it is noncoding—meaning that it does not actually provide the program or instructions for a protein that actually performs some function in the body. See chapter 4 of Keller, *The Mirage of a Space between Nature and Nurture*, for a discussion of the importance of shifts in our understandings of noncoding DNA.

30 Martin and Hine, *A Dictionary of Biology*.

31 Hammock and Young, "Microsatellite Instability Generates Diversity in Brain and Sociobehavioral Traits."

32 Hammock and Young, "Microsatellite Instability Generates Diversity in Brain and Sociobehavioral Traits"; Lim et al., "Enhanced Partner Preference in a Promiscuous Species by Manipulating the Expression of a Single Gene."

33 Burkett and Young, "The Behavioral, Anatomical and Pharmacological Parallels between Social Attachment, Love and Addiction."

34 Others counter the claims of Young's lab, arguing that mammalian monogamy is "not controlled by a single gene" (Fink et al., "Mammalian Monogamy Is Not Controlled by a Single Gene"; Heckel and Fink, "Evolution of the Arginine Vasopressin 1a Receptor and Implications for Mammalian Social Behaviour"), but these laboratories are almost never cited by the press. So this claim is not uncontested in the scientific community yet achieves the status of Truth through the reporting of the discovery of a gene. Genetic determinism has a long history of gaining traction in the United States (Terry, *An American Obsession*; Reardon, *Race to the Finish*; Hubbard and Wald, *Exploding the Gene Myth*; Conrad and Markens, "Constructing the 'Gay Gene' in the News"). This single gene narrative is disrupted later on, and especially in the Vole Genomics Initiative white papers, which make the case for complete mapping in part on the grounds of the need to move beyond the single gene approach and to account for other "regulatory elements" in the shaping of social behavior. I will turn to these complexities in chapter 5.

35 McGraw and Young, "The Prairie Vole."

36 McGraw and Young, "The Prairie Vole"; Donaldson and Young, "Oxytocin, Vasopressin, and the Neurogenetics of Sociality."

37 Hammock and Young, "Microsatellite Instability Generates Diversity in Brain and Sociobehavioral Traits."

38 See Terry, "'Unnatural Acts' in Nature," for a discussion of the difference between the modeling of homosexuality in animals for translation to human behavior in contrast to what she calls a "species-centered" approach that is sensitive to context.

39 Hernandez and Blazer, *Genes, Behavior, and the Social Environment*.

40 The diagnosis of autism has in fact been made more capacious, and a variety of scientific understandings of what has been read as social deficit, or lack of empathy, in people diagnosed with autism has developed. See Cohen-Rottenberg, "Deconstructing Autism as an Empathy Disorder."

41 This genetic data is now available through the Broad Institute and the National Center for Biotechnology Information.

42 "White Paper Proposal for Sequencing the Genome of the Prairie Vole (*Microtus ochrogaster*)," 1.

43 Rader, *Making Mice*.

44 Birke, *Feminism and the Biological Body*.

45 Hubbard, *The Politics of Women's Biology*, 12–14.

46 Davis, "New Materialism and Feminism's Anti-biologism."

47 National Science Foundation, "Variation in Vole Gene Is Bellwether for Behavior."

48 Some colonies of prairie voles in Young's laboratory are outbred with wild populations to maintain diversity ("White Paper Proposal for Sequencing the Genome of the Prairie Vole (*Microtus ochrogaster*)," 9).

49 Lim et al., "The Role of Vasopressin in the Genetic and Neural Regulation of Monogamy."

50 Pitkow et al., "Facilitation of Affiliation and Pair-Bond Formation by Vasopressin Receptor Gene Transfer into the Ventral Forebrain of a Monogamous Vole"; Bielsky et al., "The v1a Vasopressin Receptor Is Necessary and Sufficient for Normal Social Recognition."

51 The same test has been done using female animals as test subjects—researchers argue that different hormones bind with the same receptors in males and females. So it is the same neurochemical pathway that is acted on, although the evolutionary significance is different. The hormone said to control female monogamy is oxytocin, which controls maternal care behaviors. In males the hormone is vasopressin, which is said to control species-specific behaviors, like territoriality. Both males and females have both hormones, and as I mentioned in note 6, there is cross-receptivity in receptors so they do not know which hormones bind with the receptors. I discuss this in more detail in chapter 5. See Willey and Giordano, "'Why Do Voles Fall in Love?,'" for a detailed analysis of the gendered hormone story of monogamy research.

52 See Jordan-Young, *Brain Storm* (especially chapters 6 and 7), and Lloyd, *The Case of the Female Orgasm*, for detailed discussions of the limitations of scientific definitions of sex.

53 Hammock and Young, "Microsatellite Instability Generates Diversity in Brain and Sociobehavioral Traits."

54 Hollander, "Oxytocin Infusion Reduces Repetitive Behaviors in Adults with Autistic and Asperger's Disorders"; Hollander et al., "Oxytocin Increases Retention of Social Cognition in Autism"; Green and Hollander, "Autism and Oxytocin."

55 Other than technicians and others who work at Yerkes and care for the animals and the space, nonscientists are not generally admitted into the animal lab for more than a guided tour, for a variety of security reasons.

56 Hammock and Young, "Microsatellite Instability Generates Diversity in Brain and Sociobehavioral Traits"; Willey and Giordano, "'Why Do Voles Fall in Love?'"

57 See Fausto-Sterling, *Sexing the Body*, chapter 5, for a thoroughgoing discussion of the problems with this process in the study of sex differences.

58 Bennett, *Vibrant Matter*, 120.
59 Holmberg, "A Feeling for the Animal."
60 My experience with the technician who introduced me to the voles in their pre-experiment homes was somewhat different. She wore gloves but cheerfully showed me the pairs with names who had been there longest and smiled as I cooed over the new litters (so tiny!).
61 Terry, "'Unnatural Acts' in Nature," 161.
62 Roughgarden, *Evolution's Rainbow*; Terry, "'Unnatural Acts' in Nature," 154; Lloyd, *The Case of the Female Orgasm*.
63 Young and Alexander, *The Chemistry between Us*.
64 Dreger, *Hermaphrodites and the Medical Invention of Sex*; Fausto-Sterling, *Sexing the Body*; Kessler, *Lessons from the Intersexed*.
65 Markowitz, "Pelvic Politics."
66 "White Paper Proposal for Sequencing the Genome of the Prairie Vole (*Microtus ochrogaster*)," 7.
67 I owe a debt of gratitude to David Rubin for generously reading about vole chromosome evolution and explaining the biologies scientists regard as nonnormative to me. David's work on intersex offers a model of strong resistance to an "intersex exceptionalism" that would allow us to imagine that minus a few exceptions the system works just fine; I approach sex assignment in voles with that caution in mind.
68 Rubin, "'An Unnamed Blank That Craved a Name'"; Magubane, "Spectacles and Scholarship."
69 Many have argued that translational work that uses rodents to understand human behavior is flawed mainly because rodents and humans are so different. I became less and less compelled by many of these arguments the more I learned about voles. Anne Fausto-Sterling has argued that our frameworks for understanding sexuality are inadequate (even) for rodents, because they persistently ignore the capacity of animals (human and nonhuman) to learn from their experiences. See Fausto-Sterling, "Animal Models for the Development of Human Sexuality," 12–13.
70 Emens, *Monogamy's Law*, 297.
71 See Gupta, "'Screw Health,'" for an analysis of "sex for health" discourse in science and popular culture.

3. MAKING OUR POLY NATURE

1 Pigliucci, "The One Paradigm to Rule Them All."
2 Willey and Subramaniam, "Inside the Social World of Asocials."
3 Roosth and Schrader, "Feminist Theory out of Science."
4 Halberstam, *The Queer Art of Failure*.
5 Pallotta-Chiarolli, "Take Four Pioneering Poly Women."
6 Configurations of poly relationships are quite diverse—they range from "open" (non–sexually exclusive) dyadic relationships to triads and "vees" and to group

marriages and "polyfidelitous" relationships. See Kassoff, "Nonmonogamy in the Lesbian Community," and Munson and Stelboum, "Introduction," for discussions of a range of polyamorous and nonmonogamous identities and relationships.

7 See the introduction to Sedgwick, *Epistemology of the Closet*, for a more general discussion of minoritizing and majoritizing rhetoric around sexualities.

8 Emens, *Monogamy's Law*, 344, 297–300.

9 See the conference website, https://sites.google.com/site/ipachome/home, and "About the Conference," 2013, https://sites.google.com/site/ipachome/about-the-conference. The "poly researchers" listserv is a Yahoo group; membership had grown to 512 as of October 12, 2015. See Barker and Langdridge, "Whatever Happened to Non-monogamies?"

10 *Alan's List of Polyamory Events*.

11 See Burgett, "On the Mormon Question"; Aviram, "Make Love, Not Law"; Sheff, "Polyamorous Families, Same-Sex Marriage, and the Slippery Slope."

12 Sheff, *The Polyamorists Next Door*.

13 See, for example, Morrison et al., "A Comparison of Polyamorous and Monoamorous Persons." "Lovestyle" was coined in Lee, "Forbidden Colors of Love," and is widely used in poly discourse. See Ritchie and Barker, "'There Aren't Words for What We Do or How We Feel So We Have to Make Them Up.'"

14 "About the Conference."

15 "About the Conference." This particular argument is well developed in Ryan and Jetha, *Sex at Dawn*, which is frequently cited as evidence of monogamy's unnaturalness all over the blogosphere.

16 Among others, see Klesse, "Bisexual Women, Non-monogamy and Differentialist Anti-promiscuity Discourses," on the gendered racialization of promiscuity discourses; Davis, "New Materialism and Feminism's Anti-biologism," on the discursive whiteness of polyamory, and Petrella, "Ethical Sluts and Closet Polyamorists," on the neoliberal intelligibility of polyamory.

17 See Sheff and Hammers, "The Privilege of Perversities."

18 Jennifer Hamilton and Jennifer Reardon's works brilliantly model this type of approach.

19 Stepan, *The Idea of Race in Science*, 6–9; Schiebinger, *Nature's Body*.

20 Finn and Malson, "Speaking of Home Truth," 521.

21 Worth et al., "Somewhere over the Rainbow."

22 Petrella, "Ethical Sluts and Closet Polyamorists."

23 Finn and Malson, "Speaking of Home Truth."

24 Van Anders and Goldey, "Testosterone and Partnering Are Linked via Relationship Status for Women and 'Relationship Orientation' for Men"; van Anders, Goldey, and Kuo, "The Steroid/Peptide Theory of Social Bonds"; van Anders, Hamilton, and Watson, "Multiple Partners Are Associated with Higher Testosterone in North American Men and Women."

25 Van Anders, Goldey, and Kuo, "The Steroid/Peptide Theory of Social Bonds," 1266.

26 Van Anders, Goldey, and Kuo, "The Steroid/Peptide Theory of Social Bonds," 1267.

27 Van Anders and Goldey, "Testosterone and Partnering Are Linked via Relationship Status for Women and 'Relationship Orientation' for Men."

28 Finn and Malson, "Speaking of Home Truth," 520.

29 Tibbetts, "Commitment in Monogamous and Polyamorous Relationships," 8; Tweedy, "Polyamory as a Sexual Orientation."

30 Leng, Meddle, and Douglas, "Oxytocin and the Maternal Brain"; Francis, *The Oxytocin Factor*; Young, "Being Human"; Kosfeld et al., "Oxytocin Increases Trust in Humans"; Moss, "Moral Molecules, Modern Selves, and Our 'Inner Tribe.'"

31 Moss, "Moral Molecules, Modern Selves, and Our 'Inner Tribe'"; Kagan, *The Human Spark*.

32 Mandese, "Better Advertising through Chemistry." Oxytocin has been touted for its therapeutic role in human-pet relationships, wound healing, the appeal of kissing, treating depression, stress, and anxiety, among other things. See Magon and Kalra, "The Orgasmic History of Oxytocin," for a history of the hormone's many incarnations and pharmacological deployments.

33 Pfeiffer, "Oxytocin—Not Always a Moral Molecule"; "The Dark Side of the Love Hormone Oxytocin."

34 Dreu et al., "Oxytocin Promotes Human Ethnocentrism"; Radke and de Bruijn, "The Other Side of the Coin."

35 Collins, "It's All in the Family"; Cossman, "Contesting Conservatisms, Family Feuds and the Privatization of Dependency"; Engels and Hunt, *The Origin of the Family, Private Property and the State*; Fineman, "Our Sacred Institution," 387.

36 Anderlini-D'Onofrio, *Plural Loves*; Munson, *The Lesbian Polyamory Reader*.

37 Anderlini-D'Onofrio, *Gaia and the New Politics of Love*.

38 In a review essay at the end of *Plural Loves*, Maria Pallotta-Chiarolli pays tribute to the author-activists who paved the way for feminist approaches to polyamory (Pallotta-Chiarolli, "Take Four Pioneering Poly Women"). I acknowledge my debt to these writers, whose contributions have their mark on the texts I analyze here, including highly influential books like Anapol, *Polyamory*; Easton and Hardy, *Ethical Slut*; West, *Lesbian Polyfidelity*.

39 Gartrell, "If This Is Tuesday, It Must Be Dee . . . Confessions of a Closet Polyamorist," 26.

40 Loulan, "Lesbians as Luvbeins," 37.

41 Millett, *Sexual Politics*, 116.

42 Quoted in Vera, "The Polyamory Quilt," 19.

43 Overall, "Monogamy, Nonmonogamy, and Identity," 14.

44 Halberstam, for example, grapples with this problem vis-à-vis the potentiality of "wildness" as a queer analytic (Halberstam, "Wildness, Loss, Death"). Alaimo disrupts this legacy in her treatment of eros in chapter 2 of *Bodily Natures*.

45 Hammonds and Herzig, *The Nature of Difference*.

46 Williams, "Naked, Neutered, or Noble."

47 Anderlini-D'Onofrio, *Plural Loves*, 3.

48 Noël, "Progressive Polyamory." This critique has been made of not only the presumed subject of literature on polyamory but also that of queer (Johnson and Henderson, *Black Queer Studies*) and feminist (Mahmood, *Politics of Piety*) theories in general, where polyamory is increasingly being addressed.

49 Storr, "The Sexual Reproduction of 'Race.'"

50 In psychoanalytic discourse, too, Storr notes, "bisexuality" is used to describe the "original" state of both girls and boys, during the stage of phallic masturbation, during which they have both homo and heterosexual potential. See Butler, *Gender Trouble*.

51 Storr, "The Sexual Reproduction of 'Race,'" 85.

52 See, for example, McWhorter, *Racism and Sexual Oppression in Anglo-America*.

53 See the discussion of bisexuality in the introduction.

54 I hope to return to Anapol's legacy for creative feminist interventions into compulsory monogamy in the future.

55 Narayan, *Dislocating Cultures*; Volpp, "Talking 'Culture.'"

56 Hansen, *Not-So-Nuclear Families*; Lehr, *Queer Family Values*; Heinemann, *Inventing the Modern American Family*.

57 Weston, *Families We Choose*.

58 Anapol, "A Glimpse of Harmony," 113, 114.

59 Anapol, "A Glimpse of Harmony," 113.

60 Pollitt, "Whose Culture?"

61 Markowitz, "Pelvic Politics."

62 "Compersion" is a term used in poly communities and literature to refer to the feeling of joy one gets from seeing one's partner happy with someone else—it is the opposite of jealousy. See Ritchie and Barker, "'There Aren't Words for What We Do or How We Feel So We Have to Make Them Up,'" for a discussion of compersion and other concepts in "polyamorous languages."

63 Bard, "Just Like a Hollywood Movie," 191, 194.

64 Bard, "Just Like a Hollywood Movie," 194.

65 Harding, *Science and Social Inequality*, 18.

66 Hamilton, "Reconstructing Indigenous Genomes," offers a rigorous treatment of the limits of genomics ethics.

67 Bard, "Just Like a Hollywood Movie," 195, 186.

68 Anderlini-D'Onofrio, *Gaia and the New Politics of Love*, 137.

4. RETHINKING MONOGAMY'S NATURE

1 See, for example, van der Tuin and Dolphijn, "The Transversality of New Materialism," 166.

2 Foucault, "Friendship as a Way of Life," 158.

3 Rosa, "Anti-monogamy," 112–13.

4 See Butler, *Gender Trouble*, for a discussion of the performative redeployment of lesbian as a banner under which we might organize.

5 Foucault, "Friendship as a Way of Life." The strip has been compiled into thirteen collections, and some strips are also accessible online.

6 Bechdel's *Fun Home* (2006) became a *New York Times* bestseller, was reviewed widely, and won several awards. It has also received a good deal of academic attention (Chute, *Graphic Women*; Lemberg, "Closing the Gap in Alison Bechdel's *Fun Home*"), alongside her more recent *Are You My Mother?* (Bauer, "Vital Lines Drawn from Books"; Giaimo, "Unable to Remember but Unwilling to Forget").

7 Cvetkovich, "Drawing the Archive in Alison Bechdel's *Fun Home*."

8 Huffer, *Are the Lips a Grave?*, 118.

9 Bechdel, *The Indelible Alison Bechdel*.

10 Huffer, *Are the Lips a Grave?*, 119.

11 Tolmie, "Modernism, Memory and Desire," 76.

12 Ahmed, "Imaginary Prohibitions."

13 Beccalossi, "The Construction of Scientific Knowledge Regarding Female 'Sexual Inversion.'"

14 Emery, *The Lesbian Index*, 17–18.

15 Moonwomon-Baird, "What Do Lesbians Do in the Daytime?," 354, 351.

16 Smorag, "From Closet Talk to PC Terminology."

17 Willett et al., "The Seriously Erotic Politics of Feminist Laughter."

18 See Shaw, "Women on Women."

19 Shaw, "Women on Women," 93–94; see the introduction to Bechdel, *The Essential Dykes to Watch Out For*.

20 Martindale, *Un/Popular Culture*.

21 Beirne, *Lesbians in Television and Text after the Millennium*, 181.

22 Bechdel, *Dykes and Sundry Other Carbon-Based Life-Forms to Watch Out For*, 3.

23 Bechdel, *Dykes and Sundry Other Carbon-Based Life-Forms to Watch Out For*, 5.

24 See Beirne's excellent reading of Sydney's role in the strip, in *Lesbians in Television and Text after the Millennium*.

25 Gardiner, "Queering Genre."

26 See Pieper and Bauer, "Mono-normativity and Polyamory."

27 Barker and Langdridge, "Whatever Happened to Non-monogamies?"

28 Bechdel, "'Serial Monogamy.'" The protagonist is a loosely autobiographical character, like Mo, the main character in the regular strip.

29 Bechdel, "'Serial Monogamy,'" 109.

30 Bechdel, "'Serial Monogamy,'" 120.

31 Bechdel, "'Serial Monogamy,'" 126.

32 *Lynnee Breedlove's One Freak Show*, produced by Madge Darlington, Throws Like a Girl Series, San Francisco, 2007.

33 Bechdel, "'Serial Monogamy,'" 129, 130–32.

34 Bechdel, "'Serial Monogamy,'" 110.

35 Bechdel, *Dykes to Watch Out For*, 132.

36 See the preface to Bechdel, *The Essential Dykes to Watch Out For*.

37 Gatens, *Imaginary Bodies*, 105.

38 Bechdel, *The Indelible Alison Bechdel*, 73–83.

39 In December 1989, a young man systematically shot and killed fourteen women students at École Polytechnique in Montreal, citing his hatred of "feminists" (women entering male professions, like engineering) as his motivation.

40 Bechdel, *The Indelible Alison Bechdel*, 83.

41 For more detailed cast biographies, see Bechdel, "Cast Biographies."

42 Liddle, "More Than a Bookstore."

43 Bechdel, "'Serial Monogamy,'" 126.

44 See the timeline in Bechdel, *The Indelible Alison Bechdel*, 73.

45 See in particular Bechdel, *Split-Level Dykes to Watch Out For*.

46 For reflections on the activist work and legacy of the Lesbian Avengers, see Kelly Cogswell's *Eating Fire*.

47 Bechdel, *The Indelible Alison Bechdel*; Chute, *Graphic Women*; Lemberg, "Closing the Gap in Alison Bechdel's *Fun Home*."

48 See "Buyer's Remorse," in Bechdel, *Split-Level Dykes to Watch Out For*.

49 Borders Books was Barnes and Noble's corporate competitor in those days, and the success of "Bunns and Noodle" and "Bounders" is a major theme in *DTWOF*, threatening the closure of Madwimmin Books and marking a swiftly changing social and political landscape.

50 Janet Hardy used the pseudonym "Catherine Liszt" in the original publication of *The Ethical Slut*, but it has been reprinted under her real name. Recall that Anapol is the author of "A Glimpse of Harmony," one of the texts with which I engaged in chapter 3.

5. BIOPOSSIBILITY

Sections of chapter 5 were previously published as "Biopossibility: A Queer Feminist Materialist Science Studies Manifesto, with Special Reference to the Question of Monogamous Behavior," *Signs* 41, no. 3 (2016).

1 Anderson, *Ramon*. Laurie Anderson is a brilliant naturecultural thinker. See for example her *Stories from the Nerve Bible*.

2 Haraway, *When Species Meet*.

3 See, for example, Halley, *Split Decisions*.

4 Seymour, *Strange Natures*, 184.

5 Huffer, *Are the Lips a Grave?*, 87.

6 Roy, "Somatic Matters."

7 Fausto-Sterling, *Sexing the Body*; Giordano, "What's Political about Plantarflexion Muscles?"; Richardson, "Sexing the X"; Jordan-Young, *Brain Storm*.

8 Davis, "New Materialism and Feminism's Anti-biologism"; Herzig, "On Performance, Productivity, and Vocabularies of Motive in Recent Studies of

Science"; Blencowe, "Biology, Contingency and the Problem of Racism in Feminist Discourse"; Cooper, *Life as Surplus*; Pitts-Taylor, "The Plastic Brain."

9 Barad, *Meeting the Universe Halfway*.

10 Winnubst, *Queering Freedom*.

11 Lorde, "Uses of the Erotic," 56.

12 Lorde, "Uses of the Erotic," 56–57.

13 Alaimo, *Bodily Natures*, 85–87.

14 Huffer, "Foucault's Fossils."

15 See, for example, Braidotti, *The Posthuman*; van der Tuin and Dolphijn, "The Transversality of New Materialism"; Bennett, *Vibrant Matter*.

16 See the classic Hubbard and Wald, *Exploding the Gene Myth*, and the more recent Keller, *The Mirage of a Space between Nature and Nurture*, for in-depth discussions of reductive stories about gene-brain-behavior connections.

17 Lorde, "Uses of the Erotic," 53, 54.

18 Lorde, "Uses of the Erotic," 53.

19 Withers, "What Is Your Essentialism Is My Immanent Flesh!" See Ginzberg, "Audre Lorde's (Nonessentialist) Lesbian Eros," for a counter-reading of Lorde's eros as antiessentialist.

20 Lorde, "Uses of the Erotic," 54.

21 Chapkis, *Live Sex Acts*, 73.

22 See Huffer, *Are the Lips a Grave?*, for a refreshing queer feminist approach to sexual ethics that elegantly complicates a frame that dismisses feminism as moralistic.

23 Holland, *The Erotic Life of Racism*, 53–54.

24 Moore and Rivera, *Planetary Loves*.

25 See Gupta, "Compulsory Sexuality and Its Discontents," for a discussion of this riskiness in Lorde's use of "eros."

26 Huffer, *Are the Lips a Grave?*, 130.

27 Willett, *The Soul of Justice*, 180.

28 Donaldson and Young, "Oxytocin, Vasopressin, and the Neurogenetics of Sociality."

29 Insel, "The Challenge of Translation in Social Neuroscience."

30 Lim, Hammock, and Young, "The Role of Vasopressin in the Genetic and Neural Regulation of Monogamy"; Hammock and Young, "Microsatellite Instability Generates Diversity in Brain and Sociobehavioral Traits." See also chapter 2.

31 Donaldson and Young, "Oxytocin, Vasopressin, and the Neurogenetics of Sociality."

32 "White Paper Proposal for Sequencing the Genome of the Prairie Vole (*Microtus ochrogaster*)."

33 Insel, "The Challenge of Translation in Social Neuroscience."

34 Willey and Subramaniam, "Inside the Social World of Asocials."

35 Moss, "Moral Molecules, Modern Selves, and Our 'Inner Tribe.'"

36 Jordan-Young, *Brain Storm*.

37 Ahern and Young, "The Impact of Early Life Family Structure on Adult Social

Attachment, Alloparental Behavior, and the Neuropeptide Systems Regulating Affiliative Behaviors in the Monogamous Prairie Vole (*Microtus ochrogaster*)."

38 Insel, "The Challenge of Translation in Social Neuroscience."

39 Hammock and Young, "Microsatellite Instability Generates Diversity in Brain and Sociobehavioral Traits."

40 Zarembo, "DNA Tweak Turns Vole Mates into Soul Mates."

41 Hammock and Young, "Oxytocin, Vasopressin and Pair Bonding."

42 See feminist neuroscientist Sari van Anders and colleagues' discussion of the "aggression paradox" in research on bonding and hormones (van Anders et al., "The Steroid/Peptide Theory of Social Bonds").

43 Chini and Manning, "Agonist Selectivity in the Oxytocin/Vasopressin Receptor Family."

44 Bartz and Hollander, "The Neuroscience of Affiliation"; Moss, "Moral Molecules, Modern Selves, and Our 'Inner Tribe.'" See van Anders and Goldey, "Testosterone and Partnering Are Linked via Relationship Status for Women and 'Relationship Orientation' for Men," for an explication of the undertheorized importance of testosterone to pair bonding. They discuss testosterone's effects on both male and female pairing and on both territorial and nurturant bonding, in ways that complicate and challenge the gendered bonding stories of approaches that look at different hormones in male and female. Kodavanti and Curras-Collazo, "Neuroendocrine Actions of Organohalogens."

45 Donaldson and Young, "Oxytocin, Vasopressin, and the Neurogenetics of Sociality."

46 See Wilson, "Gut Feminism," for a brilliant discussion of the importance of receptors outside the brain.

47 Lolait et al., "Molecular Biology of Vasopressin Receptors"; Chini and Manning, "Agonist Selectivity in the Oxytocin/Vasopressin Receptor Family."

48 Willey and Giordano, "'Why Do Voles Fall in Love?'"

49 Dumit, "Plastic Neuroscience"; Jablonka and Lamb, *Evolution in Four Dimensions*.

50 "White Paper Proposal for Sequencing the Genome of the Prairie Vole (*Microtus ochrogaster*)," 5.

51 See, for example, Fink et al., "Mammalian Monogamy Is Not Controlled by a Single Gene"; Willey and Giordano, "'Why Do Voles Fall in Love?'"

52 "White Paper Proposal for Sequencing the Genome of the Prairie Vole (*Microtus ochrogaster*)," 4.

53 "White Paper Proposal for Sequencing the Genome of the Prairie Vole (*Microtus ochrogaster*)," 6.

54 See the afterword to Huffer, *Are the Lips a Grave?*, on queer lives in the discourse of work/life balance.

55 Sieben, "Heteronormative Pheromones?," 277.

56 The term "dis-organization" here is taken from Roy, "Feminist Theory in Science."

EPILOGUE

An earlier version of the epilogue was first presented as "Science Activism in the Lesbian Feminist Archives: Lessons for a Queer Feminist Science Studies," at the conference "Science for the People: The 1970s and Today," University of Massachusetts, Amherst, April 11–13, 2014.

1 I got in contact with Carol while writing this epilogue and discovered that a shorter version of the piece I read was later published in the *Association for Women in Science Newsletter*: Halpern, "I Dream of a Feminist Science."

2 Sandra Harding, one of the organizers of this particular symposium for the American Association for the Advancement of Science (AAAS) Annual Meeting in Houston, January 3–8, 1979, pointed me to coverage of the event in *off our backs*; see Segerberg, "Re/de/e/volving." Thank you to Karla Mantilla in her capacity as a collective member of *off our backs* for finding the article and getting it to me so quickly! Among other reflections, the article gives some attention to the theme of feminism *as* science, apparently raised by Leigh Starr at the symposium.

BIBLIOGRAPHY

Ahern, Todd H., Meera E. Modi, James P. Burkett, and Larry J. Young. "Evaluation of Two Automated Metrics for Analyzing Partner Preference Tests." *Journal of Neuroscience Methods* 182, no. 2 (2009): 180–88. doi:10.1016/j.jneumeth.2009.06.010.

Ahern, Todd H., and Larry J. Young. "The Impact of Early Life Family Structure on Adult Social Attachment, Alloparental Behavior, and the Neuropeptide Systems Regulating Affiliative Behaviors in the Monogamous Prairie Vole (*Microtus ochrogaster*)." *Frontiers in Behavioral Neuroscience* 3 (2009). doi:10.3389/neuro.08.017.2009.

Ahmed, S. "Imaginary Prohibitions: Some Preliminary Remarks on the Founding Gestures of the 'New Materialism.'" *European Journal of Women's Studies* 15, no. 1 (2008): 23–39. doi:10.1177/1350506807084854.

Alaimo, Stacy. *Bodily Natures: Science, Environment, and the Material Self*. Bloomington: Indiana University Press, 2010.

Alaimo, Stacy, and Susan J. Hekman. *Material Feminisms*. Bloomington: Indiana University Press, 2008.

Alan's List of Polyamory Events (blog). Accessed October 12, 2015. http://polyevents.blogspot.com/.

Alcoff, Linda. "Justifying Feminist Social Science." *Hypatia* 2, no. 3 (1987): 107–20. doi:10.1111/j.1527-2001.1987.tb01344.x.

Alloula, Malek. *The Colonial Harem*. Manchester: Manchester University Press, 1987.

Anapol, Deborah M. *Polyamory: The New Love without Limits; Secrets of Sustainable Intimate Relationships*. San Rafael, CA: IntiNet Resource Center, 1997.

Anapol, Deborah Taj. "A Glimpse of Harmony." *Journal of Bisexuality* 4, nos. 3–4 (2004): 109–19. doi:10.1300/J159v04n03_08.

Anderlini-D'Onofrio, Serena. *Gaia and the New Politics of Love: Notes for a Poly Planet*. Berkeley, CA: North Atlantic Books, 2010.

Anderlini-D'Onofrio, Serena. *Plural Loves: Designs for Bi and Poly Living*. Binghamton, NY: Routledge, 2005.

Anderson, Eric. *The Monogamy Gap: Men, Love, and the Reality of Cheating*. New York: Oxford University Press, 2012.

Anderson, Laurie. "Ramon." On *Strange Angels* (album). New York: Warner Brothers, 1989.

Anderson, Laurie. *Stories from the Nerve Bible: A Twenty-Year Retrospective*. New York: Perennial, 1993.

Åsberg, Cecilia, and Nina Lykke. "Feminist Technoscience Studies." *European Journal of Women's Studies* 17, no. 4 (2010): 299–305. doi:10.1177/1350506810377692.

Aviram, Hadar. "Make Love, Not Law: Perceptions of the Marriage Equality Struggle among Polyamorous Activists." *Journal of Bisexuality* 7, nos. 3–4 (2008): 261–86.

Ballon, Massie Santos. "To Have and to Vole." *Phillipine Daily Inquirer*, June 15, 2005. https://news.google.com/newspapers?id=DVY1AAAAIBAJ&sjid=ciUMAAAAIBAJ&pg=1402%2C8852080.

Barad, Karen. "Agential Realism: Feminist Interventions in Understanding Scientific Practices." In *The Science Studies Reader*, edited by Mario Biagioli, 1–11. New York: Routledge, 1999.

Barad, Karen. *Meeting the Universe Halfway: Quantum Physics and the Entanglement of Matter and Meaning*. Durham, NC: Duke University Press, 2007.

Barad, Karen. "Posthumanist Performativity: Toward an Understanding of How Matter Comes to Matter." *Signs* 28, no. 3 (2003): 801–31. doi:10.1086/345321.

Barash, David P. "Deflating the Myth of Monogamy." *Chronicle of Higher Education*, April 20, 2001. http://chronicle.com/article/Deflating-the-Myth-of-Monogamy/19296/.

Barash, David P., and Judith Eve Lipton. *The Myth of Monogamy: Fidelity and Infidelity in Animals and People*. New York: Holt, 2002.

Bard, Taliesin. "Just Like a Hollywood Movie." *Journal of Bisexuality* 4, nos. 3–4 (2004): 177–98. doi:10.1300/J159v04n03_15.

Barker, Meg, and Darren Langdridge. "Whatever Happened to Non-monogamies? Critical Reflections on Recent Research and Theory." *Sexualities* 13, no. 6 (2010): 748–72. doi:10.1177/1363460710384645.

Baron-Cohen, Simon. *Essential Difference: Male and Female Brains and the Truth about Autism*. New York: Basic Books, 2004.

Bartz, Jennifer, and Eric Hollander. "The Neuroscience of Affiliation: Forging Links between Basic and Clinical Research on Neuropeptides and Social Behavior." *Hormones and Behavior* 50, no. 4 (2006): 518–28. doi:10.1016/j.yhbeh.2006.06.018.

Bauer, Heike. "'Not a Translation but a Mutilation': The Limits of Translation and the Discipline of Sexology." *Yale Journal of Criticism* 16, no. 2 (2003): 381–405. doi:10.1353/yale.2003.0012.

Bauer, Heike. "Vital Lines Drawn from Books: Difficult Feelings in Alison Bechdel's

Fun Home and *Are You My Mother?" Journal of Lesbian Studies* 18, no. 3 (2014): 266–81. doi:10.1080/10894160.2014.896614.
Beccalossi, Chiara. "The Construction of Scientific Knowledge Regarding Female 'Sexual Inversion': Italian and British Sexology Compared, c. 1870–1920." Ph.D. diss., Queen Mary University of London, 2008. http://qmro.qmul.ac.uk/jspui/handle/123456789/1476.
Bechdel, Alison. *Are You My Mother? A Comic Drama*. Boston: Houghton Mifflin Harcourt, 2012.
Bechdel, Alison. "Cast Biographies." N.d. Website of Alison Bechdel. http://dykestowatchoutfor.com/cast-biographies.
Bechdel, Alison. *Dykes and Sundry Other Carbon-Based Life-Forms to Watch Out For*. New York: Alyson Books, 2003.
Bechdel, Alison. *Dykes to Watch Out For: The Sequel: Added Attraction! "Serial Monogamy": A Documentary*. Ithaca, NY: Firebrand Books, 1992.
Bechdel, Alison. *The Essential Dykes to Watch Out For*. Boston: Houghton Mifflin Harcourt, 2008.
Bechdel, Alison. *The Indelible Alison Bechdel: Confessions, Comix, and Miscellaneous Dykes to Watch Out For*. Ithaca, NY: Firebrand Books, 1998.
Bechdel, Alison. *Post-Dykes to Watch Out For*. Ithaca, NY: Firebrand Books, 2000.
Bechdel, Alison. "'Serial Monogamy': A Documentary." In *Dykes to Watch Out For: The Sequel: Added Attraction! "Serial Monogamy": A Documentary*. Ithaca, NY: Firebrand Books, 1992.
Bechdel, Alison. *Split-Level Dykes to Watch Out For: Cartoons*. Ithaca, NY: Firebrand Books, 1998.
Beirne, Rebecca. *Lesbians in Television and Text after the Millennium*. New York: Palgrave Macmillan, 2008.
Bennett, Jane. *Vibrant Matter: A Political Ecology of Things*. Durham, NC: Duke University Press, 2009.
Bi Academic Intervention. *The Bisexual Imaginary: Representation, Identity and Desire*. London: Cassell, 1997.
Bielsky, Isadora F., Shuang-Bao Hu, Xianghui Ren, Ernest F. Terwilliger, and Larry J. Young. "The V1a Vasopressin Receptor Is Necessary and Sufficient for Normal Social Recognition: A Gene Replacement Study." *Neuron* 47, no. 4 (2005): 503–13. doi:10.1016/j.neuron.2005.06.031.
Birke, Lynda. *Feminism and the Biological Body*. New Brunswick, NJ: Rutgers University Press, 2000.
Birke, Lynda I. A., and Arnold Arluke. *The Sacrifice: How Scientific Experiments Transform Animals and People*. Lafayette, IN: Purdue University Press, 2007.
Bland, Lucy, and Laura Doan, eds. *Sexology in Culture: Labelling Bodies and Desires*. Chicago: University of Chicago Press, 1999.
Bland, Lucy, and Laura Doan, eds. *Sexology Uncensored: The Documents of Sexual Science*. Chicago: University of Chicago Press, 1999.

Blencowe, Claire Peta. "Biology, Contingency and the Problem of Racism in Feminist Discourse." *Theory, Culture and Society* 28, no. 3 (2011): 3–27. doi:10.1177/0263276410396918.
Braidotti, Rosi. *The Posthuman*. Malden, MA: Polity, 2013.
Bravo López, Fernando. "Towards a Definition of Islamophobia: Approximations of the Early Twentieth Century." *Ethnic and Racial Studies* 34, no. 4 (2011): 556–73. doi:10.1080/01419870.2010.528440.
Brison, Susan J. *Aftermath: Violence and the Remaking of a Self*. Princeton, NJ: Princeton University Press, 2002.
Brizendine, Louann. *The Male Brain*. New York: Random House, 2010.
Bullough, Vern L. *Science in the Bedroom: A History of Sex Research*. New York: Basic Books, 1994.
Burger, Glenn, and Steven F. Kruger. *Queering the Middle Ages*. Minneapolis: University of Minnesota Press, 2001.
Burgett, Bruce. "On the Mormon Question: Race, Sex, and Polygamy in the 1850s and the 1990s." *American Quarterly* 57, no. 1 (2005): 75–102. doi:10.1353/aq.2005.0002.
Burkett, James P., and Larry J. Young. "The Behavioral, Anatomical and Pharmacological Parallels between Social Attachment, Love and Addiction." *Psychopharmacology* 224, no. 1 (2012): 1–26. doi:10.1007/s00213-012-2794-x.
Butler, Judith. *Gender Trouble: Feminism and the Subversion of Identity*. New York: Routledge, 2006.
Carter, Julian B. *The Heart of Whiteness: Normal Sexuality and Race in America, 1880–1940*. Durham, NC: Duke University Press, 2007.
Castañeda, Claudia. "Developmentalism and the Child in Nineteenth-Century Science." *Science as Culture* 10, no. 3 (2001): 375–409. doi:10.1080/09505430120074145.
Chapkis, Wendy. *Live Sex Acts: Women Performing Erotic Labor*. New York: Routledge, 1997.
Chen, Mel Y. *Animacies: Biopolitics, Racial Mattering, and Queer Affect*. Durham, NC: Duke University Press, 2012.
Chiang, Howard H. "Historicizing the Emergence of Sexual Freedom: The Medical Knowledge of Psychiatry and the Scientific Power of Sexology, 1880–1920 (1)." *Gender Forum*, no. 24 (2009). http://www.genderforum.org/issues/apparatus-xy/.
Chini, B., and M. Manning. "Agonist Selectivity in the Oxytocin/Vasopressin Receptor Family: New Insights and Challenges." *Biochemical Society Transactions* 35, no. 4 (2007): 737.
Chute, Hillary L. *Graphic Women: Life Narrative and Contemporary Comics*. New York: Columbia University Press, 2010.
Cogswell, Kelly J. *Eating Fire: My Life as a Lesbian Avenger*. Minneapolis: University of Minnesota Press, 2014.
Cohen-Rottenberg, Rachel. "Deconstructing Autism as an Empathy Disorder: A Literature Review." *Autism and Empathy*. 2012. https://autismandempathyblog

.wordpress.com/deconconstructing-autsim-as-an-empathy-disorder-a-literature -review/.
Collins, Patricia Hill. *Black Feminist Thought: Knowledge, Consciousness, and Politics of Empowerment*. New York: Routledge, 2002.
Collins, Patricia Hill. "It's All in the Family: Intersections of Gender, Race, and Nation." *Hypatia* 13, no. 3 (1998): 62–82. doi:10.1111/j.1527–2001.1998.tb01370.x.
Conrad, Peter, and Susan Markens. "Constructing the 'Gay Gene' in the News: Optimism and Skepticism in the US and British Press." *Health* 5, no. 3 (2001): 373–400. doi:10.1177/136345930100500306.
Coole, Diana, and Samantha Frost. *New Materialisms: Ontology, Agency, and Politics*. Durham, NC: Duke University Press, 2010.
Cooper, Melinda. *Life as Surplus: Biotechnology and Capitalism in the Neoliberal Era*. Seattle: University of Washington Press, 2008.
Cossman, Brenda. "Contesting Conservatisms, Family Feuds and the Privatization of Dependency." *American University Journal of Gender, Social Policy and the Law* 13, no. 3 (2005): 415–509.
Cott, Nancy F. *Public Vows: A History of Marriage and the Nation*. New ed. Cambridge, MA: Harvard University Press, 2002.
The Critical Polyamorist. "Couple-Centricity, Polyamory and Colonialism." *The Critical Polyamorist* (blog), July 28, 2014. http://www.criticalpolyamorist.com/homeblog /couple-centricity-polyamory-and-colonialism.
Cryle, Peter Maxwell, and Christopher E. Forth. *Sexuality at the Fin de Siècle: The Makings of a "Central Problem."* Newark: University of Delaware Press, 2008.
Cvetkovich, Ann. "Drawing the Archive in Alison Bechdel's *Fun Home*." *WSQ: Women's Studies Quarterly* 36, no. 1 (2008): 111–28. doi:10.1353/wsq.0.0037.
Dallos, Sally, Rudi Dallos, and Sally Foreman. *Couples, Sex and Power: The Politics of Desire*. Buckingham, England: Open University Press, 1997.
Daly, Martin, Margo Wilson, and Suzanne J. Weghorst. "Male Sexual Jealousy." *Ethology and Sociobiology* 3, no. 1 (1982): 11–27. doi:10.1016/0162–3095(82)90027–9.
"The Dark Side of the Love Hormone Oxytocin." *Popular Science*. July 23, 2013. http:// www.popsci.com/science/article/2013–07/love-hormone-isnt-anti-anxiety-drug -we-thought-it-was.
Darwin, Charles. *The Descent of Man*. New York: Digireads.com, 2004.
Davis, Noela. "New Materialism and Feminism's Anti-biologism: A Response to Sara Ahmed." *European Journal of Women's Studies* 16, no. 1 (2009): 67–80. doi:10.1177/1350506808098535.
Denike, Margaret. "The Racialization of White Man's Polygamy." *Hypatia* 25, no. 4 (2010): 852–74. doi:10.1111/j.1527–2001.2010.01140.x.
Dilno, Jen. "Monogamy and Alternate Life-Styles." In *Our Right to Love: A Lesbian Resource Book*, edited by Ginny Vida, 56–63. Englewood Cliffs, NJ: Prentice Hall, 1978.
Ditzen, Beate, Marcel Schaer, Barbara Gabriel, Guy Bodenmann, Ulrike Ehlert, and Markus Heinrichs. "Intranasal Oxytocin Increases Positive Communication and Re-

duces Cortisol Levels during Couple Conflict." *Biological Psychiatry* 65, no. 9 (2009): 728–31. doi:10.1016/j.biopsych.2008.10.011.
Donaldson, Zoe R., and Larry J. Young. "Oxytocin, Vasopressin, and the Neurogenetics of Sociality." *Science* 322, no. 5903 (2008): 900–904. doi:10.1126/science.1158668.
Dowell, Susan. *They Two Shall Be One: Monogamy in History and Religion*. London: William Collins, 1990.
Dreger, Alice Domurat. *Hermaphrodites and the Medical Invention of Sex*. Cambridge, MA: Harvard University Press, 1998.
Dreu, Carsten K. W. de, Lindred L. Greer, Gerben A. van Kleef, Shaul Shalvi, and Michel J. J. Handgraaf. "Oxytocin Promotes Human Ethnocentrism." *Proceedings of the National Academy of Sciences* 108, no. 4 (2011): 1262–66. doi:10.1073/pnas.1015316108.
duCille, Ann. *The Coupling Convention: Sex, Text, and Tradition in Black Women's Fiction*. New York: Oxford University Press, 1993.
Dudink, Stefan P. "Homosexuality, Race, and the Rhetoric of Nationalism." *History of the Present* 1, no. 2 (2011): 259–64. doi:10.5406/historypresent.1.2.0259.
Dumit, Joseph. "Plastic Neuroscience: Studying What the Brain Cares About." *Frontiers in Human Neuroscience* 8 (2014). doi:10.3389/fnhum.2014.00176.
Easton, Dossie, and Janet W. Hardy. *Ethical Slut*. New York: Random House, 2011.
Edelman, Lee. *No Future: Queer Theory and the Death Drive*. Durham, NC: Duke University Press, 2004.
Ehlers, Nadine. "Onerous Passions: Colonial Anti-miscegenation Rhetoric and the History of Sexuality." *Patterns of Prejudice* 45, no. 4 (2011): 319–40. doi:10.1080/0031322X.2011.605843.
Ehrenreich, Barbara, and Deirdre English. *For Her Own Good: Two Centuries of the Experts' Advice to Women*. New York: Random House, 2005.
Ellis, Havelock. *Sex in Relation to Society*. F. A. Davis, 1910.
Emens, Elizabeth. *Monogamy's Law: Compulsory Monogamy and Polyamorous Existence*. Rochester, NY: Social Science Research Network, March 1, 2004. http://papers.ssrn.com/abstract=506242.
Emery, Kim. *The Lesbian Index: Pragmatism and Lesbian Subjectivity in the Twentieth-Century United States*. Albany: State University of New York Press, 2002.
Engels, Friedrich, and Tristram Hunt. *The Origin of the Family, Private Property and the State*. Reissue ed. London: Penguin Classics, 2010.
Ewing, Katherine Pratt. "Naming Our Sexualities: Secular Constraints, Muslim Freedoms." *Focaal*, no. 59 (2011): 89–98. doi:10.3167/fcl.2011.590107.
Fausto-Sterling, Anne. "Animal Models for the Development of Human Sexuality." *Journal of Homosexuality* 28, nos. 3–4 (1995): 217–36. doi:10.1300/J082v28n03_02.
Fausto-Sterling, Anne. *Sexing the Body: Gender Politics and the Construction of Sexuality*. New York: Basic Books, 2000.
Ferguson, Roderick A. *Aberrations in Black: Toward a Queer of Color Critique*. Minneapolis: University of Minnesota Press, 2004.

Fineman, Martha Albertson. "Our Sacred Institution: The Ideal of the Family in American Law and Society." *Utah Law Review* 2 (1993): 387.

Fink, Sabine, Laurent Excoffier, and Gerald Heckel. "Mammalian Monogamy Is Not Controlled by a Single Gene." *Proceedings of the National Academy of Sciences* 103, no. 29 (2006): 10956–60. doi:10.1073/pnas.0602380103.

Finn, Mark, and Helen Malson. "Speaking of Home Truth: (Re)productions of Dyadic-Containment in Non-monogamous Relationships." *British Journal of Social Psychology* 47, no. 3 (2008): 519–33.

Fisher, Helen E. *Why We Love: The Nature and Chemistry of Romantic Love*. Macmillan, 2004.

Fleming, Jennifer B., and Carolyn K. Washburne. *For Better, for Worse: A Feminist Handbook on Marriage and Other Options*. New York: Scribner, 1977.

Foster, Laura A. *Critical Cultural Translation: A Socio-Legal Framework for Regulatory Orders*. Rochester, NY: Social Science Research Network, May 1, 2014. http://papers.ssrn.com/abstract=2434610.

Foucault, Michel. "Friendship as a Way of Life." In *Ethics, Subjectivity and Truth: Essential Works of Foucault 1954–1984*, vol. 1, 135–40. New York: New Press, 1997.

Foucault, Michel. *The History of Sexuality*. Vol. 1: *An Introduction*. Translated by Robert Hurley. New York: Vintage Books, 1978.

Franklin, Sarah. "Science as Culture, Cultures of Science." *Annual Review of Anthropology* 24 (1995): 163–84.

Frederickson, Kathleen. *The Ploy of Instinct: Victorian Sciences of Nature and Sexuality in Liberal Governance*. New York: Fordham University Press, 2014.

Gardiner, Judith Kegan. "Queering Genre: Alison Bechdel's *Fun Home: A Family Tragicomic* and *The Essential Dykes to Watch Out For*." *Contemporary Women's Writing* 5, no. 3 (2011): 188–207. doi:10.1093/cww/vpr015.

Gartrell, Nanette K. "If This Is Tuesday, It Must Be Dee . . . Confessions of a Closet Polyamorist." *Journal of Lesbian Studies* 3, nos. 1–2 (1999): 23–33. doi:10.1300/J155v03n01_03.

Gatens, Moira. *Imaginary Bodies: Ethics, Power and Corporeality*. New York: Routledge, 1995.

Giaimo, Genie. "Unable to Remember but Unwilling to Forget: Cognition, Perception, and Memory in the Contemporary American Memoir." Ph.D. diss., Northeastern University, 2014.

Ginzberg, Ruth. "Audre Lorde's (Nonessentialist) Lesbian Eros." *Hypatia* 7, no. 4 (1992): 73–90. doi:10.1111/j.1527-2001.1992.tb00719.x.

Giordano, Sara. "What's Political about Plantarflexion Muscles? A Feminist Investigation into the Boundaries of Muscles." Paper presented at the National Women's Studies Association annual conference, Cincinnati, Ohio, November 7–10, 2013.

Goldman, Emma. *Anarchism and Other Essays*. Mineola, NY: Dover, 1969.

Gordon, Avery F. *Ghostly Matters: Haunting and the Sociological Imagination*. Minneapolis: University of Minnesota Press, 2008.

Gordon, Avery F., and Janice Radway. *Ghostly Matters: Haunting and the Sociological Imagination*. 2nd ed. Minneapolis: University of Minnesota Press, 2008.

Gottschalk, Peter, and Gabriel Greenberg. *Islamophobia: Making Muslims the Enemy*. Lanham, MD: Rowman and Littlefield, 2008.

Gray, John. *Men Are from Mars, Women Are from Venus: The Classic Guide to Understanding the Opposite Sex*. New York: Harper Paperbacks, 2004.

Green, Joshua J., and Eric Hollander. "Autism and Oxytocin: New Developments in Translational Approaches to Therapeutics." *Neurotherapeutics* 7, no. 3 (2010): 250–57. doi:10.1016/j.nurt.2010.05.006.

Grosfoguel, Ramón, and Eric Mielants. "The Long-Durée Entanglement between Islamophobia and Racism in the Modern/Colonial Capitalist/Patriarchal World-System: An Introduction." *Human Architecture: Journal of the Sociology of Self-Knowledge* 5, no. 1 (2006). http://scholarworks.umb.edu/humanarchitecture/vol5/iss1/2.

Grosz, Elizabeth. "Matter, Life, and Other Variations." *Philosophy Today* 55 (2011): 17–27. http://cat.inist.fr/?aModele=afficheN&cpsidt=26632117.

Grosz, Elizabeth. *The Nick of Time: Politics, Evolution, and the Untimely*. Durham, NC: Duke University Press, 2004.

Gupta, Kristina. "Compulsory Sexuality and Its Discontents: The Challenge of Asexualities." Ph.D. diss., Emory University, 2013.

Gupta, Kristina. "'Screw Health': Representations of Sex as a Health-Promoting Activity in Medical and Popular Literature." *Journal of Medical Humanities* 32, no. 2 (2011): 127–40. doi:10.1007/s10912–010–9129-x.

Gupta, Kristina. "Why Do Voles Fall in Love? Interview with Feminist Science Studies Scholar Angela Willey." *Kristina Gupta, Ph.D.* (blog), June 28, 2012. http://www.kristinagupta.com/2012/06/28/why-do-voles-fall-in-love-interview-with-feminist-science-studies-scholar-angela-willey/.

Halberstam, Jack. "Wildness, Loss, Death." *Social Text* 32, no. 4 121 (2014): 137–48. doi:10.1215/01642472–2820520.

Halberstam, Judith. *The Queer Art of Failure*. Durham, NC: Duke University Press, 2011.

Halley, Janet. *Split Decisions: How and Why to Take a Break from Feminism*. Princeton, NJ: Princeton University Press, 2008.

Halpern, Carol. "I Dream of a Feminist Science." *Association of Women in Science Newsletter*, March 1982.

Halpern, Ellen L. "If Love Is So Wonderful, What's So Scary about MORE?" *Journal of Lesbian Studies* 3, nos. 1–2 (1999): 157–64. doi:10.1300/J155v03n01_17.

Hamilton, Jennifer A. "Reconstructing Indigenous Genomes: Ethical Exclusions in an Era of Genetic Indigeneity." Paper presented at the National Women's Studies Association annual conference, San Juan, Puerto Rico, November 13–16, 2014.

Hammock, Elizabeth A. D., and Larry J. Young. "Microsatellite Instability Generates Diversity in Brain and Sociobehavioral Traits." *Science* 308, no. 5728 (2005): 1630–34. doi:10.1126/science.1111427.

Hammock, Elizabeth A. D., and Larry J. Young. "Oxytocin, Vasopressin and Pair Bonding: Implications for Autism." *Philosophical Transactions of the Royal Society B: Biological Sciences* 361, no. 1476 (2006): 2187–98. doi:10.1098/rstb.2006.1939.

Hammonds, Evelynn M., and Rebecca M. Herzig. *The Nature of Difference: Sciences of Race in the United States from Jefferson to Genomics*. Cambridge, MA: MIT Press, 2009.

Hansen, Karen V. *Not-So-Nuclear Families: Class, Gender, and Networks of Care*. New Brunswick, NJ: Rutgers University Press, 2005.

Haraway, Donna. *Modest_Witness@Second_Millennium.FemaleMan©_Meets_OncoMouse™: Feminism and Technoscience*. New York: Routledge, 1997.

Haraway, Donna. "The Promises of Monsters: A Regenerative Politics for Inappropriate/d Others." In *Cultural Studies*, edited by Lawrence Grossberg, Cary Nelson, and Paula Treichler, 295–337. New York: Routledge, 1992.

Haraway, Donna. *Simians, Cyborgs, and Women: The Reinvention of Nature*. New York: Routledge, 2013.

Haraway, Donna. "Situated Knowledges: The Science Question in Feminism and the Privilege of Partial Perspective." *Feminist Studies* 14, no. 3 (1988): 575. doi:10.2307/3178066.

Haraway, Donna. *When Species Meet*. Minneapolis: University of Minnesota Press, 2008.

Harding, Sandra. "After the Neutrality Ideal: Science, Politics, and 'Strong Objectivity.'" *Social Research* 59, no. 3 (1992): 567–87.

Harding, Sandra. *Science and Social Inequality: Feminist and Postcolonial Issues*. Champaign: University of Illinois Press, 2006.

Harding, Sandra. *Whose Science? Whose Knowledge? Thinking from Women's Lives*. Ithaca, NY: Cornell University Press, 1991.

Harrison, Pam. "Novel Drug Modifies Core Autism Symptoms in Adults." *Medscape*, May 27, 2014. http://www.medscape.com/viewarticle/825711.

Heckel, Gerald, and Sabine Fink. "Evolution of the Arginine Vasopressin 1a Receptor and Implications for Mammalian Social Behaviour." *Progress in Brain Research* 170 (2008): 321–30. doi:10.1016/S0079-6123(08)00426-3.

Heinemann, Isabel. *Inventing the Modern American Family: Family Values and Social Change in 20th Century United States*. New York: Campus Verlag, 2012.

Hemmings, Clare. *Bisexual Spaces: A Geography of Sexuality and Gender*. New York: Routledge, 2002.

Hemmings, Clare. "Telling Feminist Stories." *Feminist Theory* 6, no. 2 (2005): 115–39. doi:10.1177/1464700105053690.

Hemmings, Clare. *Why Stories Matter: The Political Grammar of Feminist Theory*. Durham, NC: Duke University Press, 2011.

Herlihy, David. "Biology and History: The Triumph of Monogamy." *Journal of Interdisciplinary History* 25, no. 4 (1995): 571. doi:10.2307/205770.

Hernandez, Lyla M., and Dan Blazer, eds. *Genes, Behavior, and the Social Environment: Moving beyond the Nature/Nurture Debate*. Washington, DC: National Academies Press, 2006.

Herrn, Rainer. "On the History of Biological Theories of Homosexuality." *Journal of Homosexuality* 28, nos. 1–2 (1995): 31–56. doi:10.1300/J082v28n01_03.
Herzig, Rebecca. "On Performance, Productivity, and Vocabularies of Motive in Recent Studies of Science." *Feminist Theory* 5, no. 2 (2004): 127–47. doi:10.1177/1464700104045404.
Hird, Myra J. "Feminist Matters: New Materialist Considerations of Sexual Difference." *Feminist Theory* 5, no. 2 (2004): 223–32. doi:10.1177/1464700104045411.
Holland, Sharon Patricia. *The Erotic Life of Racism*. Durham, NC: Duke University Press, 2012.
Hollander, E. "Oxytocin Infusion Reduces Repetitive Behaviors in Adults with Autistic and Asperger's Disorders." *Neuropsychopharmacology* 28, no. 1 (2003): 193–98. doi:10.1038/sj.npp.1300021.
Hollander, Eric, Jennifer Bartz, William Chaplin, Ann Phillips, Jennifer Sumner, Latha Soorya, Evdokia Anagnostou, and Stacey Wasserman. "Oxytocin Increases Retention of Social Cognition in Autism." *Biological Psychiatry* 61, no. 4 (2007): 498–503. doi:10.1016/j.biopsych.2006.05.030.
Holmberg, Tora. "A Feeling for the Animal: On Becoming an Experimentalist." *Society and Animals* 16, no. 4 (2008): 316–35. doi:10.1163/156853008X357658.
Honig, Bonnie. "My Culture Made Me Do It." In Susan Moller Okin, *Is Multiculturalism Bad for Women?*, edited by Joshua Cohen, Matthew Howard, and Martha C. Nussbaum, 38–39. Princeton, NJ: Princeton University Press, 1999.
Hrdy, Sarah Blaffer. *Mothers and Others: The Evolutionary Origins of Mutual Understanding*. Cambridge, MA: Harvard University Press, 2009.
Hubbard, Ruth. *The Politics of Women's Biology*. New Brunswick, NJ: Rutgers University Press, 1990.
Hubbard, Ruth, and Elijah Wald. *Exploding the Gene Myth: How Genetic Information Is Produced and Manipulated by Scientists, Physicians, Employers, Insurance Companies, Educators, and Law Enforcers*. Boston: Beacon, 1999.
Huffer, Lynne. *Are the Lips a Grave? A Queer Feminist on the Ethics of Sex*. New York: Columbia University Press, 2013.
Huffer, Lynne. "Foucault's Fossils: Life Itself and the Return to Nature in Feminist Philosophy." In *Anthropocene Feminism*, edited by Richard Grusin. Minneapolis: University of Minnesota Press, 2016.
Insel, Thomas R. "The Challenge of Translation in Social Neuroscience: A Review of Oxytocin, Vasopressin, and Affiliative Behavior." *Neuron* 65, no. 6 (2010): 768–79. doi:10.1016/j.neuron.2010.03.005.
Insel, Thomas R. "Is Social Attachment an Addictive Disorder?" In "A Tribute to Paul MacLean: The Neurobiological Relevance of Social Behavior," special issue, *Physiology and Behavior* 79, no. 3 (2003): 351–57. doi:10.1016/S0031-9384(03)00148-3.
Irigaray, Luce. *Speculum of the Other Woman*. Ithaca, NY: Cornell University Press, 1985.
Israel, Jonathan I. *Radical Enlightenment: Philosophy and the Making of Modernity 1650–1750*. New York: Oxford University Press, 2001.

Iversen, Joan Smyth. *The Antipolygamy Controversy in U.S. Women's Movements, 1880–1925: A Debate on the American Home*. New York: Routledge, 1997.
Jablonka, Eva, and Marion J. Lamb. *Evolution in Four Dimensions: Genetic, Epigenetic, Behavioral, and Symbolic Variation in the History of Life*. Rev. ed. Cambridge, MA: MIT Press, 2014.
Jackson, Stevi. "Love, Social Change, and Everyday Heterosexuality." In *Love: A Question for Feminism in the Twenty-First Century*, edited by Anna G. Jónasdóttir and Ann Ferguson, 35–37. New York: Routledge, 2013.
Jackson, Stevi, and Sue Scott. "The Personal Is Still Political: Heterosexuality, Feminism and Monogamy." *Feminism and Psychology* 14, no. 1 (2004): 151–57. doi:10.1177/0959353504040317.
Johnson, E. Patrick, and Mae G. Henderson. *Black Queer Studies: A Critical Anthology*. Durham, NC: Duke University Press, 2005.
Johnston, Ian. "How Geneticists Put the Romance Back into Mating." *Scotsman*, July 30, 2005. http://www.highbeam.com/doc/1P2-13070653.html.
Jordan-Young, Rebecca M. *Brain Storm: The Flaws in the Science of Sex Differences*. Cambridge, MA: Harvard University Press, 2010.
Kagan, Jerome. *The Human Spark: The Science of Human Development*. New York: Perseus Books Group, 2013.
Kalmar, Ivan. *Early Orientalism: Imagined Islam and the Notion of Sublime Power*. New York: Routledge, 2013.
Kassoff, Elizabeth. "Nonmonogamy in the Lesbian Community." *Women and Therapy* 8, nos. 1–2 (1989): 167–82. doi:10.1300/J015v08n01_14.
Katz, Jonathan. *The Invention of Heterosexuality*. Chicago: University of Chicago Press, 2007.
Keating, AnaLouise. "Speculative Realism, Visionary Pragmatism, and Poet-Shamanic Aesthetics in Gloria Anzaldúa—and Beyond." *WSQ: Women's Studies Quarterly* 40, nos. 3–4 (2013): 51–69. doi:10.1353/wsq.2013.0020.
Keller, Evelyn Fox. *The Mirage of a Space between Nature and Nurture*. Durham, NC: Duke University Press, 2010.
Kessler, Suzanne J. *Lessons from the Intersexed*. New Brunswick, NJ: Rutgers University Press, 1998.
Kidd, Thomas S. *American Christians and Islam: Evangelical Culture and Muslims from the Colonial Period to the Age of Terrorism*. Princeton, NJ: Princeton University Press, 2009.
Kirby, Vicki. "Initial Conditions." *differences* 23, no. 3 (2012): 198–205. doi:10.1215/10407391-1892934.
Kirby, Vicki. *Telling Flesh: The Substance of the Corporeal*. New York: Routledge, 1997.
Klesse, Christian. "Bisexual Women, Non-monogamy and Differentialist Anti-promiscuity Discourses." *Sexualities* 8, no. 4 (2005): 445–64. doi:10.1177/1363460705056620.
Klesse, Christian. "'How to Be a Happy Homosexual?!' Non-monogamy and Govern-

mentality in Relationship Manuals for Gay Men in the 1980s and 1990s." *Sociological Review* 55, no. 3 (2007): 571–91. doi:10.1111/j.1467–954X.2007.00722.x.

Klesse, Christian. *The Spectre of Promiscuity: Gay Male and Bisexual Non-monogamies*. Farnham, UK: Ashgate, 2007.

Kodavanti, Prasada Rao S., and Margarita C. Curras-Collazo. "Neuroendocrine Actions of Organohalogens: Thyroid Hormones, Arginine Vasopressin, and Neuroplasticity." *Frontiers in Neuroendocrinology* 31, no. 4 (2010): 479–96. doi:10.1016/j.yfrne.2010.06.005.

Koedt, Anne. "The Myth of the Vaginal Orgasm." 1970. CWLU Herstory Website Archive. Accessed October 18, 2015. https://www.uic.edu/orgs/cwluherstory/CWLUArchive/vaginalmyth.html.

Kosfeld, Michael, Markus Heinrichs, Paul J. Zak, Urs Fischbacher, and Ernst Fehr. "Oxytocin Increases Trust in Humans." *Nature* 435, no. 7042 (2005): 673–76. doi:10.1038/nature03701.

Krafft-Ebing, Richard. *Psychopathia Sexualis: With Especial Reference to the Antipathic Sexual Instinct; a Medico-Forensic Study*. New York: Rebman Company, 1906.

Kuan, Anita. "New Study Indicates Oxytocin May Provide Treatment for Autism." April 29, 2014. http://asdnewsreview.com/asdnews/new-study-indicates-oxytocin-may-provide-treatment-for-autism/.

Lee, John Alan. "Forbidden Colors of Love." *Journal of Homosexuality* 1, no. 4 (1976): 401–18. doi:10.1300/J082v01n04_04.

Lees, Sue. *Sugar and Spice: Sexuality and Adolescent Girls*. New York: Penguin Books, 1993.

Lehr, Valerie. *Queer Family Values: Debunking the Myth of the Nuclear Family*. Philadelphia, PA: Temple University Press, 1999.

Lemberg, Jennifer. "Closing the Gap in Alison Bechdel's *Fun Home*." *WSQ: Women's Studies Quarterly* 36, no. 1 (2008): 129–40. doi:10.1353/wsq.0.0051.

Leng, Gareth, Simone L. Meddle, and Alison J. Douglas. "Oxytocin and the Maternal Brain." *Current Opinion in Pharmacology* 8, no. 6 (2008): 731–34. doi:10.1016/j.coph.2008.07.001.

Leng, Kirsten. "Cultural Difference and Sexual 'Progress': Making Sense of Ethnology's Role in Early Twentieth Century Sexual Politics." *Journal of the History of Sexuality* 25, no. 1 (2016).

Lewenstein, Bruce. "Science and the Media." In *Handbook of Science and Technology Studies*, edited by Sheila Jasanoff, Gerald E. Markle, James C. Peterson, and Trevor Pinch, 343–60. Thousand Oaks, CA: Sage, 2001.

Lewontin, Richard C., Steven Peter Russell Rose, and Leon J. Kamin. *Not in Our Genes: Biology, Ideology, and Human Nature*. New York: Pantheon Books, 1984.

Liddle, Kathleen. "More Than a Bookstore." *Journal of Lesbian Studies* 9, nos. 1–2 (2005): 145–59. doi:10.1300/J155v09n01_14.

Lim, M. M., E. a. D. Hammock, and L. J. Young. "The Role of Vasopressin in the Genetic and Neural Regulation of Monogamy." *Journal of Neuroendocrinology* 16, no. 4 (2004): 325–32. doi:10.1111/j.0953–8194.2004.01162.x.

Lim, Miranda M., Zuoxin Wang, Daniel E. Olazábal, Xianghui Ren, Ernest F. Terwilliger, and Larry J. Young. "Enhanced Partner Preference in a Promiscuous Species by Manipulating the Expression of a Single Gene." *Nature* 429, no. 6993 (2004): 754–57. doi:10.1038/nature02539.

Liu, C. J., Rebecca A. McErlean, and Mark R. Dadds. "Are We There Yet? The Clinical Potential of Intranasal Oxytocin in Psychiatry." *Current Psychiatry Reviews* 8, no. 1 (2012): 37–48. doi:10.2174/157340012798994902.

Lloyd, Elisabeth A. *The Case of the Female Orgasm: Bias in the Science of Evolution*. Cambridge, MA: Harvard University Press, 2009.

Lloyd, Elisabeth A. "Pre-theoretical Assumptions in Evolutionary Explanations of Female Sexuality." *Philosophical Studies* 69, nos. 2–3 (1993): 139–53. doi:10.1007/BF00990080.

Lolait, Stephen J., Anne-Marie O'Carroll, and Michael J. Brownstein. "Molecular Biology of Vasopressin Receptors." *Annals of the New York Academy of Sciences* 771, no. 1 (1995): 273–92. doi:10.1111/j.1749–6632.1995.tb44688.x.

Longino, Helen E. "Can There Be a Feminist Science?" *Hypatia* 2, no. 3 (1987): 51–64. doi:10.1111/j.1527–2001.1987.tb01341.x.

Longino, Helen E. *Science as Social Knowledge*. Princeton, NJ: Princeton University Press, 1990.

Longino, Helen E. "Subjects, Power, and Knowledge: Description and Prescription in Feminist Philosophies of Science." In *Feminism and Science*, edited by Evelyn Fox Keller and Helen E. Longino, 264–79. New York: Oxford University Press, 1996.

Lorde, Audre. "Uses of the Erotic: The Erotic as Power." Out & Out Books, 1978.

Loulan, Joann. "Lesbians as Luvbeins." *Journal of Lesbian Studies* 3, nos. 1–2 (1999): 35–38. doi:10.1300/J155v03n01_04.

"'Love Drug' Oxytocin Could Be Used to Improve Marriage, Researchers Argue." *Huffington Post*, June 12, 2013. http://www.huffingtonpost.com/2013/06/12/love-drug_n_3429762.html.

Ludden, David. "Orientalist Empiricism: Transformations of Colonial Knowledge." In *Orientalism and the Postcolonial Predicament: Perspectives on South Asia*, edited by Carol A. Breckenridge and Peter van der Veer, 250–78. Philadelphia: University of Pennsylvania Press, 1993.

Magon, Navneet, and Sanjay Kalra. "The Orgasmic History of Oxytocin: Love, Lust, and Labor." *Indian Journal of Endocrinology and Metabolism* 15, supp. 3 (2011): S156–S161. doi:10.4103/2230–8210.84851.

Magubane, Zine. "Spectacles and Scholarship: Caster Semenya, Intersex Studies, and the Problem of Race in Feminist Theory." *Signs* 39, no. 3 (2014): 761–85. doi:10.1086/674301.

Mahmood, Saba. *Politics of Piety: The Islamic Revival and the Feminist Subject*. Princeton, NJ: Princeton University Press, 2011.

Mandese, Joe. "Better Advertising through Chemistry: Oxytocin Is the New Dopa-

mine." *Media Daily News*, June 19, 2014. http://www.mediapost.com/publications/article/228373/better-advertising-through-chemistry-oxytocin-is.html?edition=.
Markowitz, Sally. "Pelvic Politics: Sexual Dimorphism and Racial Difference." *Signs* 26, no. 2 (2001): 389–414.
Martin, Elizabeth, and Robert S. Hine. *A Dictionary of Biology*. New York: Oxford University Press, 2008.
Martin, Emily. "The Egg and the Sperm: How Science Has Constructed a Romance Based on Stereotypical Male-Female Roles." *Signs* 16, no. 3 (1991): 485–501.
Martindale, Kathleen. *Un/Popular Culture: Lesbian Writing after the Sex Wars*. Albany: State University of New York Press, 1997.
May, Vivian M. "Disciplinary Desires and Undisciplined Daughters: Negotiating the Politics of a Women's Studies Doctoral Education." *NWSA Journal* 14, no. 1 (2002): 134–59.
McClintock, Anne. *Imperial Leather: Race, Gender and Sexuality in the Colonial Contest*. New York: Routledge, 1995.
McGraw, Lisa A., and Larry J. Young. "The Prairie Vole: An Emerging Model Organism for Understanding the Social Brain." *Trends in Neurosciences* 33, no. 2 (2010): 103–9. doi:10.1016/j.tins.2009.11.006.
McWhorter, Ladelle. *Racism and Sexual Oppression in Anglo-America: A Genealogy*. Bloomington: Indiana University Press, 2009.
Millett, Kate. *Sexual Politics*. Chicago: University of Illinois Press, 2000.
Moonwomon-Baird, Birch. "What Do Lesbians Do in the Daytime? Recover." *Journal of Sociolinguistics* 4, no. 3 (2000): 348–78. doi:10.1111/1467–9481.00120.
Moore, Stephen D., and Mayra Rivera. *Planetary Loves: Spivak, Postcoloniality, and Theology*. New York: Fordham University Press, 2011.
Morrison, Todd Graham, Dylan Beaulieu, Melanie Brockman, and Cormac Ó Beaglaoich. "A Comparison of Polyamorous and Monoamorous Persons: Are There Differences in Indices of Relationship Well-Being and Sociosexuality?" *Psychology and Sexuality* 4, no. 1 (2013): 75–91. doi:10.1080/19419899.2011.631571.
Moss, Lenny. "Moral Molecules, Modern Selves, and Our 'Inner Tribe.'" *Hedgehog Review* 15, no. 1 (2013). http://www.iasc-culture.org/THR/THR_article_2013_Spring_Moss.php.
Munson, Marcia. *The Lesbian Polyamory Reader: Open Relationships, Non-monogamy, and Casual Sex*. New York: Haworth Press, 1999.
Munson, Marcia, and Judith P. Stelboum. "Introduction." *Journal of Lesbian Studies* 3, nos. 1–2 (1999): 1–7. doi:10.1300/J155v03n01_01.
Murray, Annie. "Forsaking All Others: A Bifeminist Discussion of Compulsory Monogamy." In *Bisexual Politics: Theories, Queries, and Visions*, edited by John Dececco and Naomi S. Tucker, 293–304. New York: Routledge, 1995.
Nagel, Thomas. *The View from Nowhere*. New York: Oxford University Press, 1989.
Nair, Hemanth P., and Larry J. Young. "Vasopressin and Pair-Bond Formation: Genes to

Brain to Behavior." *Physiology* 21, no. 2 (2006): 146–52. doi:10.1152/physiol.00049.2005.

Nair, Yasmin. "Against Equality, against Marriage: An Introduction." In *Against Equality: Queer Critiques of Gay Marriage*, edited by Ryan Conrad, 15–21. Lewiston, ME: Against Equality Press, 2010.

Narayan, Uma. *Dislocating Cultures: Identities, Traditions, and Third-World Feminism*. New York: Routledge, 1997.

Nash, Geoffrey. *From Empire to Orient: Travellers to the Middle East, 1830–1926*. London: I. B. Tauris, 2005.

National Science Foundation. "Variation in Vole Gene Is Bellwether for Behavior: Study Finds 'Junk' DNA Contributes to Animal Social Interactions" (press release). July 5, 2009. https://www.nsf.gov/news/news_summ.jsp?cntn_id=104238.

Newitz, Annalee. "Love Unlimited: The Polyamorists." *New Scientist*, no. 2559 (2006): 44–47.

Noël, Melita J. "Progressive Polyamory: Considering Issues of Diversity." *Sexualities* 9, no. 5 (2006): 602–20. doi:10.1177/1363460706070003.

Okin, Susan Moller. *Is Multiculturalism Bad for Women?* Edited by Joshua Cohen, Matthew Howard, and Martha C. Nussbaum. Princeton, NJ: Princeton University Press, 1999.

Olson, Alix. "Queer(y)ing Permanent Partnership." *Wagadu* 12 (2014): 41–89.

Oosterhuis, Harry. *Stepchildren of Nature: Krafft-Ebing, Psychiatry, and the Making of Sexual Identity*. Chicago: University of Chicago Press, 2000.

Ordover, Nancy. *American Eugenics: Race, Queer Anatomy, and the Science of Nationalism*. Minneapolis: University of Minnesota Press, 2003.

Overall, Christine. "Monogamy, Nonmonogamy, and Identity." *Hypatia* 13, no. 4 (1998): 1–17.

Pallotta-Chiarolli, Maria. "Take Four Pioneering Poly Women: A Review of Three Classical Texts on Polyamory." *Journal of Bisexuality* 4, nos. 3–4 (2004): 227–34.

Papoulias, Constantina, and Felicity Callard. "Biology's Gift: Interrogating the Turn to Affect." *Body and Society* 16, no. 1 (2010): 29–56. doi:10.1177/1357034X09355231.

Parrinder, Patrick. "Eugenics and Utopia: Sexual Selection from Galton to Morris." *Utopian Studies* 8, no. 2 (1997): 1–12.

Petrella, Serena. "Ethical Sluts and Closet Polyamorists: Dissident Eroticism, Abject Subjects and the Normative Cycle in Self-Help Books on Free Love." In *The Sexual Politics of Desire and Belonging*, 151–70. New York: Rodopi, 2007.

Pfeiffer, Ulrich J. "Oxytocin—Not Always a Moral Molecule." *Frontiers in Human Neuroscience* 7, no. 10 (2013): 1–2. doi:10.3389/fnhum.2013.00010.

Pieper, Marianne, and Robin Bauer. "Mono-normativity and Polyamory." Hamburg: Research Centre for Feminist, Gender, and Queer Studies, University of Hamburg, 2005.

Pigliucci, Massimo. "The One Paradigm to Rule Them All." In *The Big Bang Theory and Philosophy*, edited by D. A. Kowalski, 128–43. Hoboken, NJ: John Wiley & Sons, 2012.

Pitkow, Lauren J., Catherine A. Sharer, Xianglin Ren, Thomas R. Insel, Ernest F. Terwilliger, and Larry J. Young. "Facilitation of Affiliation and Pair-Bond Formation by Vasopressin Receptor Gene Transfer into the Ventral Forebrain of a Monogamous Vole." *Journal of Neuroscience* 21, no. 18 (2001): 7392–96.

Pitts-Taylor, Victoria. "The Plastic Brain: Neoliberalism and the Neuronal Self." *Health* 14, no. 6 (2010): 635–52. doi:10.1177/1363459309360796.

Pollitt, Katha. "Whose Culture?" In Susan Moller Okin, *Is Multiculturalism Bad for Women?*, edited by Joshua Cohen, Matthew Howard, and Martha C. Nussbaum, 27–30. Princeton, NJ: Princeton University Press, 1999.

Price, Brooke. "Will Oxytocin Nasal Spray Treatments for Autism Really Work?" EmaxHealth, May 5, 2014. http://www.emaxhealth.com/12577/oxytocin-nasal-spray-treatment-autism-work.

Prosser, Jay. "Transsexuals and the Transexologists: Inversion and the Emergence of Transsexual Subjectivity." In *Sexology in Culture*, edited by Lucy Bland and Laura Doan, 116–31. Chicago: University of Chicago Press, 1998.

Puar, Jasbir K. *Terrorist Assemblages: Homonationalism in Queer Times*. Durham, NC: Duke University Press, 2007.

Quirk, Joe. *It's Not You It's Biology: The Science of Love, Sex, and Relationships*. Philadelphia: Running Press, 2008.

Quirk, Joe. *Sperm Are from Men, Eggs Are from Women: The Real Reason Men and Women Are Different*. Philadelphia: Running Press, 2006.

Rader, Karen Ann. *Making Mice: Standardizing Animals for American Biomedical Research, 1900–1955*. Princeton, NJ: Princeton University Press, 2004.

Radke, Sina, and Ellen R. A. de Bruijn. "The Other Side of the Coin: Oxytocin Decreases the Adherence to Fairness Norms." *Frontiers in Human Neuroscience* 6 (2012): 193. doi:10.3389/fnhum.2012.00193.

Ramazanoglu, C., and Sue Sharpe. *The Male in the Head: Young People, Heterosexuality and Power*. London: Tufnell Press, 2004.

Reardon, Jenny. *Race to the Finish: Identity and Governance in an Age of Genomics*. Princeton, NJ: Princeton University Press, 2009.

Rich, Adrienne. "Compulsory Heterosexuality and Lesbian Existence." *Signs* 5, no. 4 (1980): 631–60.

Richards, Christina. "Trans and Non-monogamies." In *Understanding Non-monogamies*, edited by Meg Barker and Darren Langdridge, 122–33. New York: Routledge, 2010.

Richardson, Sarah S. "Sexing the X: How the X Became the 'Female Chromosome.'" *Signs* 37, no. 4 (2012): 909–33. doi:10.1086/664477.

Ritchie, Ani, and Meg Barker. "Hot Bi Babes and Feminist Families: Polyamorous Women Speak Out." *Lesbian and Gay Psychology Review* 8, no. 2 (2007): 141–51.

Ritchie, Ani, and Meg Barker. "'There Aren't Words for What We Do or How We Feel So We Have to Make Them Up': Constructing Polyamorous Languages in a Culture of Compulsory Monogamy." *Sexualities* 9, no. 5 (2006): 584–601. doi:10.1177/1363460706069987.

Roberts, Celia. "Sex, Race and 'Unnatural' Difference: Tracking the Chiastic Logic of Menopause-Related Discourses." *European Journal of Women's Studies* 11, no. 1 (2004): 27–44. doi:10.1177/1350506804039813.

Robinson, Victoria. "My Baby Just Cares for Me: Feminism, Heterosexuality and Non-monogamy." *Journal of Gender Studies* 6, no. 2 (1997): 143–57. doi:10.1080/09589236.1997.9960678.

Robinson-Dunn, Diane. *The Harem, Slavery and British Imperial Culture: Anglo-Muslim Relations in the Late Nineteenth Century*. Manchester: Manchester University Press, 2006.

Roosth, Sophia, and Astrid Schrader. "Feminist Theory out of Science: Introduction." *differences* 23, no. 3 (2012): 1–8. doi:10.1215/10407391-1892880.

Rosa, Becky. "Anti-monogamy: A Radical Challenge to Compulsory Heterosexuality?" In *Stirring It: Challenges for Feminism*, edited by Gabriele Griffin, 107–20. London: Taylor and Francis, 1994.

Roughgarden, Joan. *Evolution's Rainbow: Diversity, Gender, and Sexuality in Nature and People*. Berkeley: University of California Press, 2009.

Roy, Arundhati. *The God of Small Things*. New York: Random House, 2008.

Roy, Deboleena. "Asking Different Questions: Feminist Practices for the Natural Sciences." *Hypatia* 23, no. 4 (2008): 134–56. doi:10.1111/j.1527-2001.2008.tb01437.x.

Roy, Deboleena. "Feminist Theory in Science: Working toward a Practical Transformation." *Hypatia* 19, no. 1 (2004): 255–79. doi:10.1353/hyp.2004.0013.

Roy, Deboleena. "Somatic Matters: Becoming Molecular in Molecular Biology." *Rhizomes: Cultural Studies in Emerging Knowledge* 14 (2007). http://rhizomes.net.

Roy, Deboleena, and Banu Subramaniam. "Matter in the Shadows: Feminist New Materialism and the Practices of Colonialism." In *Mattering: Feminism, Science, and Materialism*, edited by Victoria Pitts-Taylor. New York: New York University Press, 2015.

Rubin, David A. "'An Unnamed Blank That Craved a Name': A Genealogy of Intersex as Gender." *Signs* 37, no. 4 (2012): 883–908. doi:10.1086/664471.

Rusert, Britt. "Delany's Comet: Fugitive Science and the Speculative Imaginary of Emancipation." *American Quarterly* 65, no. 4 (2013): 799–829. doi:10.1353/aq.2013.0055.

Rusert, Britt. "Disappointment in the Archives of Black Freedom." *Social Text* 33, no. 4 (2015).

Rusert, Britt. "The Science of Freedom: Counterarchives of Racial Science on the Antebellum Stage." *African American Review* 45, no. 3 (2012): 291–308.

Rust, Paula C. *Bisexuality in the United States: A Social Science Reader*. New York: Columbia University Press, 2000.

Rust, Paula C. "Monogamy and Polyamory: Relationship Issues for Bisexuals." In *Bisexuality: The Psychology and Politics of an Invisible Minority*, 127–48. Thousand Oaks, CA: Sage, 1996.

Rust, Paula C. "Two Many and Not Enough." *Journal of Bisexuality* 1, no. 1 (2000): 31–68. doi:10.1300/J159v01n01_04.

Ryan, Christopher, and Cacilda Jetha. *Sex at Dawn: How We Mate, Why We Stray, and What It Means for Modern Relationships*. Reprint. New York: Harper Perennial, 2011.
Sample, Ian. "Love Is a Drug for Prairie Voles to Score." *Guardian*, December 4, 2005. http://www.theguardian.com/science/2005/dec/05/animalbehaviour.research.
Scherrer, Kristin S. "What Asexuality Contributes to the Same-Sex Marriage Discussion." *Journal of Gay and Lesbian Social Services* 22, nos. 1–2 (2010): 56–73. doi:10.1080/10538720903332255.
Schiebinger, Londa. *Nature's Body: Gender in the Making of Modern Science*. Boston: Beacon, 1993.
Schuller, Kyla. "Taxonomies of Feeling: The Epistemology of Sentimentalism in Late-Nineteenth-Century Racial and Sexual Science." *American Quarterly* 64, no. 2 (2012): 277–99. doi:10.1353/aq.2012.0023.
Scott, Joan Wallach. *The Fantasy of Feminist History*. Durham, NC: Duke University Press, 2011.
Scott, Joan Wallach. *The Politics of the Veil*. Princeton, NJ: Princeton University Press, 2010.
Segerberg, Marsha. "Re/de/e/volving: Feminist Theories of Science." *off our backs* 9, no. 3 (1979): 12–13, 29.
Seymour, Nicole. *Strange Natures: Futurity, Empathy, and the Queer Ecological Imagination*. Champaign: University of Illinois Press, 2013.
Shaw, Adrienne. "Women on Women: Lesbian Identity, Lesbian Community, and Lesbian Comics." *Journal of Lesbian Studies* 13, no. 1 (2009): 88–97. doi:10.1080/07380560802314227.
Sheff, Elisabeth. *The Polyamorists Next Door: Inside Multiple-Partner Relationships and Families*. Lanham, MD: Rowman and Littlefield, 2013.
Sheff, Elisabeth. "Polyamorous Families, Same-Sex Marriage, and the Slippery Slope." *Journal of Contemporary Ethnography* 40, no. 5 (2011): 487–520.
Sheff, Elisabeth, and Corie Hammers. "The Privilege of Perversities: Race, Class and Education among Polyamorists and Kinksters." *Psychology and Sexuality* 2, no. 3 (2011): 198–223. doi:10.1080/19419899.2010.537674.
Shehabuddin, Elora. "Gender and the Figure of the 'Moderate Muslim': Feminism in the Twenty-First Century." In *The Question of Gender: Joan W. Scott's Critical Feminism*, edited by Judith Butler and Elizabeth Weed, 102–42. Bloomington: Indiana University Press, 2011.
Shernoff, Michael. "Negotiated Nonmonogamy and Male Couples." *Family Process* 45, no. 4 (2006): 407–18. doi:10.1111/j.1545-5300.2006.00179.x.
Sieben, A. "Heteronormative Pheromones? A Feminist Approach to Human Chemical Communication." *Feminist Theory* 12, no. 3 (2011): 263–80. doi:10.1177/1464700111417664.
Silverman, Chloe. *Understanding Autism: Parents, Doctors, and the History of a Disorder*. Princeton, NJ: Princeton University Press, 2011.
Smorag, Pascale. "From Closet Talk to PC Terminology: Gay Speech and the Politics of

Visibility." *Transatlantica*, no. 1 (July 28, 2008). http://transatlantica.revues.org/3503?&.

Somerville, Siobhan B. *Queering the Color Line: Race and the Invention of Homosexuality in American Culture*. Durham, NC: Duke University Press, 2000.

Steet, Linda. *Veils and Daggers: A Century of National Geographic's Representation of the Arab World*. Philadelphia: Temple University Press, 2000.

Stelboum, Judith P. "Patriarchal Monogamy." *Journal of Lesbian Studies* 3, nos. 1–2 (1999): 39–46. doi:10.1300/J155v03n01_05.

Stepan, Nancy. *The Idea of Race in Science: Great Britain, 1800–1960*. London: Macmillan, 1982.

Stepan, Nancy Leys. "Race and Gender: The Role of Analogy in Science." *Isis* 77, no. 2 (1986): 261–77.

Stepan, Nancy Leys, and Sander L. Gilman. "Appropriating the Idioms of Science." In *The Racial Economy of Science*, edited by Sandra Harding, 170–93. Bloomington: Indiana University Press, 1993.

Storr, Merl. "The Sexual Reproduction of 'Race': Bisexuality, History and Racialization." In *The Bisexual Imaginary: Representation, Identity and Desire*, 73–88. London: Cassell, 1997.

Subramaniam, Banu. "And the Mirror Cracked! Reflections of Natures and Cultures." In *Feminist Science Studies: A New Generation*, edited by Maralee Mayberry, Banu Subramaniam, and Lisa H. Weasel, 55–62. New York: Routledge, 2001.

Subramaniam, Banu. *Ghost Stories for Darwin: The Science of Variation and the Politics of Diversity*. Chicago: University of Illinois Press, 2014.

Subramaniam, Banu. "Moored Metamorphoses: A Retrospective Essay on Feminist Science Studies." *Signs* 34, no. 4 (2009): 951–80. doi:10.1086/597147.

TallBear, Kim. "Dear Indigenous Studies, It's Not Me, It's You. Why I Left and What Needs to Change." In *Critical Indigenous Studies: Engagements in First World Locations*, edited by Aileen Moreton-Robinson. Tucson: University of Arizona Press, forthcoming.

Terry, Jennifer. *An American Obsession: Science, Medicine, and Homosexuality in Modern Society*. Chicago: University of Chicago Press, 1999.

Terry, Jennifer. "'Unnatural Acts' in Nature: The Scientific Fascination with Queer Animals." *GLQ: A Journal of Lesbian and Gay Studies* 6, no. 2 (2000): 151–93.

Thornhill, Randy, and Craig T. Palmer. *A Natural History of Rape: Biological Bases of Sexual Coercion*. Cambridge, MA: MIT Press, 2001.

Tibbetts, Lana. "Commitment in Monogamous and Polyamorous Relationships." *Social Work* 521 (2001). http://sw.oxfordjournals.org/.

Tolmie, Jane. "Modernism, Memory and Desire: Queer Cultural Production in Alison Bechdel's *Fun Home*." *TOPIA: Canadian Journal of Cultural Studies*, no. 22 (March 29, 2011). http://pi.library.yorku.ca/ojs/index.php/topia/article/view/31865.

Tweedy, Ann E. "Polyamory as a Sexual Orientation." *University of Cincinnati Law Review* 79 (2010): 1461.

Uvnäs Moberg, Kerstin. *The Oxytocin Factor: Tapping the Hormone of Calm, Love, and Healing*. Translated by Roberta Francis. Boston: Da Capo, 2003.

van Anders, Sari M., and Katherine L. Goldey. "Testosterone and Partnering Are Linked via Relationship Status for Women and 'Relationship Orientation' for Men." *Hormones and Behavior* 58, no. 5 (2010): 820–26. doi:10.1016/j.yhbeh.2010.08.005.

van Anders, Sari M., Katherine L. Goldey, and Patty X. Kuo. "The Steroid/Peptide Theory of Social Bonds: Integrating Testosterone and Peptide Responses for Classifying Social Behavioral Contexts." *Psychoneuroendocrinology* 36, no. 9 (2011): 1265–75. doi:10.1016/j.psyneuen.2011.06.001.

van Anders, Sari M., Lisa Dawn Hamilton, and Neil V. Watson. "Multiple Partners Are Associated with Higher Testosterone in North American Men and Women." *Hormones and Behavior* 51, no. 3 (2007): 454–59. doi:10.1016/j.yhbeh.2007.01.002.

van der Tuin, Iris, and Rick Dolphijn. "The Transversality of New Materialism." *Women: A Cultural Review* 21, no. 2 (2010): 153–71. doi:10.1080/09574042.2010.488377.

Vera, Anne Dal. "The Polyamory Quilt." *Journal of Lesbian Studies* 3, nos. 1–2 (1999): 11–22. doi:10.1300/J155v03n01_02.

Vida, Ginny. *Our Right to Love: A Lesbian Resource Book*. Englewood Cliffs, NJ: Prentice Hall, 1978.

Volpp, Leti. "Talking 'Culture': Gender, Race, Nation, and the Politics of Multiculturalism." *Columbia Law Review* 96, no. 6 (1996): 1573. doi:10.2307/1123327.

West, Celeste. *Lesbian Polyfidelity: A Pleasure Guide for All Women Whose Hearts Are Open to Multiple Sensualoves, Or, How to Keep Nonmonogamy Safe, Sane, Honest and Laughing, You Rogue!* San Francisco: Booklegger, 1996.

Weston, Kath. *Families We Choose: Lesbians, Gays, Kinship*. New York: Columbia University Press, 1997.

"White Paper Proposal for Sequencing the Genome of the Prairie Vole (*Microtus ochrogaster*)." N.d. http://www.genome.gov/Pages/Research/Sequencing/SeqProposals/VoleWhitePaper_and_LOS.pdf.

Willett, Cynthia. *The Soul of Justice: Social Bonds and Racial Hubris*. Ithaca, NY: Cornell University Press, 2001.

Willett, Cynthia, Julie Willett, and Yael D. Sherman. "The Seriously Erotic Politics of Feminist Laughter." *Social Research: An International Quarterly* 79, no. 1 (2012): 217–46.

Willey, Angela. "Biopossibility: A Queer Feminist Materialist Science Studies Manifesto, with Special Reference to the Question of Monogamous Behavior." *Signs* 41, no. 3 (2016).

Willey, Angela. "'Christian Nations,' 'Polygamic Races' and Women's Rights: Toward a Genealogy of Non/monogamy and Whiteness." *Sexualities* 9, no. 5 (2006): 530–46. doi:10.1177/1363460706069964.

Willey, Angela. "Constituting Compulsory Monogamy: Normative Femininity at the Limits of Imagination." *Journal of Gender Studies* (forthcoming). doi:10.1080/09589236.2014.889600.

Willey, Angela. "The Science of Love behind the Science of Rape." *Feminist Wire*, February 17, 2013. http://thefeministwire.com/2013/02/oped-the-science-of-love-behind-the-science-of-rape/.

Willey, Angela. "'Science Says She's Gotta Have It': Reading for Racial Resonances in Woman-Centered Poly Literature." In *Understanding Non-monogamies*, edited by Meg Barker and Darren Langdridge, 34–45. New York: Routledge, 2010.

Willey, Angela, and Sara Giordano. "'Why Do Voles Fall in Love?': Sexual Dimorphism in Monogamy Gene Research." In *Gender and the Science of Difference: Cultural Politics of Contemporary Science and Medicine*, edited by Jill A. Fisher, 108–25. New Brunswick, NJ: Rutgers University Press, 2011.

Willey, Angela, and Banu Subramaniam. "Inside the Social World of Asocials: White Nerd Masculinity, Science, and the Politics of Reverent Disdain." *Feminist Studies*, forthcoming.

Willey, Angela, Banu Subramaniam, Jennifer A. Hamilton, and Jane Couperus. "The Mating Life of Geeks: Love, Neuroscience, and the New Autistic Subject." *Signs* 40, no. 2 (2015): 369–91. doi:10.1086/678146.

Williams, Carla. "Naked, Neutered, or Noble: The Black Female Body in America and the Problem of Photographic History." In *Skin Deep, Spirit Strong: The Black Female Body in American Culture*, 182–200. Ann Arbor: University of Michigan Press, 2002.

Wilson, Elizabeth A. "Gut Feminism." *differences* 15, no. 3 (2004): 66–94.

Wilson, Elizabeth A. *Neural Geographies: Feminism and the Microstructure of Cognition*. New York: Routledge, 1998.

Wilson, Elizabeth A. *Psychosomatic: Feminism and the Neurological Body*. Durham, NC: Duke University Press, 2004.

Wilson, Elizabeth A. "Underbelly." *differences* 21, no. 1 (2010): 194–208. doi:10.1215/10407391-2009-027.

Wing, Adrien Katherine. "Polygamy in Black America." In *Critical Race Feminism: A Reader*, 2nd ed., 186–94. New York University Press, 2003.

Winnubst, Shannon. *Queering Freedom*. Bloomington: Indiana University Press, 2006.

Withers, Deborah M. "What Is Your Essentialism Is My Immanent Flesh! The Ontological Politics of Feminist Epistemology." *European Journal of Women's Studies* 17, no. 3 (2010): 231–47. doi:10.1177/1350506810368907.

Witte, John, Jr. *From Sacrament to Contract: Marriage, Religion, and Law in the Western Tradition*. 2nd ed. Louisville, KY: Westminster John Knox Press, 2012.

Worth, Heather, Alison Reid, and Karen McMillan. "Somewhere over the Rainbow: Love, Trust and Monogamy in Gay Relationships." *Journal of Sociology* 38, no. 3 (2002): 237–53. doi:10.1177/144078302128756642.

Yeng, Sokthan. "Foucault's Critique of the Science of Sexuality: The Function of Science within Bio-Power." *Journal of French and Francophone Philosophy* 18, no. 1 (2010): 9–26. doi:10.5195/jffp.2010.169.

Young, Larry J. "Being Human: Love: Neuroscience Reveals All." *Nature* 457, no. 7226 (2009): 148. doi:10.1038/457148a.

Young, Larry, and Brian Alexander. *The Chemistry between Us: Love, Sex, and the Science of Attraction*. New York: Penguin, 2012.

Young, Larry J., Miranda M. Lim, Brenden Gingrich, and Thomas R. Insel. "Cellular Mechanisms of Social Attachment." *Hormones and Behavior* 40, no. 2 (2001): 133–38. doi:10.1006/hbeh.2001.1691.

Young, Larry J., and C. Smith. "Molecules That Mediate Monogamy" (interview). *The Naked Scientists: Science and Radio Podcasts*, February 15, 2009. http://www.thenakedscientists.com/HTML/content/interviews/interview/1058/.

Young, Larry J., and Zuoxin Wang. "The Neurobiology of Pair Bonding." *Nature Neuroscience* 7, no. 10 (2004): 1048–54. doi:10.1038/nn1327.

Zarembo, Alan. "DNA Tweak Turns Vole Mates into Soul Mates." *Los Angeles Times*, June 17, 2004. http://articles.latimes.com/2004/jun/17/science/sci-monogamy17.

INDEX

addiction, 54, 57
agenital realism, 15
Ahmed, Sara, 17–18
Anapol, Debora, 88–90, 118
Anderlini-D'Onofrio, Serena, 84, 92
animals. *See* nonhuman animals
anthropomorphism, 60, 66
antibiologism, 17–19
antimonogamy: as distinct from non-monogamy, 96; dyke ethics of, 97, 113–15, 119
archives: Haslam Collection on Polyamory, 76–77; Lesbian Herstory Archive, 141–44
asexuality, 8. *See also* compulsory sexuality
autism, 54, 135, 157n40; oxytocin as treatment for, 51–52, 63, 156n28; as scientific proxy for bonding, 53–55, 57–59, 61, 68

Barad, Karen, 15–16
Bechdel, Alison. See *Dykes to Watch Out For*
belonging: biological conceptions of, 82; coupled forms of, 28; economy of, 121; ethics of, 131; new naturecultural forms of, 122–23; social, 3, 74, 83, 93; systems of, 41, 96. *See also* kinship; relationships
biology. *See* biopossibility; disciplinarity; neuroscience
biopossibility, 123–25, 127–34, 137–39
bisexuality, 5–11, 86–88, 149n48. *See also* polyamory
black feminist theory, 10, 129
Breedlove, Lynnee, 104

Christian marriage, 27, 30–38, 41
colonial sexual science, 1–22. *See also* postcolonialism; sexology
compulsory heterosexuality, 4
compulsory monogamy: challenged by polyamory, 74–76, 93; and politics of science, 11, 59; as problem for feminism, 4–5; as reinforced by homo/bi/trans-phobia, 8–9; as undermining friendship, 96
compulsory sexuality, 8, 11, 85, 96
consensual nonmonogamy, 75; as multidisciplinary object of knowing, 77. *See also* nonmonogamy; polyamory

coupling: denaturalization of, 111; polyamory, 96, 118; science of, 12, 47–59, 67–69. *See also* pair bonding; social monogamy
cross-receptivity, of hormones and receptors, 56, 136

Darwinism, 30–34, 154–55n51. *See also* evolutionism; neo-Darwinian evolution
desire, 3–14, 23, 42–43, 85, 127–31. *See also* mononormative embodiment
disciplinarity, 3–5, 19–22, 74, 124, 148n12
double alterity, 29
DTWOF. See *Dykes to Watch Out For*
dyke ethics, 97–102, 113–15, 119–23, 131, 145
dyke science, 141–46
Dykes to Watch Out For (DTWOF; Bechdel), 97; kinship and community in, 107–15; mononormativity in, 101–7; polyamory in, 116–18; timeline, 107–8. *See also* dyke ethics; *Serial Monogamy*

Ellis, Havelock, 29, 41–42; on monogamy and evolutionary development, 37–39; on monogamy and marriage, 34–36
embodiment: mononormative, 98–99, 101–7, 115; as naturecultural or material-discursive phenomenon, 4, 9–10, 14–16, 19–22, 124–25; and postcolonial legacies, 30–34, 42–43; as theorized through Lorde's erotic, 125–31. *See also* biopossibility; desire
Emens, Elizabeth, 4, 75–76
epigenetics, 132–33
epistemic authority, 11, 14–16, 19, 28–31, 144–45. *See also* science
epistemic racism, 31–36, 39–41, 154n33
epistemology, 128, 133, 137, 145; and dyke ethics, 98–99, 101, 118; feminist, 124, 141, 145; and "the natural," 76, 80, 91, 95; and religion, 42. *See also* epistemic authority; epistemic racism; ontology
erotic, the. *See* Lorde, Audre
ethics: of belonging, 131; naturecultural, 128. *See also* dyke ethics
ethnocentrism hormone, 83
ethnography, laboratory. *See* laboratory ethnography
evolutionism: in monogamy gene research, 46, 53–58, 69–71, 137, 157n34, 158n51, 159n67; in polyamory discourse, 76–92; and sexology, 30–34, 38–41, 147n3, 154–55n51; and social monogamy, 47–50, 76, 150n61. *See also* epigenetics; neo-Darwinian evolution; plasticity; temporality
extrapair copulation, 49–50

femininity, 7, 89–90. *See also* gender
feminist science, 14–15, 141–46
feminist science studies, 10–16; genealogies of, 144–45; and materialism, 18–19
Fisher, Helen, 49
Foucault, Michel, 26, 28–29, 79, 96–97, 122–23
friendship: and biopossibility, 138; in DTWOF, 107–15; and dyke ethics, 23, 97–98, 121, 145; as juxtaposed to coupling, 8, 70–72, 86, 132
"Friendship as a Way of Life" (Foucault), 97, 122
futurity, 123

gender, 98–101, 135–36; and neuroscience of monogamy, 47, 50–58, 67–71; and polyamory, 80, 85–90; and race, 6–14, 37–38, 47, 71–79, 110–13, 135
genetics and monogamy, 51, 57, 131–32, 157n34; markers in voles, 134, 136. *See also* epigenetics; neuroscience

Haraway, Donna, 1–2, 4, 15–17, 125
Harding, Sandra, 14–16, 91–92, 167n2
harem, in the colonial imagination, 32–33
Haslam Collection on Polyamory, 76–77
heteronormativity, 8, 76, 102, 130
heterosexuality, naturalization of, 4
Holland, Sharon, 129
hormones, 124, 133, 158n51, 166n44. *See also* oxytocin; vasopressin
Huffer, Lynne, 118, 123, 150n65, 153n17, 165n22; on love, 98, 130

Insel, Tom, 133–34
International Conference on Polyamory and Mononormativity, 102
International Conference on the Future of Monogamy and Nonmonogamy, 76–77
intersex, 26, 71, 87, 159n67
Islamophobia, 30, 32–33, 153n19

jealousy, 11, 135
joy, 122, 126–27

Kenneth R. Haslam Collection on Polyamory, 76–77
Kerista Commune, 77–78
kinship, 56, 104, 107–15
Krafft-Ebing, Richard von, 29–34, 39–41, 56. See also *Psychopathia Sexualis*

laboratory ethnography: observation of experiments, 63–67, 159n67; protocol for study of, 52–53. *See also* Young, Larry
lesbian, 97–100, 141–42, 145. *See also* dyke ethics
Lesbian Herstory Archive, 141–42, 144
lesbian kinship, as feature of dyke anti-monogamy, 104
Lesbian Polyamory Reader, The (Munson and Stelboum), 84–86
Lorde, Audre, 122; as a materialist, 125–31, 137–38
love, 6–9, 34, 37, 49; and polyamory, 77–93; and queer feminism, 130; science of, 45–50, 70
lovestyle: bi and poly, 84, 92, 108; monoamory, 77

marriage, 4–6, 10, 77; Christian, 27, 30–38, 41; the secularization of, 26–27, 36–37, 42–44
"Marriage and Divorce" (Ellis), 42
materialism, 17–23; of Audre Lorde, 125–31; queer feminist, 26, 122, 124–25. *See also* biopossibility; disciplinarity
McClintock, Anne, 27–28
measurement, of monogamy and pair bonding, 60, 63–66
microsatellite DNA, 55–56, 156–57n29
monogamy: heterosexual, 32; sexual, 47–48, 101, 155n6; social, 47–50, 54–56, 155n6; super and simple, 75, 111, 153n4. *See also* compulsory monogamy; monogamy gene; pair bonding
monogamy gene, 22, 46, 50–59, 63–64, 131–38. *See also* neuroscience
mononormative embodiment, 97–99, 101–7, 115–18
Myth of Monogamy, The (Barash and Lipton), 25, 49

natural history, of monogamy, 49
naturecultural, 4; approaches, 17–23; dyke ethics as, 98–99; monogamy as, 42–44. *See also* biopossibility; materialism
neo-Darwinian evolution, as explanation for human sexuality, 76, 84, 92

neuroscience, 46–51, 64, 80–82, 131–38; social, 125, 133–34. *See also* epigenetics; genetics
new materialism, 17–18, 124, 127, 131
nondyadic relationships. *See* nonmonogamy; polyamory
nonhuman animals, 63, 157n38, 161n32; in evolutionary thought, 38–39, 41, 55; as experimental subjects, 49, 53, 55, 159n60, 159n69. *See also* voles
nonmonogamy, 13–15, 40, 73–75, 79–92; as distinct from antimonogamy, 96. *See also* polyamory

ontology, 23, 128, 137, 145
orgasm, 12, 61, 150n65
oxytocin, 49, 56, 61, 68; connecting monogamy to polyamory, 82; as enabling pair bonding behavior, 136; as "ethnocentrism hormone," 83; as maternal hormone, 135; and monogamy, 82, 134–38, 158n51; potential links to autism, 51–52; receptors in voles, 134–36

pair bonding, 47–49; measurement of, 60; multipoint (nonexclusive), 80–82; same-sex, 68–70. *See also* compulsory sexuality; coupling; social monogamy
partner preference test, 63–66
plasticity, 47, 55, 92, 124, 134. *See also* epigenetics
polyamory, 74–75, 82, 84–92; archive about, 76–77; fictional narrative on, 88, 90–91; science of, 80–82; as theme in *DTWOF*, 115–19; types of, 159n6
polyfidelity, 77
polygamy, 32–35, 77, 147n7, 154n38
postcolonialism: feminist theories of, 10, 124, 145; and sexuality studies, 26–30; and structural racism, 91–92
privatization, 42, 82, 115, 124, 145
pseudoscience, 28
Psychopathia Sexualis (Krafft-Ebing), 29–36, 39–41, 46, 56

queer animal behavior, 67, 70–72, 157n38
queer empathy, 123
queer feminist materialism, 26, 122, 124–25

race. *See* racialization; racism
racialization, 10, 13; of autism, 53–55; of love, 37–38; of monogamy, chapter 1; in polyamory discourse, 85–93. *See also* evolutionism
racism, 30, 42, 87, 100; as effect of oxytocin, 83; epistemic, 31–36, 39–41, 154n33; and postcolonialism, 91–93. *See also* racialization
reflexivity, 14, 95, 100, 123
relationships: alternative, 8, 78, 80; archival holdings on, 76–77, 141–42; and compulsory sexuality, 96; and evolution of humans, 47, 76; lesbian, 97; and naturalization of monogamy, 72, 78; polyfidelity, 77; sexual desire and, 8; types of poly, 159n6; women's, 7. *See also* belonging; friendship; kinship; lovestyle
research laboratory. *See* Young, Larry
Rosa, Becky, 8, 96–97
Roy, Deboleena, 17, 123–24

same-sex pair bonds, of voles, 69–70
science: feminist, 3–5, 10, 14–18, 42, 135; of monogamy, 50–59, 63–64, 131–38; politics of, 11–16, 42, 133; and pseudoscience, 28; of racialized gender, 13. *See also* dyke science; epistemology; feminist science studies; neuroscience
Science and Social Inequality (Harding), 14–16, 91–92

scientists, study of. *See* laboratory ethnography
Serial Monogamy (Bechdel), 102–7
sexology, discourses of, 1–23, 28–29, 31. *See also* colonial sexual science; Ellis, Havelock; Krafft-Ebing, Richard von
sexual difference, 10, 13, 69–70, 159n67. *See also* intersex
sexuality, 26, 40–44; and colonization, history of, 27–34; displaced in *DTWOF*, 115–19; as interpretive grid for bonding, 47, 59; Lorde's critique of, 122, 125–31, 137–38; polyamory as, 74–80; primitive, 88–92; science of, 68–71. *See also* asexuality; bisexuality; compulsory sexuality
sexual monogamy, versus social monogamy, 47–50
simple monogamy, 75
social belonging, 3, 74, 83; forms of, 93
social brain, study of, 56
social monogamy, versus sexual monogamy, 47–50
social neuroscience, 125, 133–34
Sprinkle, Annie, 146
Studies in the Psychology of Sex (Ellis), 29, 34–40
super monogamy, and simple monogamy, 75, 106

temporality (evolutionary), 40–41, 92, 136–37
trans critiques of monogamy, 9–10, 99
translational research, as opposed to basic research, 58

Understanding Non-monogamies, 76
"Uses of the Erotic" (Lorde), 23, 122–28, 130, 138

van Anders, Sari, 80–82
vasopressin, 49, 61; as hormone of sociality, 138; receptors in voles, 56, 134–36
Vole Genomics Initiative, 58–59
voles, 45, 58–59, 132, 134; as experimental test subjects, 60, 62–67; genomic sequencing of, 71; meadow vole, 132, 134; monogamous versus promiscuous, 58; prairie vole, 45, 58–59, 132, 134. *See also* partner preference test; Young, Larry

whiteness, 10, 13, 79, 122–23; and autism, 54–55; in *DTWOF*, 110; and sexology, 30–32. *See also* racialization
Wilson, Elizabeth, 18–19
Winnubst, Shannon, 122–23
Witte, John, Jr., 1, 25
women's identity formation, and monogamy, 7–8
worlding, 123, 145

Yerkes National Primate Research Center. *See* Young, Larry
Young, Larry: on the monogamy gene in voles, 131–32; neuroscience laboratory of, 46–50; on same-sex pair bonds of voles, 69–70; and Vole Genomics Initiative, 58–59. *See also* laboratory ethnography; partner preference test; voles